THE ORIGINS OF WAR

Arther Ferrill **THE ORIGINS OF**

with 68 illustrations, maps and battle plans

WAR

FROM THE STONE AGE TO ALEXANDER THE GREAT

THAMES AND HUDSON

To Gretchen and Chester Starr
In Admiration and Affection

HALF-TITLE PAGE: The origins of war can be traced back into prehistory. These Neolithic Spanish archers appear to be wearing some kind of protection (early armor?), probably made of leather, for their chests, loins and knees. TITLE PAGE: Ramesses II in his war chariot at the battle of Kadesh (c. 1285 BC).

© 1985 Thames and Hudson Ltd, London

First published in the USA in 1985 by Thames and Hudson Inc., 500 Fifth Avenue, New York, New York 10110

Library of Congress Catalog Card Number 84-51642

Printed and bound in the German Democratic Republic

Contents

Preface

There is an inevitable quaintness about ancient warfare, an element of romance and glory, of bloodshed and savagery, the use of bows and arrows, of cavalry without stirrups, of slings, spears, swords and javelins, all of which give it a fairy-tale aura of limitless antiquity and almost total irrelevancy to modern times. In fact, the high degree of sophistication attained in ancient warfare is rarely given its due, except for the way in which ancient armies shaped the fate of rising and falling empires. Although ancient warriors did fight without benefit of stirrups and gunpowder, one of the themes of this book is that the developments that led to the tactically integrated army of Alexander the Great laid the foundation and shaped the practice of modern warfare down to the time of Napoleon. Western medieval armies could not have held their ground in the face of Alexander's attack. Even the introduction of gunpowder led to remarkably few changes in the practice of warfare until the rifled infantry weapon became standard in the middle of the nineteenth century. In the final chapter I shall try to show how the commonplace features of Alexander's generalship, had they been applied on the field by his admirer, Napoleon, would have led to a French victory at Waterloo.

At the beginning of this century Hans Delbrück opened his *History of the Art of War Within the Framework of Political History* with the observation that military history begins with the history of man, but that the military historian should not start 'at the point when the first more or less recognizable events begin to emerge from the twilight of the prehistoric era, but rather at the point where the source material begins to provide a full and valid glimpse into the events.' For Delbrück that meant the Persian Wars, and probably in 1900 his view was justified. But the present century has seen so much advancement in our knowledge of prehistory and the ancient Near East that now, as we approach the end of the century, Delbrück's attitude is no longer valid. It is, however, still widely practised; General Sir John Hackett's justly acclaimed and recently published book, *The Profession of Arms* (1983), begins with Spartan warfare.

Furthermore, the tendency to begin military history with Greek heavy infantry, the so-called hoplite phalanx, has led to significant misunderstanding of the main features of ancient military history. In the period before Alexander there were two independent lines of military development. One of them starts in the Late Palaeolithic and extends down through prehistoric times to Egypt and Mesopotamia and culminates in the empires of Assyria and Persia. Another begins in Greece around 700 BC with the emergence of the hoplite phalanx at a time when Greece was isolated from developments in the Near East. For 200 years these two lines evolved side by side but apart from one another, and they started tentatively to come together during the Persian Wars of the early fifth century. Greece learned much about the use of cavalry, skirmishers, and light infantry from Persia, and Persia learned the use of heavy infantry from Greece, until finally, Philip and Alexander blended the best of the two traditions and carried military strategy and tactics to a point rarely achieved and much less often exceeded by generals down to the time of Napoleon.

I have tried in this book to look at war generally in terms of actual combat on land and sea. As a result readers can expect to find little here on the 'causes' of war or on the broader political, economic and social results. The omission is not intended as a reflection on the historical importance of causes and results, but my purpose in this book has been, wherever possible, to elucidate the less frequently analyzed, more purely military, aspects of war.

I owe thanks to a large number of friends and colleagues. Fritz Levy read each chapter and offered many valuable and judicious comments that have made this a better book, as did Captain Michael Byrne of the United States Military Academy at West Point. Carol Thomas, Solomon Katz, Jon Bridgman, Maclyn Burg, Donald Treadgold and Scott Lytle each read some of the chapters. Chester Starr and Thomas Kelly, to whom I owe so much, responded willingly, as they always do, when I asked for help. Finally, Kathleen Harrison did a superb job of typing.

Arther Ferrill

Chapter One
Prehistoric Warfare

What is War?

'I am tired and sick of war. Its glory is all moonshine. . . . War is hell.' WILLIAM TECUMSEH SHERMAN, 19 June 1879

And so it is – vividly so for those of my friends who suffered, some of them horribly, in World War II, in Korea, and in Vietnam. 'I can still hear the horses screaming,' says a veteran of the campaign against Hitler. The Germans had used horses from the beginning of World War II, but, as the war ground to an end, and fuel was scarce, they began to rely even more heavily on the animals for transporting artillery. The sounds of the dying horses reverberated over the battlefields.

Reflections of intensely personal human feelings, of pain and tragedy, darken the pages of modern warfare. Cavalié Mercer, a captain of artillery, remembered some years after the battle of Waterloo how the loud, shrill agony of a gunner whose arm had just been shattered struck him 'to the very soul'.[1] A sentence from John Keegan's masterpiece of military history, *The Face of Battle* (1976), describing the 'disaster' of Waterloo, summarizes the 'hellishness' of war with an eloquence vivid in its portrayal of reality: 'Within a space of about two square miles of open, waterless, treeless and almost uninhabited countryside, which had been covered at early morning by standing crops, lay by nightfall the bodies of forty thousand human beings and ten thousand horses, many of them alive and suffering dreadfully.'[2]

We shall often have occasion in the pages of this book to examine ancient warfare in the light of Waterloo. Napoleon and the Iron Duke fought the last battle between major powers in the history of warfare in which Alexander the Great (356–323 BC) would not have been out of place. To be sure, the introduction of the stirrup in the Early Middle Ages and of gunpowder in the Late Middle Ages made some

9

substantial differences, but not as many as most twentieth-century readers might assume. At Waterloo Napoleon did have artillery, but Alexander's catapults were nearly their equal in range and destructiveness. Napoleon's army numbered some 72,000 men whereas Alexander had about 75,000 fighting troops by the time he crossed the Khyber Pass into India. The battle of Waterloo was actually fought on a smaller scale, geographically and tactically, than the battle of the Hydaspes in the Punjab in July of 326 BC.

After Waterloo, by the time of the Crimean War and the American Civil War, technological change took warfare far beyond the conception of ancient generals. The railroads and highly developed firearms increased mobility and firepower beyond the wildest imagination of the Persian conqueror, Cyrus the Great, or Alexander, but in 1815 Napoleon and Wellington could move their armies no farther or faster than Alexander. Napoleon is famous for his view that an army travels on its stomach, but Alexander understood that as well. Although the tin can goes back to the Napoleonic Wars, it was in fact little used, and Alexander's logistical system functioned nearly as smoothly and with as much sophistication as Napoleon's.[3] As for the musket of the early nineteenth century, Alexander's archers and slingers could not compete in penetrating power but they could get off more shots (it took about twenty seconds to reload the musket), and they had a greater effective range. As John Keegan says of Napoleonic marksmanship, 'even at fifty yards a large proportion of musketeers clean missed their target – it reinforces suspicions that many musketeers did not aim at all, or at least did not aim at a particular human target.'[4]

The medieval battles of Crécy and Agincourt were minor engagements by Alexander's standards. With his balanced striking force of heavy infantry, light infantry, cavalry and skirmishers he would have made short work of the victorious English armies of the vaunted longbow. And the gunpowder employed at Agincourt would not have deterred him. Between Alexander and Napoleon, a period of more than 2,000 years, there is an amazing continuity of military technology, ruptured at the end only by the Industrial Revolution of the nineteenth and twentieth centuries.

Those who have experienced war have sometimes been amused, sometimes annoyed, by scholars who insist on defining it. 'War is Hell' is good enough for one who has been under fire. Unfortunately the historian and the archaeologist, looking for the *origins* of a complicated pattern of social behaviour (in this case warfare), must have an acceptable definition, at least a working definition, particularly, as in this case, when the search extends into the darkness of prehistory. For one thing is certain – the origins of war are prehistoric. By the beginning of recorded times, at the earliest appearance of civilization, war was an established pattern of behaviour in Mesopotamia and in Egypt.

In military science it is widely accepted that definitions are notoriously difficult or stupidly arbitrary.[5] For example, there is a superb article under 'Warfare' in the latest edition of *Encyclopaedia Britannica* which illustrates the problem of distinguishing between such basic military terms as 'strategy' and 'tactics', a fact long known to professional military historians. Maréchel Bosquet's famous comment about the Charge of the Light Brigade – *C'est magnifique, mais ce n'est pas la guerre* ('It's magnificent, but it's not war') – illustrates the point nicely. Obviously any definition of war will be subject to modification, exception, and dispute.

At the risk of grotesque simplification let me suggest that 'organized warfare' can best be defined with one word. The word is *formation*. Not all military writers would use exactly the same term, but they generally agree on the basic idea. When warriors are put into the field in formation, when they work as a team under a commander or leader rather than as a band of leaderless heroes, they have crossed the line (it has been called 'the military horizon') from 'primitive' to 'true' or 'organized' warfare.[6] Primitive warfare consists of ambushes, feuds, skirmishes, whereas organized warfare involves genuine battle of the kind detailed in Edward Creasey's classic *Fifteen Decisive Battles of the World* (1851). The basic formations used down to the time of Napoleon have been the column, the line, the square and the circle. The latter two are basically defensive formations. Deployment into the column for marching and into the line for attack is, regardless of weapons or military technology, the *sine qua non* of warfare.

The point is colourfully made in the description of a relatively minor event during the battle of Waterloo. The Scots Greys, attacking French infantry, were carried away by success and pursued too far and carelessly. One of their staff officers wrote:

Our men were out of hand. Every officer within hearing exerted themselves to the utmost to *reform* the men; but the helplessness of the Enemy offered too great a temptation to the Dragoons, and our efforts were abortive . . . *If we could have formed a hundred men* we could have made a respectable retreat, and saved many; but *we could effect no formation*, and were as helpless against their attack as their Infantry had been against ours. Everyone saw what must happen . . . It was in this part of the transaction that almost the whole loss of the Brigade took place.[7]

John Keegan also emphasizes the importance of formation (which implies discipline) by stressing its opposite:

Inside every army is a crowd struggling to get out, and the strongest fear with which every commander lives – stronger than his fear of defeat or even of mutiny – is that of his army reverting to a crowd through some error of his making . . . Many armies, beginning as crowds, remain crowdlike throughout their existence . . . Tactically quite unarticulated, they were vulnerable to the attack of any drilled, determined, homogeneous force . . . The replacement of crowd armies by nuclear professional armies was one of the most important, if complex, processes in European history.[8]

Now that we have at least a rough idea of what we are looking for, of what warfare is, we can sever the historian's lifeline to written sources and take the plunge into the darkness and the mysteries of prehistory in the search for the origins of war.

Prehistoric Warfare in Modern Scholarship

The beginnings of organized warfare, the deployment of the column and the line, the invention of strategy and tactics, the use of massive defensive fortifications, and the development of a military weapons technology with its long-, intermediate- and short-range weapons can all be traced back into prehistoric times. Warfare, except for its various modern refinements, cannot be credited to civilized man, although we shall see that the ancient civilizations of the Near East and Greece added powerful new ingredients to the war machine they inherited from Neolithic times.

Strangely, modern archaeologists and anthropologists have generally ignored the development of warfare in prehistory.[9] As one observer has said about modern studies of primitive war, 'Anthropologists, sociologists, and other social scientists have largely confined their writing to deprecating war rather than attempting to understand this behavior pattern which has played such a tremendous role in human affairs.'[10] Modern scholars have written at considerable length about the social, economic, political and religious structure of prehistoric societies, but their consideration of prehistoric war has focused on its ceremonial significance and on its role in shaping political institutions, or they have often seen it in demographic terms as the by-product of early population pressures.[11]

Prehistoric warfare, however, was as independently important in early society as the discovery of agriculture, the development of proto-urban settlements and the emergence of organized religious systems. Indeed, we shall see that the Neolithic Revolution is in many ways characterized by an explosive revolution in man's war-making capacity, that the appearance of proto-urban settlements in some areas was influenced at least as strongly by warfare as it was by the discovery of agriculture. In fact, though the cultivation of plants occurred in many places for numerous reasons, in a few places it may actually have been war rather than agriculture that led to the earliest Neolithic settlements.

Some of the first features of war can be traced back beyond these settlements of the Neolithic Age to Early and Middle Palaeolithic times. The use of the spear, fire, stones and clubs against animals is well attested. Such weapons must sometimes have been used against man as well, though in fact there is little evidence from all but Late Palaeolithic sites of anything that can be called organized warfare. Feuds and quarrels undoubtedly led occasionally to violence and killing. A few hominid and early human skeletons reflect violent death, but whether as a result of war or warlike action cannot be determined. Still, a review of the evidence will show that organized warfare appeared at least by the end of the Palaeolithic Age.

The Australopithecines

'Man is a predator whose natural instinct is to kill with a weapon.' ROBERT ARDREY, *African Genesis* (New York 1961), p. 316

Within the last generation marvellous new discoveries of the traces of early man-like creatures (sometimes called 'premen') have occurred in Africa.[12] By 1975 archaeologists and physical anthropologists had turned up about forty Australopithecine skulls proving, they have argued, the existence of at least two if not three hominid species at the dawn of man's evolutionary development, in a period that extends roughly from 1,000,000 to 5,000,000 years ago. These discoveries have generated tremendous controversy, and one of the most raging has swirled about the apparent aggressive nature of man's early biological ancestors. Has man from the beginning been biologically programmed for war?

To be sure, the controversy actually predates the discovery of Australopithecine remains. Rousseau painted a charming picture of the life of the Noble Savage uncontaminated by the evils of civilization, in response to Hobbes' often-quoted description of primitive life as 'nasty, brutish and short'. Early in this century William James argued in an essentially pacifist essay that 'History is a bath of blood', and that there was an element of inheritance in man's warlike drives:

> The earlier men were hunting men, and to hunt a neighboring tribe, kill the males, loot the village, and possess the females was the most profitable, as well as the most exciting way of living. Thus were the more martial tribes selected, and in chiefs and peoples a pure pugnacity and love of glory came to mingle with the more fundamental appetite for plunder . . . Modern man inherits all the innate pugnacity and all the love of glory of his ancestors.[13]

Sigmund Freud, in *Civilization and its Discontents* (1930) and in a famous letter to Albert Einstein, observed that man's 'desire for aggression has to be reckoned as a part of his instinctual endowment. . . .' As Freud said in the letter to Einstein,

> You are amazed that it is so easy to infect men with the war fever, and you surmise that man has in him an active instinct for hatred and destruction, amenable to such stimulations. I entirely agree with you. I believe in the existence of this instinct and have been recently at pains to study its manifestations. . . . The upshot of these observations, as bearing on the subject in hand, is that there is no likelihood of our being able to suppress humanity's aggressive tendencies.[14]

These views, for the most part, were deeply disturbing to pacifists. Margaret Mead joined the argument with an essay entitled 'Warfare is only an Invention – not a Biological Necessity'.[15]

A major escalation of the controversy came with the discovery of *Australopithecus* (literally, 'Southern Ape') by Raymond Dart in 1924, and its subsequent interpretation by him. In an article entitled, 'The Predatory Transition from Ape to Man', published in 1954, Dart argued, perhaps too colourfully and polemically, that Australopithecines were meat-eaters, cannibals, and armed hunters.[16] The small brain of the Australopithecine (*c.* 400–500 cubic centimetres) was, according to Dart,

> demonstrably more than adequate for the crude, omnivorous cannibalistic, bone-club wielding, jaw-bone cleaving Samsonian phase of human

emergence. . . . The loathsome cruelty of man forms one of his inescapable, characteristic and differentiative features; and it is explicable only in terms of his carnivorous and cannibalistic origin. . . .

In a later book, *Adventures with the Missing Link* (1959), Dart analyzed an Australopithecine jaw and concluded that it was 'bashed in by a formidable blow from the front and delivered with great accuracy just to the left of the point of the jaw.' The weapon, he believed, was an antelope humerus. Australopithecines were in his view definitely nasty creatures: 'They were murderers and flesh hunters; their favourite tool was a bludgeon of bone, usually the thighbone or armbone of an antelope.'[17]

Conceivably the issues raised by Dart about man's genetic drive to kill might have remained in the obscurity of academic books and journals had it not been for his enthusiastic disciple, Robert Ardrey, who in the last twenty-five years has published several popular books on the subject beginning with *African Genesis* (1961).[18] Nor should one overlook the importance of Konrad Lorenz's *On Aggression* (1966).[19] Lorenz had won a Nobel Prize for his earlier work on animal behaviour, and his views on the animal nature of aggression in man carried respected authority. Inevitably they provoked a counterattack. Ashley Montagu's *The Nature of Human Aggression* (1976) and Richard E. Leakey's *Origins* (1979) are typical.[20] They clearly demonstrate that the evidence for Dart's view of aggression among Australopithecines is shaky – to say the least. But they also go on to argue the opposite view – that early man was generally peaceful and cooperative: 'An objective assessment must surely admit that the weight of evidence is in favor of a relatively peaceable past.'[21]

In fact, however, the evidence is too scanty to prove either case. Perhaps as time goes by and new discoveries contribute to a better understanding of early man, prehistorians will be able to reconstruct with some reasonable accuracy certain features of Australopithecine society. At the present time that is simply impossible. Nor, as we move down into the last million years, does certainty increase very rapidly. *Homo erectus* (Java Man and Peking Man), living perhaps 400,000 to 600,000 years ago, is a shadowy figure. Konrad Lorenz described Peking Man as 'the Prometheus who learned to preserve fire [and] used it to roast his brothers: beside the first traces of the regular use of fire lie the mutilated and roasted bones of *Sinanthropus pekinensis* himself.'[22] The view is an established one, although it is expressed less graphically in many textbooks, but in fact of all the human bones and bone fragments found at Choukoutien only one fragment showed evidence of burning, and that one is doubtful.[23]

Still, Peking Man was without doubt a skilled slayer of animals, and he did have the use of fire. At the Choukoutien site there are about thirty metres of deposits, including the bones of the mammoth and the rhinoceros, as well as many other large animals.[24] It requires some skill simply to butcher such beasts; to kill them with a wooden spear is a tricky and very dangerous act, but Peking Man had obviously mastered the art of killing big game. Did he ever turn his spear, or other instruments of the hunt, against another man? Probably. But to imagine organized armies of Peking Men marching across China 500,000 years ago is to go far beyond the available evidence.

Palaeolithic Tools and Weapons:
From *Australopithecus* to *Homo Sapiens Neanderthalensis*

Weapons and warfare are obviously closely interrelated although, theoretically, crafted weapons are not strictly necessary for war. Man can kill in organized formations with his bare hands, and weapons in the form of sticks, stones, and animal bones are provided in sufficiently lethal form by nature. Nevertheless by the beginning of the last ice age, some 70,000 years ago, when Neanderthal Man had spread over a vast area, one of the major weapons of war had been invented – the spear, which continued in use down to the twentieth century in the form of the bayonet.[25] It could also be used for throwing as a javelin. Sharpened to a thin, almost needle-like point, the wooden spear or javelin was a fearsome weapon for use against the throat, breast or abdomen. There is in fact until the final stages of the Palaeolithic Age no conclusive evidence that any of the so-called prehistoric tools or hunting weapons were used against man at all. The hand-shaped pebble choppers of Olduvai Gorge and the better-crafted ones from Choukoutien were obviously not devised for murder since a blow on the head with a club or animal bone would have been more effective.

Indeed, the pebble chopper (and its later development, the hand-axe) was in the words of a prominent authority 'the predominant tool in the equipment of the Early Stone Age hunters of Africa, western Europe and southern Asia.'[26] It had virtually no military use. As early man discovered that he could produce sharp stone flakes from striking flint or quartz, he acquired blades for cutting, but these probably also had no immediate use in fighting. The club, spear and thrown stone represented short-, intermediate- and long-range firepower down through Neanderthal times. Although there is little direct evidence of struggle among men, one Neanderthal skeleton reveals a hole in the pelvic section that seems to have been made by a spear.[27]

The Cave Paintings

In the late Palaeolithic Age (35,000 to 12,000 BC), the age of the cave paintings, of Cro-Magnon Man, of *Homo sapiens sapiens*, there were new developments in man's offensive capability. Spear points of stone and bone are common, and spearthrowers comparable to the atlatl of the New World have been found in France. The spearthrower in essence extended man's forearm and gave the spear greater range, accuracy and penetrating power.

The cave paintings, however, reflect very little evidence of warfare or of advances in weapons technology. There are several thousand scenes of animals, and, on the whole, they are idyllically peaceful. Only about 130 depictions altogether may be of men – the figures are too crudely drawn to permit certainty – and a few of the men (sometimes referred to as 'anthropomorphs', meaning that they might possibly be men) seem to be dead or dying from wounds. Still, most of the 130 anthropomorphs are shown in peaceful scenes.[28]

Does this Palaeolithic painting (left) represent a man killed by an animal in the hunt or perhaps by a spear? Palaeolithic cave paintings rarely depict men at all, and there is no definite evidence of warfare in them.
Is this so-called anthropomorph from a Palaeolithic painting at Cougnac (right) actually a man, and has he been pierced by lances or by arrows? There is no certain evidence of the bow and arrow in Palaeolithic cave art.

Has this prehistoric bison, painted on the cave walls at Niaux in the Pyrenees, been wounded with arrows, darts or spears? Or do the arrow-like symbols have sexual significance? Authorities cannot agree.

Some students of the cave paintings have seen evidence of the bow and arrow, but on close examination that evidence seems at best inconclusive. The bow and arrow were probably not known to the cave painters, and the few slashes that appear to be arrows are either symbols with some special meaning – some authorities have argued that they have sexual significance – or meaningless doodles.[29] Of all the Palaeolithic cave paintings only one illustrates what may be arrows, but there are no depictions of bows, and the 'arrows', if they are not male sex-symbols, as many believe, could just as easily represent spears or darts.

The Origins of War:
The Epipalaeolithic and the Neolithic

In the Epipalaeolithic and Proto-Neolithic periods (also known collectively as the Mesolithic Age), 12,000 to 8000 BC, there was a revolution in weapons technology that has only a few modern parallels – the invention of gunpowder, the locomotive, airplanes, tanks, and the atomic bomb. Four staggeringly powerful new weapons make their first appearance, weapons (along with the Palaeolithic spear) that would dominate warfare down to the present millennium:

18

the bow, the sling, the dagger (or the short, short sword), and the mace. This new, revolutionary weapons technology was combined with the invention of military tactics and, by historical standards, produced true warfare.

Where the bow and arrow were invented nobody knows, but sometime probably in the (very) late Palaeolithic Age (12,000 to 10,000 BC) they appeared and spread rapidly around the Mediterranean.[30] Neolithic cave paintings clearly reveal their use against men as well as animals.[31] This war-like function must have developed earlier, but perhaps too late to be represented in the Palaeolithic cave art of France and Spain. The range of firepower was extended dramatically. The spear, when used as a throwing weapon, that is, as a javelin, had a range of about fifty yards. The bow and arrow doubled that.[32] Moreover, it was an inexpensive weapon – at least the simple bow of the Neolithic Age was. Anyone could make one and kill from a concealed position at a distance. When a group of people acted together and fired on command, they could unleash a mighty barrage of fire, and a single warrior could carry far more arrows than spears.

Clearly by Neolithic times the bow and arrow were used in the hunt (Spanish Levant).

Much more important for the history of warfare, there is evidence for the application of strategy and tactics by the beginning of Neolithic times, the use of organized troops according to plan. It is generally assumed, probably correctly, that strategy and tactics in human warfare emerged out of the complex hunting patterns of Palaeolithic man. There is considerable evidence that organized groups of men, almost certainly under the command of a leader, helped to stampede large animals over cliffs or to draw them into bogs.[33] What is known of the hunting habits of primitive societies surviving into modern times confirms this assumption.

There is solid evidence, as solid as the Neolithic Age ever produces, of the deployment of the column and the line. One authority has said,

Those people who do not avail themselves of these two sociologic devices are below the military horizon without argument. Their fighting can be nothing but a scuffle, regardless of the amount of bloodshed, and cannot be called a war. . . . The line is the simplest tactical formation, and a sociologic trait without which there can be no true war.[34]

Neolithic archers here seem to be 'organized', working together cooperatively against a herd of deer. The techniques of organized hunting were probably also used in prehistoric warfare.

(Right) In a Neolithic painting from the Spanish Levant marching warriors carry bows and arrows. The leader is apparently differentiated from the men in file behind by a distinctive headdress. Neolithic warriors knew the use of the 'column' for marching.

This Neolithic execution scene from the Spanish Levant shows archers organized into a firing line and, presumably, firing on command. The deployment of troops into column and line is one of the most significant features of early, organized warfare.

The appearance of the column and the line, which imply command and organization, is synonymous with the invention of tactics. In the accompanying illustration, note that the leader of the column has a distinctive headdress setting him apart from his followers. There is also a scene of a line of executioners surely firing on command.

There are some tantalizing depictions of what may represent the first appearance of armour. Archers are shown with clothing or protection of one type or another. The dress is usually described as shoulder cape, loincloth and knee-bands, but it is equally possible that they are protective coverings, made of leather or bark, for the breast, the genitals and the legs.

Even more intriguing is a scene of archers fighting that illustrates in an embryonic fashion for the Neolithic period the double envelopment, a movement of one line around, and attacking the wings of, the enemy line. It is on a very small scale, four warriors against three, and it would be absurd to make much of it, but it does show for the 'army of four' the two warriors in the centre advancing against the 'army of three' while the other two on the wings of the 'army of four' seem to make flanking attacks. Of course it is possible that the 'order of battle' is apparent rather than real, that it was spontaneous rather than planned. On the other hand, if Late Palaeolithic and Neolithic man deployed the column and the line and executed flanking manoeuvres, with his new weapons he could put powerful armies (rather than an 'army of four') into the field. We shall see later, when we examine early Neolithic fortifications, that there is compelling evidence that he did.

Neolithic war. Pictorial evidence of man fighting against man is as old as the Neolithic Age, as this painting from Spain reveals: Note that the 'army of four' is attempting to direct flanking fire against the 'army of three' in what may be the earliest evidence of 'envelopment' in battle.

The devastating effect of early weapons is amply illustrated by a burial site along the Nile in ancient Nubia. It is on the Sudanese side of the Egypt-Sudan border at Jebel Sahaba, less than two miles north of Wadi Halfa. The prehistorians of ancient Egypt refer to the site as 'Cemetery 117'. Discovered in the 1960s, it belongs to the Qadan culture (12,000 to 4500 BC), usually referred to as Epipalaeolithic, but possibly Proto-Neolithic, at least in its extensive use of microliths and its experimentation with agriculture.[35]

There were fifty-nine excavated burials at Site 117, and the skeletal remains are generally in a good state of preservation. Signs of staggering human savagery greeted the excavators. Included in the graves of about forty per cent of the skeletons were small flake points (microliths), probably arrowheads since they seem too small for spears or darts. Points were actually embedded in the bones of four of the dead men and women (some of whom suffered several wounds). In two of these cases the points were found in the sphenoid bones in the skull, and they must have entered from under the lower jaw. That probably means that the individuals were wounded and disabled, lying on their backs, in agony, heads thrown backwards, when they were shot through the throat with the bow and arrow.

Although these remains may reflect a simple execution rather than war, some of the multiple wounds are frightening to imagine. Burial no. 44, a young adult female, had twenty-one chipped-stone artifacts in her body .Three of them found in front of, inside, and behind the mandible, must have been attached as point and barbs on an arrowshaft that was shot into her mouth. Essentially she had been hit over her entire body. Overkill may be a modern concept, but it was an ancient practice. Burials 20 and 21, two adult males, showed six and nineteen wounds respectively, including for no. 21 two stone artifacts in the skull.

It is possible that many of the remaining sixty per cent of Cemetery 117 died from wounds also. Presumably arrows could sometimes be extracted from the dead with points intact, and in that case there would be no archaeological evidence of death by violence. Seven of the skeletons show fractures of the arms that are characteristically produced when the arm is used to parry a blow. These fractures had healed before death, but they illustrate the dangers of life for the people of Cemetery 117. Altogether at the site there were skeletons of eleven children, twenty adult males, twenty-one adult females, and seven adults, sex unknown. Roughly the same percentage (about forty-five per cent) of men and women were clearly killed by microliths, and four of the eleven children (just over thirty-six per cent). We may have in this site the first extensive skeletal evidence for warfare in prehistoric times. It is possible that the dead with multiple wounds were simply executed, but it is far more likely, since the percentage of executions in the group would be incredibly high, that they died from an act of war. Whether it was organized war or simply a primitive ambush or skirmish, we cannot know, and the victims cannot now care. Even in historical combat the survivors often have only the vaguest perception of what happened around them. I am reminded of one of the survivors of the battle of Waterloo who was asked the next day for an account of the fighting: 'I'll be hanged if I know anything about the matter,' he said, 'for I was all day trodden in the mud and ridden over by every scoundrel who had a horse.'[36] The people of Cemetery 117 may have felt much the same, at least those who survived for peaceful burial, although their foe was probably infantry rather than cavalry.

Before proceeding to Neolithic fortifications, let us consider the simultaneous appearance, along with the bow, of other offensive weapons, the dagger, the sling, and the mace. All three have been found at Çatal Hüyük in Anatolia dating from about 7000 B.C.[37] Several beautifully wrought stone daggers, some ceremonial but others clearly functional, were turned up in the excavations, and one of them was found in a leather sheath.

One of the main long-range weapons in the Neolithic arsenal was the much-neglected sling, deadlier than the early simple bow and with greater range and accuracy.[38] The biblical story of David and Goliath vividly illustrates its power.

> And David put his hand in his bag, and took thence a stone, and slang it, and smote the Philistine in his forehead, that the stone sunk into his forehead; and he fell upon his face to the earth.
>
> So David prevailed over the Philistine with a sling and with a stone, and smote the Philistine, and slew him; but there was no sword in the hand of David.
>
> I SAMUEL 17: 49–50; *Anchor Bible* translation

The sling is depicted in the Neolithic art of Çatal Hüyük, and at other Anatolian sites piles of rounded slingstones have been found. Many Neolithic Anatolian settlements (Hacılar is merely one example) show no evidence for the bow at all, but the inhabitants made projectiles of baked clay for the sling.[39] In later, historic times the sling was used all over the Mediterranean, and among primitive societies it can be found throughout the world.[40] It could have a range of approximately 200 yards, and greater distances are not unheard of. Xenophon in the *Anabasis* claimed that his Rhodian slingers outdistanced Persian archers and fired with greater accuracy.[41] Early in this century a scholar wrote of the Tanala tribe in Madagascar that 'at 50 yards slings are as dangerous as firearms in native hands'.[42] In the nineteenth century a French archaeological expedition was attacked by natives near Susa with 'poor-quality muskets, pistols, lances, and the far more dangerous slings'.[43] A heavy, fist-sized stone slung from the sling can smash skulls or break arms, ribs, and legs. It could be effective, in later times, even against an armoured warrior.

It is often said that the sling was less effective than the bow in tactical operations because slingers required too much space in the line.[44] To avoid hitting the person standing next to them as they slung their weapon, slingers were stationed farther apart than archers and did not form a compact line. But slings need not be long, and Trajan's Column in Rome shows slingers in close formation.

This depiction (left) from the early Neolithic settlement at Çatal Hüyük in modern Turkey shows that the sling was used in Neolithic times.
Slingers in the Roman army of the Emperor Trajan (right) used relatively large, heavy stones that could probably smash bones under armour. The short slings made it possible for slingers to fight in tight formation as shown here in a scene from Trajan's Column.
A bone-handled flint dagger from Çatal Hüyük (facing page) was probably a 'ceremonial' weapon – too nice to be used in actual fighting – but others with wooden hilts were undoubtedly lethal in close, hand-to-hand combat.

Ancient Roman slingers, for whom we have some evidence in the military writings of Vegetius, were trained to release the projectiles in the first toss of the sling.[45] We know that in the Roman Republic there were regular cohorts of slingers in the legion while the Romans relied on their allies or on mercenaries for the bow.[46] It is true that the sling requires more practice for effective use than the bow, but its use was more widespread in the ancient Mediterranean than is commonly believed.[47] In competition with the simple bows of the Neolithic period the sling could easily hold its own as a military weapon, though for hunting big animals the piercing arrow may have been more effective since it would cause death by bleeding.

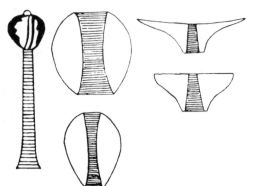

Maces could be made in many shapes. Depicted here are apple-, pear-, and saucer-shaped ones. The one with a handle comes from Egypt.

Bashing weapons on wooden handles – stone maceheads, axes and adzes – also became common in the Late Palaeolithic and Neolithic. As technological advances over their Palaeolithic club and hammer predecessors, they are not nearly as important as the bow and the sling, but it does not take much imagination to realize what they could do to skulls, particularly before the development of the metal helmet.

Neolithic Fortifications

When V. Gordon Childe wrote of the 'Neolithic Revolution', he had in mind the discovery of agriculture rather than a military act, but the development and application by Epipalaeolithic or Proto-Neolithic man of a mighty, offensive arsenal of spears, bows, slings, maces, axes and daggers caused what may have been an equally dramatic and significant change in man's relationship with man. That change and the over-all importance of prehistoric warfare are best seen in the spread of fortified sites all around the eastern Mediterranean from 8000 to 4000 B C.

One of the world's leading Neolithic archaeologists, James Mellaart, has argued in the last decade that Childe was wrong in suggesting that the discovery of agriculture led to permanent settlements, to Neolithic villages and towns which later developed into civilized cities. Mellaart points out that there were many 'permanent' settlements during the Palaeolithic:

The large number of Upper Palaeolithic sites, caves, rockshelters or open settlements, provides a potent argument against the old theory of aimless wandering as a characteristic of the period. The presence of numerous rock sanctuaries in western Europe should have immediately dispelled such ideas; territoriality and circumscribed culture areas were probably not much different from those in later times. Agriculture did not produce permanent settlements, though one cannot deny that it helped to stabilize patterns that were already in the making.[48]

Furthermore, Mellaart believes that Childe was mistaken in seeing the Neolithic period as the precursor of the 'Urban Revolution' or the appearance of civilization in the Near East. According to him, cities develop from the beginning of the Neolithic Age:

Long-lived settlements that generated their own economic growth on the basis of their economy, such as Jericho, Mureybet, Çatal Hüyük, Beidha, Alikosh, Tepe Guran, Tell es-Sawwan, Eridu, Hacılar, Siyalk and Byblos, I would regard as cities. Each of these may be seen as the centre of a city-state, even if it had no dependent towns and villages, for it must have controlled territory, however small, for its economic needs. . . . Indeed, archaeology has shown that cities came into being as early as towns and villages and the first demonstrable signs of the cultivation of plants and the herding of animals emanate not from villages, but from the important primary sites, cities such as those mentioned above.[49]

In calling these early Neolithic sites cities Mellaart has probably gone too far to suit most prehistorians.[50] Some of the sites had fewer than one thousand souls. But Mellaart is surely right in focusing attention on the 'primary sites' whether or not they can be called cities. Agriculture and the domestication of animals do seem to be associated with them. What he and other archaeologists have failed to notice, however, is that many of them are fortified sites – not necessarily walled, but fortified.[51]

There was in the Near East at the beginning of the Neolithic Age a genuine burst of organized warfare as important for the history of the area as Alexander's conquest of Persia in the fourth century B C or the march of Islam in the seventh century AD. Early Neolithic man, to protect himself from the firepower of the new offensive weapons system, began to build fortifications. Those fortified sites are the most impressive archaeological remnants of the military explosion, revealing dramatically the impact of war on man's culture. In some places there is reason to assume that the massive fortifications of various types led to, indeed required, the discovery of agriculture and the domestication of animals.

One reason archaeologists have ignored military influences in the Neolithic Revolution, in addition to the general reluctance of professionals in the field to deal directly with warfare on its own terms as a major facet of human culture, is that the military nature of early Neolithic architecture is not always readily apparent. Walls are not the only form of fortification, and many Neolithic sites, which seem to consist simply of a cluster of private dwellings, were actually architecturally designed for the purpose of protection against attacking forces.

One of the earliest of all known Neolithic settlements, Jericho, has classic, massive walls and tower(s), a bastion of defence against the new long-range weapons.[52] The Pre-pottery Neolithic A settlement (8350–7350 BC) was surrounded by a wall ten feet thick and thirteen or more feet high. There was a solid, colossal tower, thirty-three feet in diameter and twenty-eight feet high with a stairway through the centre and access through a door at the bottom. Although the entire wall has not been excavated, it probably encircled an area of about ten acres and had a length of about 765 yards. There were possibly other towers.

The population of Jericho at this stage was probably around 2,000, and, if there were 500 to 600 fighting men it would have been possible to station one defender for every yard of the wall.[53] There is no evidence of domesticated animals, but in the oasis environment created by the Jericho spring early Neolithic deposits have revealed traces of the domestic (rather than wild) forms of two-row hulled barley and emmer wheat and carbonized seeds of lentil and fig.[54] The Jericho oasis was clearly choice land for the hunting community that settled there. Most prehistorians have assumed that the introduction of agriculture permitted the accumulation of wealth that required walls for defence, though the archaeological evidence does not permit anyone to say that agriculture was introduced before the walls.

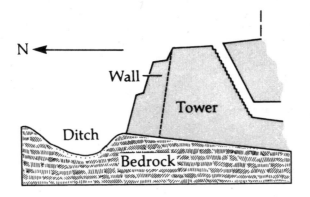

Cross section of the ditch, wall and tower at Jericho. The Pre-pottery Neolithic stone tower on the inside of the wall is preserved to a height of twenty-eight feet. An enclosed staircase leads down through the centre.

It makes equal sense to assume that the walls came first. It was as a hunting site that Jericho attracted settlers. Animals were drawn into the area by the abundant water supply. To protect themselves against the encroachment of archers and slingers the inhabitants of Jericho built massive walls and by doing so tied themselves down irrevocably to their site. The cultivation of crops may have followed naturally. It is widely known that modest experiments in agriculture had occurred in the Palaeolithic Age, and once man built walls for protection he could more easily store reserves of food and more safely work the land around his site.[55]

Militarily the walls provided substantial though not iron-clad security. Jerichoans were archers themselves and from their walls, with reserves of food and water, they could expect to repel invaders. Before the introduction of battering rams and the invention of mining tactics a walled city should have been defensible against scaling, unless the attackers greatly outnumbered the defenders. A surprise attack through the gates at night would likely have been the most successful tactic against a walled settlement, but presumably the inhabitants maintained a night patrol. The very existence of such large walls, especially since they are combined with towers, is evidence of some considerable military sophistication. But one should not push the argument too far. The tower that has been excavated was built *inside* the wall, not as part of the wall projecting to the outside. So the Jerichoans could not take advantage of the flanking fire that the slight architectural adjustment would have given them.

Jericho was not unique as prehistorians once suggested.[56] Other early Neolithic sites were walled or at least fortified. Çatal Hüyük is an excellent example of a fortified settlement without strong encircling walls. For a population of something like 5,000 to 6,000 there were interconnected houses, sharing common walls, built on a standardized rectangular plan with access into each house by ladder through a hole in the roof. The structures date from 7100 to 6300 BC, and the architectural style had a clearly military significance.[57] As one observer has said, 'since the blank wall of the houses presented a continuous unbroken front toward the outside, they formed an effective defensive system that obviated the need of additional walls for the town's protection. An attacker who managed to break the outside wall at any point would find himself not inside the town but inside a single room. . . .'[58]

Perhaps the most vivid way to illustrate the military nature of architecture at Çatal Hüyük is to emphasize the utter defencelessness of individual, unconnected structures in open settlements. Once villagers in such settlements entered their homes for the night, unless they posted an outside guard, their lives were in considerable jeopardy if an enemy preyed in the area. They would be surrounded and trapped in their huts or houses, taken one at a time by attackers. One authority has described the danger:

The old way of making war among the Bering Eskimo was to lie in wait around a village until night, then to steal to every house and barricade the doors from the outside. The men of the village being thus confined, the attackers could leisurely shoot them with arrows through the smoke holes. This reveals a rather simple method.[59]

Neolithic man, at least in the Near East (but also in much of America), proved not so simple. At Hacılar and Mersin the contiguous architecture of Çatal Hüyük was supplemented with strong outside walls. Other Neolithic settlements adopted the same defensive strategy pursued at Çatal Hüyük and simply relied on contiguous dwellings to provide their outside perimeter. In Mesopotamia around 5000 BC Tell es-Sawwan was surrounded by a buttressed fortification

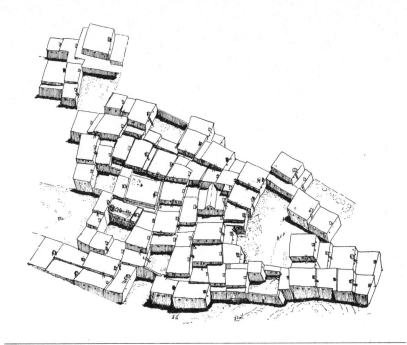

A reconstruction of the southeast corner of the Neolithic mound of Çatal Hüyük (after Mellaart), which shows a system of contiguous walls that served as a fortification. Entry into each unit was through a hole in the roof. Presumably ladders could be retracted when an enemy approached.

wall. By about 4500 BC defensive architecture had taken great strides. At Yalangach in the Transcaspian Lowlands the walls had round towers facing outwards from the walls thus providing a platform for flanking fire against attackers.

Enough evidence has been produced to demonstrate that warfare was a major feature of life in prehistoric times, at least from the Late Palaeolithic onwards. Since there are no written documents from the Stone Age, we have no heroes, no generals, no battles to describe in the way modern military historians can analyze Waterloo. Warriors, perhaps of the kind immortalized in Homer's *Iliad* and *Odyssey*, must have figured prominently in Neolithic times, but the only definite Neolithic military tradition surviving into historic times and embodied in the literature of the early civilizations is the reputation of the walls of Jericho.[60] The earliest civilizations inherited from prehistoric ages a legacy of weapons development, offensive and defensive strategies and tactics, and a sense of territoriality. As soon as man learned how to write, he had wars to write about.

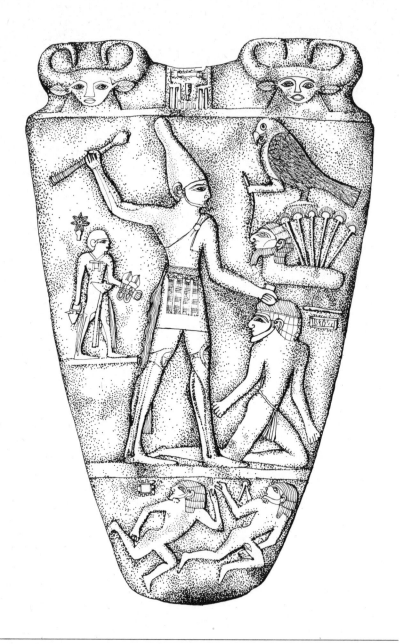

The unification of ancient Egypt was fashioned in war. The palette of Narmer (reverse), c. 3100 BC, shows the new king sacrificing an opponent with a mace to the falcon of Horus. The papyrus plants represent Lower Egypt.

Chapter Two
Ancient Near Eastern Warfare: the Copper-Bronze Age

Although most military historians have paid slightly more attention to warfare in the ancient Near East than to the origins of war in prehistoric times, ancient Near Eastern war remains a much-neglected subject.[61] The major military historians of our era, such as Liddell Hart and J.F.C. Fuller, have found considerable inspiration in the study of Graeco-Roman warfare while neglecting its forerunners.[62] The evidence, especially the literary evidence, is admittedly sparse. Such works as have been published (the best known is probably Yigael Yadin's monumental, two-volume *The Art of Warfare in Biblical Lands* (1963)) are based largely on archaeological remains and emphasize developments in fortification and weapons technology that are revealed by the archaeologist's spade.[63]

This lack of interest in the dynamics, of the strategy and tactics, of ancient Near Eastern warfare in favour of technological developments has led to misinterpretation of the main features of ancient military history. Historians have often ironically observed that the Persian army defending the empire against Alexander's invasion in the fourth century BC contained in the centre of its line a Greek hoplite phalanx, implying that the ancient Near East had learned an important military lesson from the Greeks. Much more ironic is the fact that Alexander's army owed a vastly greater debt to Persia than the Persian army to Greece. The use of siege warfare, cavalry, and skirmishers was a product of ancient Near Eastern warfare, and classical Greek armies were drastically deficient in those skills. Ancient Near Eastern logistics had for centuries permitted the conquest of vast empires and the movement of armies over enormous distances. In the period from 700 to 500 BC Greeks made striking advances in philosophy, literature, art and politics, but they were slow learners of the art of land warfare.

Only after borrowing extensively from Persian military practice (500 to 336 BC) was the Greek world able to place in the field an independent army that had a chance of making it to Babylon.[64]

As we shall see later in this chapter, one reason for neglecting the development of early ancient warfare has been the probably misleading assumption of Egyptologists that Egypt in the Old Kingdom (2650–2150 BC) was isolationist and because of her peculiar geography required no standing army. Defensive policies, however, are not inherently less militaristic than offensive ones, as any student of Japanese history knows, and, if it is true that Egyptian pharaohs of the Old Kingdom were less expansionistic than their successors in the Middle and New Kingdoms, it does not follow that they were less militaristic.[65]

The one cardinal fact of early Egyptian history is that the birth of civilization on the Nile was fashioned in war, and the kingdom of the pharaohs was maintained by military force. The evidence of archaeology and the artistic and literary records of the first dynasties testify to the importance of armies. Almost every student of antiquity has heard of the famous slate palette of Narmer (or Menes), the first of the pharaohs, dating to about 3100 BC, yet few Egyptologists emphasize the military, as opposed to political, representation on that palette of Egypt's birth as a nation.[66] In gruesome detail it depicts the new ruler, who had moved from the south to conquer the delta, uniting the two kingdoms of Egypt in a bloodbath. On one side Narmer wears the crown of Upper Egypt as he despatches an opponent to an early reward with a mace. Also shown is the falcon of Horus, representing Narmer, holding a rope attached to the head of a bearded enemy that protrudes from six papyrus plants, the symbol of Lower Egypt. On the other side, wearing the crown of Lower Egypt, Narmer reviews under the standards of his divisions the headless dead killed by his troops. The union of the two halves of Egypt is symbolized by the two long-necked creatures which are restrained from fighting. At the upper right is Narmer's ship, and at the bottom of both sides are small illustrations of fortified sites.

Although this palette clearly reveals the importance of organized warfare at the outset of Egyptian history, it is not in fact the earliest such representation. From late predynastic Egypt there survives a palette that shows seven fortified and buttressed towns besieged with battering rams. The symbols inside the fortifications presumably

The palette of Narmer (obverse) shows the king examining the headless bodies of his enemies under the standards of his army. The two long-necked creatures in the middle represent the two halves of Egypt restrained from fighting. At the bottom the bull of Narmer destroys the fortified site of the foe.

identify the locations, though they cannot be read today. The animal attackers, according to the late Sir Alan Gardiner, 'represent distinct provinces warring together as a coalition'.[67] On the opposite side the booty of war – oxen, donkeys, rams and olive oil (represented by a grove of olive trees) – serves to justify the attack. The symbol at the right of the trees identifies the war-ravaged land as Libya.

There is similar evidence for the early militarization of Mesopotamia, though we shall defer consideration of it for a later section of this chapter. What is obvious is that with the birth of civilization we have records of the use of large national armies on a scale far greater than anything we can imagine for prehistoric times. Partly this development was due to the tremendous population explosion brought about by the irrigation and cultivation of the great river valleys. Partly it may be attributed to the political power and authority of the new rulers who were a major by-product of that complex phenomenon, the origins of the state.

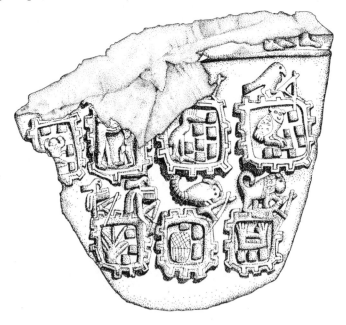

The palette of the Fortresses (late predynastic Egypt) shows animals, which probably represent an alliance, besieging fortified towns. The palette is early evidence of the use of fortifications in Egypt.

A word about scale may help to illustrate the historical significance of these early armies. There is reference in the Old Kingdom to an army of 'many tens of thousands' which most Egyptologists too eagerly dismiss as an exaggeration, but, exaggeration or not, by the time of the New Kingdom (1550–1070 BC) the pharaohs could certainly place an army of 20,000 into the field, as they did early in the thirteenth century BC at the battle of Kadesh. The Hittites countered with an army of 17,000. Accustomed as we are in the twentieth century to wars involving millions of troops, it is easy to forget that throughout most of the history of the Western world, well down into modern times, an army of 20,000 was a major striking force. At the battle of Crécy (1346) Edward III deployed 20,000 men victoriously, and at Agincourt (1415) 6,000 to 7,000 Englishmen defeated a French force of 25,000. In the seventeenth century, during the Thirty Years War, Gustavus Adolphus, the King of Sweden, revolutionized modern warfare with an army of some 20,000. Much later, at the battle of New

The opposite side of the palette of the Fortresses shows the booty of war – cattle, asses, rams and incense trees. On the lower right is the symbol for 'the land of the throw-stick', Libya.

Orleans (1815), 4,000 Americans under General Jackson defeated Major-General Sir Edward Pakenham and 9,000 British troops.[68] Ancient Near Eastern armies were competitive, at least in size, with many major armies of later times, and, after the invention of logistics (organized supply), the armies of Egypt and Mesopotamia could be sent on campaign many hundreds of miles from home base. Before we consider the strategic and tactical use of these military forces, however, it is necessary to examine the new weapons technology made possible by man's discovery of the use of metals.

Metals and Weapons

'We are reluctant to admit that essentially war is the business of killing, though that is the simplest truth in the book.' S.L.A. MARSHALL, 1964

In prehistoric times, perhaps as early as about 6000 BC, in Anatolia at least, Neolithic man began to experiment with the use of copper. Developments were naturally slow, and it was not until the fourth millennium BC that the extraction and smelting of metals yielded a major new technology usually characterized as the Bronze Age. The beginnings of the Bronze Age are roughly contemporary with the appearance of civilization in the Near East, and one of the main features of the new period, metal weapons, made warfare a much more lethal activity than it had been in Neolithic times.

Weapons analysts have usually divided the instruments of offensive attack into three broad categories – long-, intermediate- and short-range firepower. Firepower is an obviously anachronistic concept for ancient weapons, but it is much too useful to abandon simply for the sake of History.[69] If one assumes that firepower, or killing offensive capacity, can be delivered with a spearpoint, an arrow, a javelin, or a sword, even though no gunpowder is used, then the term has a place in ancient warfare. An older and more accurate division of weapons into only two categories – shock weapons, used for striking and thrusting in hand-to-hand combat, and missile weapons for shooting or throwing against the enemy – may still occasionally be found in some discussions of ancient warfare, and we shall use both the modern and the old-fashioned distinctions as they seem appropriate.[70]

Shock – direct, hand-to-hand, body-to-body contact – rarely occurs in present-day warfare despite the romantic portrayal of bayonet charges in World War II movies. The rifle, the machine-gun, the flame-thrower and the hand-grenade, as well as other ingenious devices, have all but eliminated shock weapons, except when one side runs out of ammunition, but ancient warfare was often decided by shock, man directly against man, with the mace or the battle-axe, spears and swords, chariots and cavalry attacks. Intermediate- and long-range weapons, javelins, bows, slings and catapults were normally used for skirmishing at the outset of a battle; they rarely brought an end to conflict. That came only when the opposing armies engaged in shock with one another. Nor should we be misled by the ages-old fascination with long-range superweapons. Throughout history armies that have specialized in shock have often defeated armies relying on intermediate- or long-range firepower.

Man's use of metals transformed the weaponry of shock. Stone maces are very nearly as good as metal ones, although they break more easily on impact, but metal battle-axes are infinitely superior to stone. The brittleness of stone is simply not suitable for sharpened striking edges, but metal not only made such edges possible – it permitted a wide variety of shapes. The introduction of the metal helmet virtually eliminated the mace from the ancient battlefield in favour of the battle-axe which could pierce or cut at least some armour, depending on its quality. To judge from Egyptian and Mesopotamian remains the piercing axe, with its long, thin blade and deep penetrating power, was the preferred weapon.

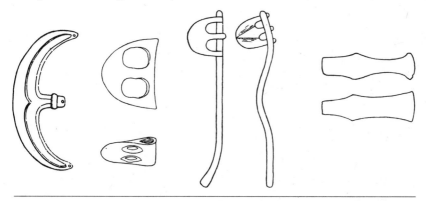

Battle-axes appeared in the ancient Near East in many shapes. Illustrated here are epsilon, eye, and duck-bill axeheads, tang and socket axes, and lugged axeheads.

Ironically it was the invention of the wheel rather than the use of metals that led to the most important new weapon of the Bronze Age, the war chariot.[71] It appeared first in Mesopotamia in the third millennium BC, a thousand years before its introduction into Egypt by the Hyksos. Early Mesopotamians used asses rather than horses to pull it, and the earliest wheels were solid, not spoked. Sometimes notches were carved around the outer rim of the wheel to give it more traction. By the second millennium BC the horse-drawn, spoked, war chariot was the élite striking arm of ancient armies, and it was used primarily as a mobile firing platform rather than as a means of transportation from base to battlefield. It combined speed or mobility with stability, but, depending on the construction, as in a four-wheeled chariot, the greater the stability the less the speed. The more popular, light, two-wheeled chariots of the age of chariot warfare (1700–1200 BC) were fast, but they were more unstable as a firing platform, and they delivered less firepower, unit for unit.

The period also saw the development of the composite bow, a powerful offensive weapon.[72] It was made of wood, animal horn, sinews and glue, required great strength to string, and had an effective range in trained hands of 250–300 yards, greater than that of the medieval English longbow. With the composite bow and the new, metal arrowheads the archer became the premier infantryman of ancient Near Eastern armies, though the ability to close with shock weapons was still generally essential.

Egyptian archers on the practice range (from a New Kingdom tomb painting in Thebes), guided by instructors, use a composite bow (right) and the easier simple bow (left). Specialized training in the Egyptian army was intensive.

A light, two-wheeled Sumerian chariot (c. 2800 BC) drawn by asses. The studded wheels are made from three boards. Since this chariot carried no warrior, and the driver appears unarmed, it must have been used mainly for sending messages, or for ceremonial purposes. Based on a model of a copper original from Tell Agrab.

An early representation (c. 2800 BC) from a Mesopotamian vase of a four-wheeled chariot with horses. This chariot carried two men.

A scene from the 'Standard of Ur', third millennium BC, *shows Sumerian infantrymen in line with pikes and body armour. The bow was not as common in early Mesopotamia as in Egypt. Even the warriors on the four-wheeled chariots used pikes or javelins. Note that the wheels are made of two slabs of wood fastened together with braces.*

Indeed, the importance of shock is best illustrated in the ancient art of Mesopotamia which shows, more than that of Egypt, the role of the spear or pike. Sumerians are depicted in close order advancing with chariot support, carrying the thrusting spear in the manner of the later Greek hoplite phalanx. Metal spearpoints added to their power. The advantages of combining mobility (chariots) and security (pikemen) with short-, intermediate- and long-range firepower (spears, javelins and bows) were recognized early in the ancient Near East, though the Greeks of the classical period were slow to learn the possibilities.

As we have seen, there were undoubtedly forms of personal, defensive armour in prehistoric times, but the Bronze Age saw great strides in that area of military technology. Shields of various designs and construction, plus metal scale armour (the coat of mail), offered at least some protection against the fearsome new weapons. Almost every conceivable variety of shield, from round to figure-of-eight, depending partly on the weapons opponents were expected to use, appeared in the Bronze Age. Helmets underwent many styling changes in response to the appearance of new offensive instruments of death,

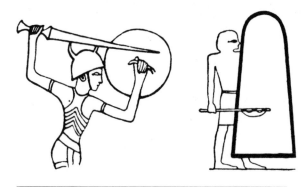

In the ancient Near East shields of many shapes and sizes were designed. The round shield, left, was used by the Sea Peoples. The long shield in the middle is Egyptian, and the 'figure-of-eight' shield is Hittite.

but no helmets of the ancient Near East seem to have covered the entire face, probably because of the hot climate.

One other offensive weapon requires special mention in this survey of the new technology. The use of metal made the fighting sword possible, and it spread rapidly and widely around the Near East. In Neolithic times daggers had been made from stone, but stone was generally too brittle for the longer sword, although there are some surviving examples of stone swords. Bronze made it possible to fashion thrusting and cutting swords, and they appeared in a multiplicity of forms. However, even bronze was not strong enough for a genuinely stout sword with a firm cutting edge, and although swords were common for ceremonial purposes and occasionally for fighting, significant military use of the new weapon required a harder metal and would not come until the development of iron technology.[73]

Out of the new weapons technology of the Bronze Age and the consolidation of the ancient Near Eastern states emerged an organized armaments industry. Wall paintings from Egypt show arsenals for the manufacture of bows, arrows, shields, chariot wheels, and other

In ancient Egypt the pharaohs maintained their own arsenals. Above is a scene from a Middle Kingdom arsenal, and paintings of New Kingdom ones have survived as well. In this scene (from a painting at Beni-Hasan) craftsmen are making bows and arrows.

artifacts of war. Despite the enormous increase in man's war-making capacity, however, Bronze Age warriors faced, as surely as we do today, the great dilemma of military innovation, the so-called 'offence-defence inventive cycle'.[74] The three indispensable ingredients of warfare – mobility, security and firepower – are so interrelated that a change in one requires corresponding changes in the others. A soldier is more mobile in the field if he wears no armour, but he is less secure; he has more firepower if he carries a heavy and immobilizing supply of weapons; if he gains security with heavy armour, he loses both mobility and firepower. Generals of antiquity, including those of the Bronze Age, ignored this cycle at their peril.

The Grand Strategy of Ancient Egypt

'Grand strategy' is an elusive concept. It often shades into simple strategy, and, insofar as purely political and economic considerations impinge on it, its connections with military planning sometimes seem remote.[75] Nevertheless, for our purposes, conceding that nothing is ever as simple as simple definitions make it appear, we can regard grand strategy as the overall plan for defending the security and integrity of the state, including–when necessary or desirable the expansion of territory over which the state rules. Diplomatic and economic means as well as military may be used in the implementation of a state's grand strategy.

Military grand strategists from the time of Napoleon to the end of World War II have generally emphasized the need to maintain a

44

powerful, offensive, striking army designed to win decisive victories in major conflicts. This 'offensive' approach to national security is usually associated with the great German military theoretician, Clausewitz, although he is merely the best known of a large group including Jomini, du Picq, Marshal Foch, and Liddell Hart.[76]

Offensive notions, however, have not always dominated grand strategy. Since 1945, because of the development of powerful new weapons, grand strategists have emphasized the need to avoid major conflicts and to accept an almost permanent state of 'limited' wars and diplomatic conflict in which the possession of a deadly, nuclear arsenal is used for psychological rather than for directly military purposes. Recently Edward N. Luttwak in a brilliant book, *The Grand Strategy of the Roman Empire*, has shown that Roman imperial grand strategy, though highly militaristic, tended to be more defensive than offensive and that to understand it properly one must break from the influence of Clausewitz.[77]

In this context, the grand strategy of ancient Egypt is particularly interesting, because over the centuries it changed from defensive militarism in the Old Kingdom to aggressive, offensive imperialism in the New Kingdom. As we have seen earlier in this chapter, the first pharaoh of the united Egypt seized control in a brutal display of military force, smashing Lower Egypt with his army and taking possession of it. But once the internal disposition of Egyptian affairs was settled by force, the pharaohs of the Old Kingdom pursued a defensive rather than an offensive grand strategy. This does not mean, contrary to what Egyptologists have so often said, that the Old Kingdom required no standing army. As great an authority as Sir Alan Gardiner, while stating the traditional view that the peaceful Egypt of the Old Kingdom required only a 'police force' rather than a standing army, conceded that the description was based on an argument from silence. In fact, although evidence from the Old Kingdom is sparse, it is not silent, and it suggests that Egyptian grand strategy was militaristic even though it was essentially defensive.

Studies by other Egyptologists, if they have not yet found their way into the standard texts, show that the pharaohs of the Old Kingdom maintained a standing army and a system of forts and were capable of conducting reasonably complicated sieges against fortified sites.[78] That is the clear implication of the early palettes, and it is reinforced by the ruins of a rough stone wall at Buhen (Fourth Dynasty), a salient gatehouse at Hierakonpolis, and a siege scene of the Fifth Dynasty at Dishâsha which shows soldiers using battering poles and scaling ladders. Siege operations are much too complicated for a simple 'police force', and literary documents also strongly imply the existence of a standing army.[79] The most famous is a biography of Weni, a high-ranking Egyptian official of the Old Kingdom, which suggests that in addition to the regular troops and a body of Nubian mercenaries the pharaohs had a system of conscription that produced, as the occasion required, armies of 'many tens of thousands'.[80] There was certainly also a system for calling up local militia which presumably had some military training.[81] Despite evidence for occasional wars in the Sinai and even beyond, as well as activity along the Nubian frontier, it appears that the pharaohs of the period pursued a grand strategy of preclusive security, were content with the defence of the Nile civilization, and relied on a small standing army and on the natural geographical isolation of Egypt for frontier defence.

Virtually nothing is known about the tactical organization of the military forces of the Old Kingdom, but hieroglyphic texts do reveal the title of general, of 'overseer of soldiers', and for Dynasties I–VII there is some information on at least fifteen Egyptian generals.[82] We know the command assignments of about ten of these officers, many of whom were active in the Sinai, but expeditions south into Nubia were conducted by 'caravan leaders' who must have been professionals in the style of fighting required on the Nubian frontier. Ironically the Weni who commanded the 'many tens of thousands' was a civil administrator undoubtedly appointed to the task to manage the formidable problems of supply for a large army. In addition in this period there was an 'overseer of the two arsenals' and an 'overseer of desert blockhouses and royal fortresses', sometimes also called 'overseer of the affairs of the fortresses'. The fortresses certainly guarded the flanks of the Delta and the Nubian frontier, while the blockhouses stretched up the Nile to protect against sporadic attacks by desert people down the wadis into the valley.

When the Old Kingdom collapsed around 2150 BC in a surge of anarchy and feudalism, there followed a period of chaos (The First Intermediate Period, *c.* 2150–2040 BC) in which the nomarchs or governors in Egypt raised private armies, probably based on the local militia and the national system of conscription applied regionally. Out of the turmoil emerged the pharaohs of the Middle Kingdom (*c.*

2050–1640 BC), based at Thebes in Upper Egypt, who restored order and adopted a new grand strategy for the Egyptian state while they reorganized the army. Generally the Middle Kingdom was even more militaristic than the Old, and the new army forged by the pharaohs of the Twelfth Dynasty was much more professional.

Although the rulers of the Middle Kingdom were forced to acquiesce in the private armies of the great nomarchs, they raised a national standing army strong enough to restrain private wars, and they were able to deploy the armies of their barons (nomarchs) alongside the national army as the occasion required.[83] Recruitment officers spread over the land claiming one man in a hundred within the provinces for the pharaoh's army. There was a 'general of Upper and Lower Egypt', or a 'generalissimo', to whom the regular generals of the state army reported. The texts reveal another new officer, 'commander of the shock troops', who probably controlled assault units. Finally, a kind of Praetorian Guard of 'retainers' (which served as a palace guard in peacetime and as an élite corps under the pharaoh in war) was organized in the Middle Kingdom.

Military clerks appear in abundance, and perhaps an organized intelligence service developed, since one general has the title 'Master of the Secrets of the King in the Army'. Terms for 'company' or 'regiment' and for 'garrison troops' are found in the texts, and the army itself seems to have been divided into two corps consisting of the 'young men', who were organized into two sub-units, the 'recruits' and the 'warriors', and a corps of shock troops. The 'recruits' were conscripts, but the 'warriors' and the shock troops were certainly professional soldiers.[84] Though precise details of the tactical organization of Middle Kingdom armies are lacking, it is obvious that military specialization underwent rapid development and increased to a remarkable extent the tactical flexibility of Egyptian generals.

With this new army the pharaohs of the Middle Kingdom embarked on an innovative grand strategy for the defence of the frontiers of Egypt. It is possible, and perhaps probable, that the troubled First Intermediate Period witnessed a decline in frontier defences in the northeast and that marauders from Palestine, the so-called Asiatic Sandpeople, occasionally threatened the Delta. In any event the pharaohs of the age abandoned the system of preclusive security, in which the frontiers of Egypt had constituted a first and last line of defence, and marched with their armies at least as far as Shechem in

Samaria, where they followed a strategy of search and destroy, knocking out the strongholds of the Asiatic nomads. How far north they went is disputed, but it is possible that they reached the mouth of the Orontes. Significantly the pharaohs apparently regarded these excursions as primarily strategic rather than imperialistic, since there is no evidence that any attempt was made to garrison or annex Palestinian territory, although the lure of booty may occasionally have drawn them into the region. They did strengthen their fortifications at the isthmus of Suez with the 'Walls of the Prince' (a system of forts rather than walls), but they clearly treated this perimeter as a last line of defence and were prepared to advance hundreds of miles beyond it with their armies to assure the security of Egypt.[85]

In the south, where the danger of Nubian attack was an ever-present threat, the Egyptians moved from the First to the Second Cataract of the Nile during the Middle Kingdom. Their strategy in this area differed somewhat from that in the northeast. Here they had a last line of defence at the First Cataract, represented partly by a massive wall that stretched for four miles between the southern and northern landing places on the cataract, protecting the overland road where the Nile was obstructed.[86] From the First Cataract to the Second there were at least fourteen fortresses and seven more within the forty-mile course of the Second Cataract. These structures were large and had a purely military purpose; the pharaohs of the Middle Kingdom made no attempt to colonize the territory between the cataracts. Strategy on the southern frontier involved a classic defence-in-depth perimeter between the First and Second Cataracts, with reasonably strong determination to prevent penetration of the first line of defence at the Second Cataract.

In general the grand strategy of the Egyptian Middle Kingdom was less expansionistic than historians have realized. In the northeast it was based upon holding the frontiers of the Old Kingdom by strengthening the fortifications and using them as a base for large-scale search and destroy missions by their mobile army in Palestine. In the south the pharaohs also accepted the Old Kingdom frontier of the First Cataract but strengthened it by extending a series of forts to the Second Cataract and creating a militarized zone where the Egyptian army controlled the river and the countryside and, based on the First Cataract, was in a much stronger position to defend the southern frontier. To be sure, booty from Palestine and the gold of Nubia made both strategies remunerative as well as militarily sound. This diversified grand strategy served the Middle Kingdom well and resulted in a period of peace, stability and prosperity.

Egypt was toppled, however, at the end of the Middle Kingdom by the appearance of the mysterious and fearsome Hyksos whose arrival inaugurated the Second Intermediate Period (1640–1550 BC). They gained control of Lower Egypt, and the period of their predominance was regarded by later Egyptians as a great humiliation. They seem to have come into the Delta from the east where late in the Middle Kingdom there must have been a decline in frontier defences, but there are many unanswered questions about the Hyksos, and for our purposes it is sufficient to note that their contribution to the military history of ancient Egypt was enormous. They introduced the war chariot, which would soon become the primary offensive striking instrument of the Egyptian army, and several new weapons and fortification procedures.[87]

In the sixteenth century BC the founder of the Eighteenth Dynasty, Ahmose, drove the Hyksos from the Delta and launched the New Kingdom of Egyptian History. Under Ahmose and his successors, particularly Thutmose III and Ramesses II, the New Kingdom abandoned the defensive grand strategy of earlier periods, and the pharaohs deployed an army that regularly reached into Syria and Ethiopia. Partly this was the result, as Egyptologists have argued, of

Eighteenth-dynasty Egyptian troops in Ethiopia (Punt) are led in column (or file) by their officer. The file leader carries a bow-case. The assistant leader (at the rear of the file) keeps the men in order. All the soldiers (except the officer) are armed with spear and battle-axe.

49

the major military reorganization of Theban rulers provoked by the Hyksos presence in the Delta and inspired to a considerable extent by innovations introduced by the Hyksos. Simple imperialism undoubtedly also played a role in Egyptian policy, but the main cause of Egyptian aggression in the Near East and up to the Fourth Cataract in the south was the realization that the grand strategy of the Middle Kingdom was no longer appropriate for the new military conditions now prevailing.

While pharaohs of the Middle Kingdom could safely rely on a strategy of search and destroy behind the 'Walls of the Prince' at Suez, in the New Kingdom Egypt faced far stronger opponents in Syria-Palestine. The Asiatic Sandpeople were replaced in the area by large and powerful kingdoms, such as that of the Hurrians of Mitanni, and the Hittite Empire in Anatolia supported an army large and mobile enough to represent a genuine threat in Syria to Egypt's efforts to dominate that zone. With the emergence of other powerful states in the Near East, diplomacy began to play an important role in the grand strategies of all the competing nations. As a result the Egyptian pharaohs were forced to maintain a much larger and more mobile army for use beyond Suez and to develop a system of allies, or client kings, simply to guarantee the military integrity of the Nile. The domination of the Hyksos had shown Egyptians that easterners were a genuine threat to their civilization. Equally in the south the disruptions of the Hyksos period had led to the loss of territory between the Second and First Cataracts and to the renewal of the Nubian threat.

Thutmose III (1479–1425) was the greatest of the conquering pharaohs, and he did more than any other ruler to establish a new grand strategy for Egypt. Earlier Thutmose I (1504–1492) had advanced with Egyptian armies to the Euphrates, and even earlier than that Ahmose had reasserted Egyptian control in the south, but conditions in both areas remained unsettled. Hatshepsut (1473–1458), regent during Thutmose III's minority, was more concerned with domestic affairs during her reign than with foreign adventures, and Egypt's northeastern frontier was threatened by a coalition of the princes of Palestine under the leadership of the King of Kadesh. Thutmose III, when he acceded to full power in 1458 BC, moved out with his army, and in a great battle at Megiddo defeated the king and stormed the city; but during the course of his reign he was forced to lead about fifteen expeditions into Syria-Palestine. Later Ramesses II (1290–1224) would duplicate Thutmose's achievements on the field of battle.

The grand strategy of the New Kingdom broke sharply from the military traditions of the Old and Middle Kingdoms as the Egyptian pharaohs relied almost exclusively on mobile armies and foreign alliances rather than on fortifications and defensive perimeters for the maintenance of their hegemony in Syria-Palestine. During the age of the Hyksos, fortifications in the south had been lost to the Nubians, and, when Egyptian armies returned to the area in the New Kingdom, they found them destroyed and cluttered with sand and garbage.[88] As they moved up to the Fourth Cataract, they built only a few new, defensive fortresses, relying instead on the size and mobility of their army for defence. Even in Syria-Palestine there were rarely 'permanent' garrisons. One interesting feature of the New Kingdom is that grand strategy became a matter for debate within the court as some pharaohs, who could be called 'doves', attempted to return Egypt to its more isolationist tradition. The 'hawks' were more often in the ascendant, but inconsistency made their aggressive grand strategy less effective over the long run than it might otherwise have been.

Notwithstanding frequent controversies between 'hawks' and 'doves', the army of the New Kingdom was one of the greatest and most efficient military forces in the history of the world, thoroughly professional in spirit, though conscripts were often used, with a command structure and system of tactical organization that make the armies of classical Greece look puny in comparison. Much has been written on this army (especially by Alan Richard Schulman, *Military Rank, Title, and Organization in the Egyptian New Kingdom* (1964)), and the description that follows will necessarily focus only on the major features, but they should be sufficient to show the remarkable developments in warfare in the Bronze Age since prehistoric times, and to reveal as well why the pharaohs of the New Kingdom were so confident in their field armies that they could neglect defensive fortifications.[89]

The pharaoh often served as commander-in-chief, almost always in the great campaigns, although other generals were occasionally in command of independent, minor operations. The pharaoh's vizier acted as war minister, and the generals of the Egyptian army formed a

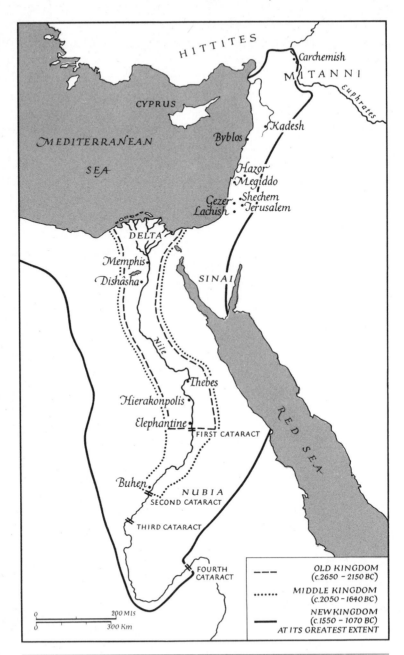

Map of ancient Egypt.

council of war, probably at home and definitely in the field, in much the same manner as Alexander the Great was later served by his high-ranking Macedonian officers. Early in the New Kingdom the field army consisted of divisions of about 5,000 men, including contingents of chariotry and infantry, though the number may have varied depending on the occasion. The divisions clearly had tactical independence, with their own names drawn from the religion of Egypt – the division of Amon, for example – and their own standards. The commanding officer of a division had twenty company commanders (the 'standard bearers'), and each company consisted of 250 men. Companies were divided into units of fifty men each under platoon leaders known as 'the great ones of the fifty'.

Ancillary units were probably incorporated into an Egyptian army division (or 'host') under the commanding general. An 'assault-officer' seems to have outranked the company commanders while the 'commander of chariot warriors' was apparently equal in rank to the 'standard bearer' of the company. Ordinarily mercenary foreign troops under an Egyptian officer served alongside native Egyptians in the armies of the New Kingdom. It is likely that by the time of Ramesses II the chariots were organized as a separate arm independent of the infantry.

The Egyptian army of the New Kingdom was a highly organized, tactically flexible, striking force, and under Ramesses II we know that four divisions, about 20,000 men altogether, were put into the field at Kadesh. A reflection of the national burdens associated with Egypt's aggressive grand strategy is that for at least one pharaoh of the late New Kingdom (Ramesses III) recruitment officers demanded one man in ten from the native population (excluding temple employees) compared with the standard of one in a hundred during the Middle Kingdom. Although there is no way of knowing the size of the regional armies of the nomarchs in the Middle Kingdom, it is nevertheless certain that conscription became an ever greater demand on the manpower reserves of New Kingdom Egypt.

Strategy and Tactics: the Battles of Megiddo and Kadesh

It remains now to see how the Egyptian army actually functioned in the field, and fortunately there are records of two great Bronze Age battles that are complete enough to permit a reconstruction of the strategy and tactics of the New Kingdom in the specific context of historical strife: the battle of Megiddo (1458 BC) and the battle of Kadesh (1285 BC). Both battles were fought before the time of the Trojan War of the Late Bronze Age Aegean, and contemporary Egyptian accounts, literary and pictorial, make a reliable analysis of the strategic and tactical complexities of Bronze Age warfare much less difficult than the task of determining what the poet Homer knew about Mycenaean fighting.

The terms 'strategy' and 'tactics' are so commonly used and misused that we should pause for a moment to consider their meaning before examining their application on the ancient field of battle. Military analysts know that the distinctions between strategy and tactics are often slippery, that they are sometimes so interrelated that they become blurred.[90] Still, for reasons of clarity, the word 'strategy' is normally used to refer to the military plan for the conduct of a war or a campaign, while 'tactics' is reserved for battle plans. It is probably impossible to eliminate some of the abuses to which the words have been subjected; 'Fabian tactics of delay' should more properly be called the 'strategy of exhaustion', because the plan of Fabius Maximus for dealing with Hannibal was much more strategic than tactical; likewise 'search and destroy' is a strategic rather than a tactical approach to warfare, as General Westmoreland and Admiral U.S. Grant Sharp well knew, though the expression, 'search and destroy tactics' gained wide currency in the Vietnam era.[91] Popular misuse of the terms merely adds to the difficulty of employing them properly, but we shall try to reserve strategy for 'game plan' and tactics for the 'plays', to rely on the common (and often inappropriate) analogy between war and American football.

In 1458 BC, in the first year of his reign after the end of Hatshepsut's regency, Thutmose III decided to deal directly with growing problems in Syria-Palestine that threatened the integrity of Egypt's northeastern frontier, so long neglected by Hatshepsut.[92] Earlier the King of Kadesh apparently hoped to take advantage of the change in leadership in Egypt by moving south from the Orontes in alliance with local princes, and by seizing Megiddo in Palestine which dominated the main line of communication overland between Egypt and Mesopotamia at a critical point in the Fertile Crescent. His offensive strategy was to penetrate the Egyptian sphere of influence and secure military control

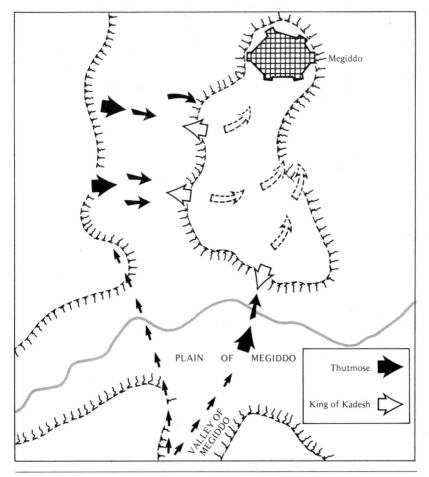

The battle of Megiddo, 1458 BC.

of Megiddo, a strongly fortified site where he could maintain his advantageous strategic position with defensive tactics. Thutmose countered by advancing northwards rapidly with his army in the hope of achieving both strategic and tactical surprise and defeating the King of Kadesh with offensive tactics.

That speed was part of Thutmose's strategy is revealed by the fact that it took only nine days for the army to move from Egypt to Gaza, which would have required an average march of about fifteen miles per day, a pace that rivals Alexander's marches and demands a sophisticated logistical support system. When Thutmose reached the vicinity of Megiddo, he summoned his war council to discuss the final approach. There were three possible routes. One was through a narrow and steep pass leading directly to Megiddo, and the other two were less difficult routes that wound around to approach Megiddo either from the north or the south.

Thutmose's generals believed that the narrow, direct approach had to be avoided at all costs, because it would be necessary for the Egyptians to move in line of column against a defending force waiting for them in line of battle. 'What is it like', they said,

to go on this road which becomes so narrow? It is reported that the foe is there, waiting on the outside, while they are becoming more numerous. Will not horse have to go after horse, and the army and the people similarly? Will the vanguard of us be fighting while the rear guard is waiting here [behind] unable to fight?[93]

Thutmose decided, however, that to avoid giving the enemy an advantage in morale, he had to move directly against their position: 'They will say, these enemies whom Re abominates: "Has His Majesty set out on another road because he has become afraid of us?" – so they will speak.'

The pharaoh's decision was a wise one, and it was possibly based on reports from his intelligence service. Apparently the King of Kadesh expected the Egyptians to avoid the direct route for the same sound, tactical reasons advanced by the Egyptian generals in the war council, and he had despatched units of his defending force to guard the other approaches. As Thutmose neared the end of his chosen path, his generals urged him to halt the advance to permit the rear of the column to move up so that the entire army could attack the enemy:

Let our victorious lord listen to us this time, and let our lord guard for us the rear of his army and his people. When the rear of the army comes forth for us into the open, then we shall fight against these foreigners, then we shall not trouble our hearts about the rear of an army.

Thutmose understood the need to concentrate his forces and to attack in massed formation in line of battle, so this time he deferred to the advice of his generals. Because the King of Kadesh was uninformed about the Egyptian tactical plan and had assumed a tactically defensive position around Megiddo, Thutmose executed the extremely difficult manoeuvre of deploying his troops from line of column into line of battle without interference from his opponent. He divided his army into three battle groups, one to attack the defenders in the north, another in the south, and the main group under the pharaoh's personal command to strike directly at the centre of the enemy army in front of Megiddo. The battle began at dawn, and the Egyptian army drove back the defending forces all along their line into the protection of the walled city. The rout was so decisive that the inhabitants closed their gates and used ropes made of clothing to haul the defenders back over the walls.

Clearly Thutmose should have pressed his advantage and stormed the city in its state of panic, but unfortunately his army began to loot the camps outside the city in search of booty. The official record reveals a recognition that the army failed to maintain military 'mission and aim': 'Now if only His Majesty's army had not given up their hearts to capturing the possessions of the enemy, they could have captured Megiddo at this time.' Yigael Yadin argues that this was 'an occurrence which is typical of many undisciplined and untrained troops,' but his judgment is too harsh. As John Keegan has shown in *The Face of Battle*, looting was a problem for highly organized armies of medieval and modern times, and in antiquity the vaunted Persian army against Alexander at Gaugamela fell victim to the temptation at even greater cost than to the pharaoh's army at Megiddo. The principle of maintenance of mission and aim is easier to state than to apply in the field, and Julius Caesar was more than once exasperated by one of the most highly trained and disciplined forces in military history when his legions ignored mission and aim. At Megiddo the result was that Thutmose had to settle for a formal siege during which the city fell after seven months. Despite the lost opportunity to bring the war to a rapid conclusion Egyptian tactical success outside the city ultimately enabled the pharaoh to win the war.

About 200 years later, in the 1280s BC, Ramesses II conducted a similar campaign to the north, this time against the city of Kadesh on the Orontes and the King of the Hittites who had moved from Asia Minor into the area with an army of 17,000.[94] Ramesses' army of 20,000 advanced all the way to Kadesh in a stunningly rapid march that took only a month. His strategic goal was to end Hittite interference in the Egyptian sphere of influence in Syria by striking far away from his home base in Egypt to defeat and destroy the enemy's main force in the field.

He arrived to within fifteen miles of Kadesh at a hill overlooking the city near Shabtuna, encamped for the night and departed the next morning, presumably hoping to seize Kadesh by the end of the day. The Egyptian army was divided into four divisions of 5,000 men each named after the gods Amon, Ra, Ptah, and Sutekh and consisted of chariots, archers, spearmen and axe-wielders. Ramesses crossed the Orontes near Shabtuna, and at that time two 'deserters' from the Hittites, who claimed that the enemy was still far away and had not yet arrived at Kadesh, were brought to the pharaoh. In fact they were spies sent by the Hittite king Muwatallis. Upon receipt of this information Ramesses moved ahead with his bodyguard to establish a camp northwest of the city while his army advanced from the south in a line of column several miles long.

As Ramesses sat on a golden throne in his camp awaiting the arrival of his army, two captured Hittite scouts revealed under torture that a great force of Hittites was hidden to the east of Kadesh. By this time the leading division of Ra had approached from behind near the southeast of Kadesh. Before Ramesses knew what was happening, the Hittites crossed the Orontes from the southeast and hit the exposed flank of the division of Ra with their chariots which were heavier than the Egyptian ones, three-man rather than two-man vehicles. The division of Ra broke in panic and fled up against the division of Amon which as a result also seems to have fallen into confusion and incipient flight.

According to the Egyptian account, at this point Ramesses personally mounted his chariot and rushed forward by himself into the thick of the foe. Surrounded by 2,500 enemy chariots, he singlehandedly defeated the Hittites. In fact, though the exploit is often dismissed as sheer fable on the part of the 'braggart warrior', it is likely that Ramesses rallied his troops by an amazing display of personal bravery on the field just as Caesar did later on more than one occasion.[95] The heavier Hittite chariots must have made pursuit difficult, and with their lighter chariots Ramesses' forces were able to escape some of the devastating effect of the Hittite attack. Because of their greater manoeuvrability it was easier for them to regroup than the Hittites realized. At least some of the Hittite troops had begun to loot the Egyptian camp, but the last-minute arrival of the pharaoh's mercenary troops who had been summoned earlier from the coast caught the Hittites by surprise. This permitted Ramesses to regroup

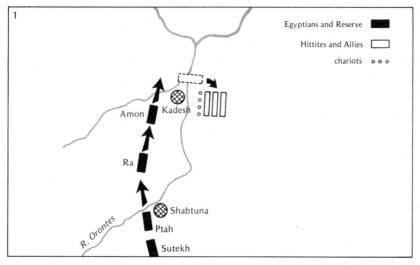

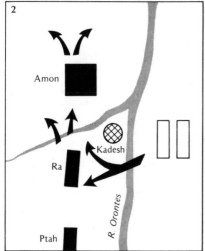

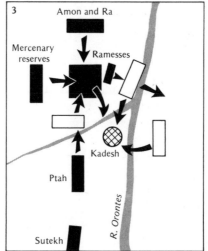

The battle of Kadesh, 1285 BC – three phases.

the divisions of Amon and Ra and drive the Hittites, now north of the city, back across the Orontes.[96]

Near nightfall the division of Ptah came up from the south, and the Hittites decided to move into Kadesh for protection. The division of Sutekh did not appear in time to participate in the battle. Under these circumstances, so far north from his base, Ramesses was not strong enough to conduct a siege against such a powerful force behind firm walls, and he withdrew his army and accepted a strategic defeat, or at least a stalemate, despite his tactical success, and Egypt and the Hittites later negotiated an alliance or non-aggression pact. When Wellington said after Waterloo that his victory was 'a near run thing', he was correct, but Ramesses more than 3,000 years earlier had come closer to the edge of defeat.

The strategic and tactical significance of these New Kingdom battles, especially if they are considered to be representative of the warfare of their period, is staggering. The size of the armies, their tactical organization, the use of chariots and other specialized units and the quality of generalship all show a degree of military sophistication that would be hard to match in many later historical periods. If one makes an allowance for the technological limitations of the Bronze Age, it is not difficult to conceive that the quality of generalship found in some of the Egyptian pharaohs was competitive with the best generalship of any period down to modern times.

This may best be illustrated by some interesting parallels between Waterloo and Kadesh. In both cases an army moving up from the south hoped to destroy a northern force, and, just as Napoleon intended to have dinner in Brussels after defeating Wellington, so Ramesses undoubtedly expected to have his evening meal in Kadesh. They were both disappointed in their dinner plans, but here the resemblance between Napoleon and Ramesses ends. Wellington was at or near the front throughout the battle of Waterloo, apparently indifferent to the risk of personal injury, but Napoleon stayed some distance behind his army watching the action through his field-glasses, angry because Marshal Ney had started the cavalry attack too soon, yet unable to prevent it because he was so far removed from the fighting.[97] At Kadesh Ramesses threw himself into the thick of the battle and rallied his troops while the Hittite king Muwatallis stayed behind on the eastern side of the Orontes and was not present to hold his troops to mission and aim after their initial and highly successful assault on the flanks of Ramesses' advancing column. The last-minute arrival of Blücher at Waterloo is reminiscent of the rescue of Ramesses by his mercenary units. Napoleon had no fortified Kadesh to fall back upon, and he was destroyed; Muwatallis had selected a site so strong that even in defeat he could avoid destruction.

Babylonian Warfare

Although developments in warfare in southern Mesopotamia from the fourth to the second millennium BC are every bit as fascinating and important as those in Egypt, we shall survey them only briefly here, emphasizing the contrasts with Egyptian warfare, because in the following chapter on the Assyrians and Persians it will be possible to describe Mesopotamian warfare at the highest stage of its evolution. Historians have traditionally argued that geography made Egypt more secure and peaceful than Mesopotamia, which was exposed to frequent invasions and upheavals. Geography was important, but its chief significance was that the peculiar stretch of land along the tube of the Nile was for the most part not urbanized, and the state that emerged there was a nation free from the rivalries of numerous, competitive city-states. Early Mesopotamia, especially in the Sumerian period of the fourth and third millennia BC, rarely benefited from large territorial organization under a single leader. Warfare was more frequent and strategically less decisive.

The chariot, which appeared much earlier in Mesopotamia than in Egypt, was widely used as early as 3000–2500 BC, and the highly mobile two-man, two-wheeled chariot of the Egyptian New Kingdom did not appear before centuries of development and refinement had taken place in Mesopotamia.[98] The war chariots of Sumer were heavier, larger, and slower, and the four-wheeled chariots transported four men: the driver, the warrior, and two shield-bearers to protect the warrior. Warriors were armed with javelins and spears rather than with the bow. The chariots were less mobile and delivered less firepower than those of the second millennium, and they were probably not used tactically in the same way. Later chariots could be deployed for shock attacks against the flank of an enemy, whereas the earlier ones drawn by asses were difficult to turn sharply and had to be brought much closer to the enemy formation to deliver effective fire. With the development in later times of the spoked wheel and the rear axle, giving rise to the two-man chariot drawn by horses, the war chariot became a much more fearsome weapon.

The bow seems to have been used more frequently in Egypt and at an earlier date than in Mesopotamia. Even the Sumerian infantryman was normally armed only with javelins and spears, with daggers and swords for closing with the enemy, though the battle-axe was also an important weapon. Akkadians under Sargon the Great (2334–2279 BC) introduced the bow, but it fell into disuse again until the unification of Lower Mesopotamia in the First Dynasty of Babylon by Hammurabi (1792–1750 BC). Siege warfare and fortification became a more important branch of military science in Mesopotamia, though it was highly developed in Egypt too, mainly because the capture of towns or cities was a common strategic goal. Frontier defences as such, other than walled cities, show none of the organization of Middle and New Kingdom frontiers.

Biblical Warfare

In Palestine during the period of the Judges and the united monarchy of Saul, David and Solomon (*c.* 1200–900 BC) warfare was a standard feature of life, and, because biblical accounts of the fighting have survived, much is known of the various struggles with the Philistines and the Canaanites.[99] The Song of Deborah in the Book of Judges 5 tells of the campaign to control the Valley of Jezreel against a Canaanite army of horse-drawn chariot squadrons. The tribal armies of Israel, called up only in such a military emergency, seized the high ground and fell on the chariots as they became bogged down in the floodwaters of the River Kishon. Gideon's efforts to secure control of the eastern half of the valley (Judges 6–8) with a picked force of 300 men against the Midianites in their camp illustrate Israelite mastery of the tactics of surprise and planning in a military situation that resembled guerrilla warfare. Israelite forces of the period of the Judges were unusually varied, containing units of archers, spear and javelin men, and – significantly – slingers, but they lacked war chariots which were probably introduced into Israelite warfare by David, although some modern historians believe that Saul was the first Israelite leader to use them.

Saul's method of warfare differed little from that of the period of the Judges. Deploying small forces and relying on ambushes, he struggled with the Philistines from his fortified camp at Gibeah. In the Valley of Elah he won a decisive victory over his enemy when both sides agreed to stake all on a duel of champions, David and Goliath, but after David became king, Israelite warfare changed fundamentally. He took Jerusalem from the Jebusites by storm and used it as a base against the Philistines, the Edomites, the Ammonites and the Moabites. In establishing a strong strategic base he gave up the guerrilla tactics of his predecessor and could no longer rely on surprise since his movements could be more easily watched. This forced him to develop a large regular army, supplemented when necessary by the old tribal militia. The new, mobile army which also included mercenaries served Israel well under both David and Solomon. Under Solomon there was an extensive expansion of Israelite chariotry and the construction of fortified bases at Hazor, Megiddo, and Gezer. The fortifications were solid and architecturally highly advanced, and Solomon was able to station contingents of his army in critical points along the main lines of communication outside Jerusalem for the strategic defence of his kingdom. Finally, the division of the kingdom after Solomon created an altogether new strategic problem as Assyrians and Persians confronted the Jews with military forces too large to oppose with any chance of success.

In looking back over the entire period of Bronze Age warfare certain features stand out emphatically. To return to one of the themes of the first chapter, it is obvious that the techniques of organized warfare had been developed and were ready for extensive application at the beginning of historic times as man crossed the boundary of the prehistoric world into civilization. The societies of the Tigris-Euphrates and Nile valleys were forged from the outset in war, and the skill of war was one of the most important distinguishing characteristics of the early civilizations. By the end of the period large armies of 20,000 men, intricately organized on a tactical basis with an elaborate and effective command structure, supported by an efficient logistical system and armaments industry, guided by generals showing an impressive grasp of strategy and tactics, competed with one another around the eastern coast of the Mediterranean and into Mesopotamia. Organized reconnaissance services, commissariat, tactically specialized units of heavy and light infantry, and chariot squadrons attained a stage of sophistication and long-range importance, as we shall see, that are all too often ignored by historians who believe that the history of ancient warfare began with Greek heavy infantry, the so-called hoplite phalanx.

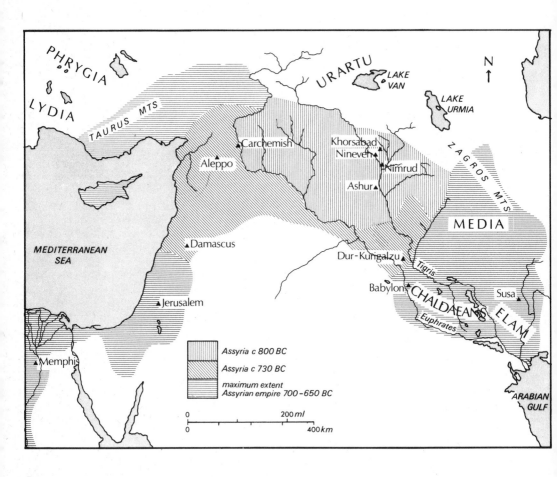

Map of Assyrian conquests: with their iron army, the Assyrians
created the world's first empire.

Chapter Three
Assyria and Persia: the Age of Iron

'In the most polite and powerful nations, genius of every kind has displayed itself about the same period; and the age of science has generally been the age of military virtue and success.' EDWARD GIBBON, *The Decline and Fall of the Roman Empire*

Although some would challenge the inclusion of Assyria among 'the most polite' nations of the world, historians have emphasized Assyria's role in ancient Mesopotamia as a unifier and preserver of culture and as a dynamically innovative creator of new lines of human achievement. These new lines include warfare as well as architecture and sculpture. If the formula, Assyria is to Babylon as Rome is to Greece, has as much validity as it does widespread acquiescence, it suggests the need to look carefully at Assyrian military policy and practice for decisive changes in the art of war.[100]

Before the rise of Assyria, Mesopotamia's city-state structure denied the inhabitants of the Tigris-Euphrates valleys the advantages of national unity so clearly represented in ancient Egypt. Only twice, and then briefly, had Mesopotamia been organized under a single, powerful leader – first, in the twenty-fourth century BC under the Akkadian, Sargon I, and later, in Babylon in the eighteenth century BC under the famous law-giver, Hammurabi. In the 400 years after that prince the mysterious and relatively weak Kassites maintained a feeble hold on Babylon, although the Hittites at least once actually took the city temporarily, while in northern Mesopotamia the Hurrians in the kingdom of Mitanni became the dominant power. Assur, the earliest capital of Assyria, was situated in mid-Mesopotamia on the Tigris, and for most of the second millennium BC Assyrian kings were vassals of Babylon, occasionally of Mitanni. Beginning around 1350 BC, however, Assyrian rulers grew stronger while Babylonian and Hurrian kings became weaker. In the twelfth century Elamites from Iran toppled the Kassites in Babylon, and power shifted to Assyria under

Tiglath Pileser I (1114–1076), who defeated the Hurrians and sent armies all the way to Phoenicia as well as south to Babylon.[101]

When Tiglath Pileser I died, Assyria suffered an eclipse of power that rapidly turned into deep disintegration as nomadic tribesmen, mountaineers and the so-called Sea Peoples threw the eastern Mediterranean into a Dark Age of invasions lasting roughly from 1200 to 900 BC. In the Aegean Minoan, Mycenaean and Hittite civilizations were destroyed, and Egypt was drastically weakened. The entire Fertile Crescent became a power vacuum in which the smaller nations of the Philistines, the Canaanites and the Israelites were able to achieve a kind of independence and vitality that would not have been possible in the earlier days of the great powers. Finally, out of the chaos the Assyrian state, which had clung tenaciously to a stretch of territory along the Tigris about 100 miles long, reemerged around 900 BC as a major nation and began to create an empire that eventually absorbed much of the ancient Near East.

The rise of Assyria coincided with one of man's great technological advances. The Iron Age began around 1200 BC, and it is likely, to judge from the Bible, that the Philistines had an initial advantage over the Hebrews in the period 1200 to 1000 BC because of their knowledge of the new iron technology.[102]

There was no smith to be found in all the land of Israel, for the Philistines had said to themselves, 'The Hebrews might make swords or spears!' So all Israel would go down to the Philistines to repair any of their plowshares, mattocks, axes, or sickles. The price was a paim for plowshares and mattocks and a third of a shekel for picks and axes or setting an ox-goad. So at the time of the battle of Michmash neither sword nor spear was available to any of the soldiers who were with Saul and Jonathan – only Saul and Jonathan had them.

I SAMUEL 13: 19–22; *Anchor Bible* translation

Although iron had been used for jewelry and ceremonial weapons before 1200 BC, it was pure wrought iron, softer than bronze, because ancient smiths did not learn how to generate the heat needed to melt iron for casting (1530°C.). But eventually, through trial and error, they discovered how to introduce carbon into red-hot iron to produce carburized, or steel-like iron. The process is complicated and not fully understood. It involves heating and reheating, or tempering, to reduce brittleness. By 900 ancient Near Eastern smiths had developed the procedures, and Assyria armed her warriors with the advanced weapons of the new iron technology.[103]

Iron rapidly became synonymous with brute strength. The Behemoth of Job 40:18 had bones 'as hard as hammered iron', and a Babylonian Wisdom text says, 'Woman is a sharp iron dagger that cuts a man's throat'.[104] One of the most important features of the change from the Bronze Age to the Iron Age is that iron may be found in abundance around the earth while tin, especially alluvial tin, necessary for turning copper into bronze, is relatively rare. The new weapons were better, and no metals shortage could deplete an arsenal.

Assyrian Grand Strategy

'The Assyrian came down like the wolf on the fold.
And his cohorts were gleaming in purple and gold.'
LORD BYRON, 'The Destruction of Sennacherib'

We can excuse the poet's reference to gold, representing as it does the imagery of wealth, rapaciousness, might and glory; the distinctive metal of the new age, as we have seen above, was iron. In the period from 900 to 612 BC the Assyrians with their iron army built the world's first empire by conquering the ancient Near East and organizing it into provinces under the active supervision of the Assyrian kings. The Egyptian state of the New Kingdom has often been called an empire, but the pharaohs of the era ruled directly only over the Nile and attempted to maintain merely a sphere of influence or hegemony in Syria-Palestine. The Assyrian kings incorporated conquered peoples into their state and had to provide for the firm defence of the entire region. They were therefore confronted with the need to develop a new grand strategy in which the defence of the Assyrian homeland in Upper Mesopotamia was simply a part of a much broader security system.

The essential features of Assyrian grand strategy appear early and were firmly in place by the reign of Tiglath Pileser III (744–727). At the beginning of the period of Assyrian revival King Adadnirari II (911–891) faced strategic problems on three fronts. One was the mountainous region of Urartu to the north, earlier controlled by the Hurrians, a constant menace to the integrity of the Assyrian Empire. Another was represented by fiercely independent Babylon in the south, complicated by the threat from aggressive Elamites in the Persian highlands. The third was westward towards the sea, a front that brought Assyria face to face with the Israelites.[105] In a series of annual campaigns that began more as raids than as wars of conquest the kings of the ninth century dealt with varied success with their frontier problems in this 'Assyrian triangle', creating, as Leo Oppenheim has said, 'more or less ephemeral empires'.[106] Assurnasirpal II (883–859) and his son Shalmaneser III (858–824) were particularly aggressive and successful, but the great age of the Assyrian Empire came in the eighth and seventh centuries under Tiglath Pileser III, Sargon II (721–705), Sennacherib (704–681), Esarhaddon (680–669), and Assurbanipal (668–627), all of whom sought to hold the territory they conquered.

Tiglath Pileser III took Babylon and Damascus; Sargon II waged many wars and exiled the leaders of the Kingdom of Israel; Sennacherib took Cilicia in southeast Anatolia and moved the capital of the Assyrian Empire to Nineveh; Esarhaddon seized Egypt and united most of the ancient Near East under Assyrian rule. Assyrian grand strategy was designed to deal with a twofold problem: how to hold the conquered provinces in subjugation and how to defend the imperial frontiers. Unlike the Roman Empire, the Assyrians could not count on the loyalty of their provincials and did not have the luxury of dispersing their military forces along the frontiers of the provinces. Although they placed garrisons at strategic points within their empire, they always maintained a strong central reserve directly under the command of the king. In this way the needs of internal as well as external security shaped Assyrian grand strategy.

One result of internal threats to the Assyrian Empire was the adoption by the kings of a conscious policy of terrorism as part of their grand strategy. To keep their subjects in check Assyrian kings openly declared a savage and furious policy of military retaliation for acts of disloyalty. Babylon was often battered and once, under Sennacherib, totally destroyed. His account of the destruction of that great city inevitably reminds the reader of the Romans at Carthage:

Like the on-coming of a storm I broke loose, and overwhelmed it like a hurricane. . . . With their corpses I filled the city squares. . . . The city and its houses, from its foundation to its top, I destroyed, I devastated, I burned with fire. The wall and outer wall, temples and gods, temple towers of brick and earth, as many as there were, I razed and dumped them into the Arahtu Canal. Through the midst of that city I dug canals, I flooded its site with water, and the very foundations thereof I destroyed. I made its destruction more complete than that by a flood. That in days to come the site of that city, and its temples and gods, might not be remembered, I completely blotted it out with floods of water and made it like a meadow.[107]

Babylon, however, like Carthage, could be destroyed but not obliterated, and it rose again with the stubbornness of a weed to continue its obstinate resistance to the hated Assyrians.

Although the Assyrians did face serious difficulties in unifying the Near East, even today the great narratives of Assyrian reprisal, placed in prominent public locations for all to see, send a chill down the spine. A famous example, inscribed on the entrance to a temple in the royal residence of Assurnasirpal II, relates the awesome vengeance of the king against the rebellious city of Suru, and we are made to understand, as Assurnasirpal intended, that revolt was a mistake:

While I was staying in the land of Kutmuki, they brought me the word: 'The city of Suru of Bit-Halupe has revolted, they have slain Hamatai, their governor, and Ahiababa, the son of a nobody, whom they have brought from Bit-Adini, they have set up as king over them.' With the help of Adad and the great gods who have made great my kingdom, I mobilized my chariots and armies and marched along the bank of the Habur. . . . To the city of Suru of Bit-Halupe I drew near, and the terror of the splendor of Assur, my lord, overwhelmed them. The chief men and the elders of the city, to save their lives, came forth into my presence and embraced my feet, saying: 'If it is thy pleasure, slay! If it is thy pleasure, let live! That which thy heart desireth, do!' Ahiababa, the son of a nobody, whom they had brought from Bit-Adini, I took captive. In the valor of my heart and with the fury of my weapons I stormed the city. All the rebels they seized and delivered them up. . . . Azi-ilu I set over them as my own governor. I built a pillar over against his city gate, and I flayed all the chief men who had revolted, and I covered the pillar with their skins; some I walled up within the pillar, some I impaled upon the pillar on stakes, and others I bound to stakes round about the pillar; many within the border of my own land I flayed, and I spread their skins upon the walls; and I cut off the limbs of the officers, of the royal officers who had rebelled. Ahiababa I took to Nineveh, I flayed him, I spread his skin upon the wall of Nineveh. . . .[108]

This gruesome document is nearly as revolting as photographs of Nazi concentration camps, and it has few parallels in history. It is not insignificant to note that the rebel leaders of the city of Suru surrendered without a struggle on the arrival of the king and his army outside their city, yet Assurnasirpal spared neither the leaders nor the city. Surrender, even unconditional surrender, could not ameliorate the punishment for rebellion against Assyria.

If the document seems too vividly colourful and cruel, it is not by virtue of that fact exceptional or atypical. Even Assyrian pictorial art illustrates in all too ghastly a fashion the folly of resistance to Assyrian armies. Its portrayal of burning cities, of women and children captured by Assyrian warriors, of the vanquished foe in flight and death, of piles of human heads is also part of the grand strategy of the Assyrian Empire – to hold conquered populations in subjection by terrorism applied and advertised. Associated with the use of military force and the propaganda of terror is the well-known Assyrian practice of the wholesale transportation of leaders from one region of the empire to another. The captivity of the Israelites and their deportation into Mesopotamia are a famous example. Assyrian kings were much more aggressive than Babylonian rulers or Egyptian pharaohs in the use of terrorist symbolism and psychology to advance their grand strategy.

The bulwark of Assyrian grand strategy, however, was the incredibly effective field army that swept away all obstacles and planted its standards in Anatolia, the Levant, Egypt and Babylon. Unfortunately there is no major, modern study of the Assyrian army, though sufficient evidence exists for the writing of one, and we can only hope that Assyriologists will soon fill the void.[109] Nevertheless, the general lines of its organization and deployment may be traced, and on a few points where there are recent systematic studies it is possible to show the complexity and tactical sophistication of the Assyrian military establishment.

The army with which the Assyrians pursued their grand strategy was an integrated force of heavy and light infantry, consisting of spearmen, archers, slingers, storm troops, and engineers. The Assyrians were the first major power to use regular cavalry units, but chariotry remained the élite striking force of their army. Although there was a standing, central army, conscription was imposed on all the provinces, and the provincial militia could be called up for the greatest wars. Assyrian sculptural reliefs show that the army functioned as well in mountainous terrain as on the level plain, something that even in modern times only really able forces can do. Assyrian commanders were conscious of the need to maintain a military force with sufficient tactical flexibility to meet the strategic demands of fighting in the widely differing geographical circumstances of the Assyrian triangle. In addition, as we shall see below, the Assyrians mastered the art of siege warfare with an efficiency not matched until the invention of catapults and the campaigns of Alexander the Great. The size of the full Assyrian army is not known, but recent estimates have put it in the range of 100,000 to 200,000 men.

If those estimates are too high, it is at least certain that Assyrian kings mobilized the largest armies the ancient Near East had ever seen.[110]

Horse Recruitment and Siege Warfare

Organization is the *sine qua non* of warfare. Organization in its broadest sense – including logistics, conscription, armament, command structure, tactical formation, and military engineering – shapes grand strategy, strategy and tactics. Compared with the relatively simple system of military organization that prevailed in the Greek world in the age of the hoplite phalanx, the ancient Near Eastern kingdoms of Egypt, Assyria and Persia stand out like towering giants. Since it would be impossible in a survey of this sort to touch upon all features of Assyrian military organization, we shall concentrate on two aspects of it, by way of example: the supply of military horses and the techniques of siege warfare.

There is much more to cavalry and chariot warfare than the romance and glory of the charge at the gallop. One of the main problems, in addition to feeding and training the animals, as well as the men, is how to get the horses in the first place. They are not simply there, especially in the ancient world where the horse was not used extensively in agriculture. (An agricultural draft horse is unlikely to make a good cavalry mount in any event.) The Assyrians mastered the problems of horse recruitment as well as any great power in history, considering the fact that they were not a nomadic horse nation.

A vast collection of surviving letters, numbering more than 2,000, sent by the kings' agents in the provinces to the kings themselves, illustrates sometimes in microscopic detail the active attention of Assyria's rulers to matters of horse recruitment. A recent study of those letters reveals that Assyrian horse supply was supervised by high-ranking governmental officers called *mušarkisus*, usually two to a province, appointed by the central government and reporting directly to the king rather than to the provincial governors.[111] The *mušarkisu* travelled constantly from village to village in the provinces collecting horses for the king. He was assisted by scribes and other helpers and sometimes worked only for a single branch of the horse army, i.e., for the 'palace chariotry', or 'the cavalry bodyguard'.

An extensive collection of 'Horse Reports', written daily to the king (probably Esarhaddon) in a concentrated period of three months early in an uncertain year, has been carefully analyzed by J.N. Postgate in a fascinating book, *Taxation and Conscription in the Assyrian Empire* (1974). The reports were written by the officer in charge of the royal stables near Nineveh, and often he asks the king directly to make a decision about the disposition of the horses: 'The horses of the Melidaean(s) which came in today before the king – are they to stay in the arsenal –, or are they to come out or to stay.'[112] Twenty-seven such daily reports show that some 2,911 animals arrived in Nineveh (about 100 per day), and that they came from provinces all over the empire.

From other documents it is possible to determine that the chariot men of the king's army spent the winter months in their villages in the provinces and cared for their own horses, so these 'Horse Reports' deal with additional supplies for the king's forces. The bureaucratic machinery for collection and subsequent disposal of horses to the central army and to corrals in the provinces reflects not only a highly organized system for the supply of animals, but also for the provision of food for their upkeep. Of the 2,911 animals mentioned in the 'Horse Reports', 27 are described as 'stud horses', 1,840 as 'yoke' or chariot horses (sometimes divided into two different breeds, Kusaean or Nubian horses and Mesaean or Iranian horses), and 787 as riding or cavalry horses. In addition some 136 mules were received. If the system of military administration of the Assyrian army was as highly developed in other branches as it was in the provision of animals for the chariotry and cavalry, and it almost certainly was, we can safely assume that Assyrian advances in the art of warfare from 900 to 612 BC, a period that overlaps and is contemporary with the emergence of the phalanx in Greece (*c.* 700–500 BC), were more significant than military historians have generally realized.

The problems of horse supply have plagued many modern nations. At Waterloo, 2,500 years after the fall of Assyria, Napoleon is considered to have performed a near miraculous feat in procuring enough horses to mount a cavalry of 20,000.

That Napoleon could in two months collect 20,000 horsemen for his invasion of Belgium, after providing for the Army Corps guarding the other frontiers of France, and having had a nucleus of 8,000 horses only on which to start the mobilization, is one of the many proofs of his marvellous genius; but the inevitable hurry, and consequent want of training, accounts in a great measure for the want of success attained by the French Cavalry.[113]

It would be absurd to argue that the horse strength of the Assyrian army was as great as that of Napoleonic armies, but a quick calculation shows that, if an Assyrian king received more than 100 new war horses a day for three months in addition to the large number, whatever it may have been, permanently assigned to the provinces and the central army, the mechanics of horse recruitment had reached a remarkably high level.

Perhaps a word is in order about one of the great mysteries of Assyrian military history, the fact that Assyrians were the first to deploy cavalry forces, yet they retained chariotry as a more important arm. Cavalry, because of its greater mobility, is in virtually every respect except the delivery of firepower superior to chariotry. The war chariot would soon disappear from the field of battle nearly altogether, only to reappear later in rare and unusual instances where its inferiority to cavalry was invariably demonstrated. Why, then, did the Assyrians retain chariots in preference to cavalry? It was once thought that the early horses were not large enough to carry a rider, but recent research suggests that this is not the case. Possibly the lack of the horseshoe made the use of cavalry in rough terrain, where it would have been deployed more often than chariots, too expensive in animals, since it caused a breakdown in the horses' hooves. Or, more

Assyrian chariot and cavalryman of the time of Assurbanipal. Although the Assyrians were the first to use cavalry systematically in warfare, they continued to rely primarily on the war chariot. The vehicle here has a driver, archer and two shield-bearers to protect them.

likely, we may see here simply another instance of the well-known, conservative tendency of the military mind, reluctant to abandon the traditional way of fighting even when change seems desirable, a tendency that is often most notable in otherwise highly successful armies.[114]

That the Assyrians were usually capable of change is best illustrated in their innovative mastery of siege warfare. Yigael Yadin has demonstrated through careful analysis of Assyrian sculptural reliefs the revolutionary developments Assyrians effected in the art of the siege.[115] The rise of powerful armies in the second and first millennia BC had spurred a corresponding emphasis on fortified sites, particularly in the smaller states of the Fertile Crescent that could not hope to maintain field armies large enough to resist the land forces of the great powers. There are, however, numerous ways of taking fortified cities, and the Assyrians organized their army so that it was equally effective in conventional battle and in the siege, a feat of military organization that Greek armies could not possibly have matched in the age of the phalanx. Amazingly the Assyrians seem to have mastered all aspects of siege warfare, and their approach to the capture of fortified sites shows a manifold variety of tactical techniques.

The best way to take a city is to approach it in such force that it surrenders before any other military action occurs. We have seen that Suru under Assurnasirpal did just that and, in the fourth century BC, Alexander took Babylon by simply marching in force against it. Various devices were used by Assyrian generals to avoid the dangerous cost of penetration by direct assault. If the defenders of a city refused to open the gates, it was sometimes possible through the use of ruse to infiltrate. The story of the Trojan Horse is the most famous example, and the fear of ruse in ancient Near Eastern warfare is clearly indicated in the biblical account of the siege of Samaria (II Kings 7:10–11), when the king refused to believe that the attackers had abandoned their camp.

When such stratagems failed, the next step was to storm the fortifications, assuming the attacking forces had sufficient strength to assure some prospect of success. Assyrian generals had at their disposal the specialized troops that were necessary to storm a city in several different ways, either singly or collectively. One way was to breach the walls with a battering ram. As early as Assurnasirpal

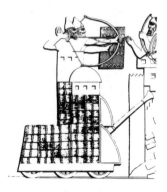

The mobile tower and battering ram of Assurnasirpal (left) with six wheels was heavy and difficult to move. The lighter, mobile ram of Sennacherib (right) was easier to use against the enemy wall. Note that the warrior uses water to douse fire (probably from a flaming arrow).

Assyrian sculptured reliefs illustrate the use of battering rams on wheeled, mobile towers that could be moved up against the wall and at the same time offered protection to the wielders of the ram. The towers were large enough to contain archers for use against the counterattacking force on the city wall. The early, multiple-wheeled Assyrian siege towers were too heavy and immobile, but by the time of Tiglath Pileser III lighter, four-wheeled towers were deployed, sometimes several of them together, against the same point on the wall (which was in fact normally the gate, since it was relatively weaker). If it proved necessary to build a ramp to help move the siege towers against the fortifications, Assyrian engineers were prepared to do so. A special member of the battering-ram team was responsible for putting out fires when the enemy threw lighted torches onto the towers. Other Assyrian storm troopers were trained to use poles or pikes against weak points in the walls, and special shields or screens were designed to protect them while they worked. Pikemen sometimes held large screens for the archers to use as cover while they delivered supporting fire in aid of the besiegers. Assyrians also often used the flaming torch to bring a fortified site to its knees.

Clearly the Assyrians were prepared to move through walls with their battering rams, but they were also trained to go over the walls with scaling ladders, or by building earthen ramps. Sometimes this

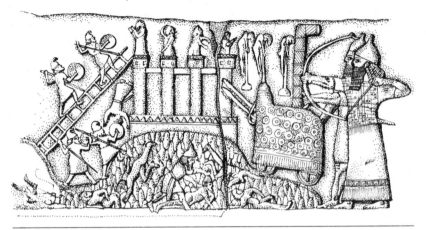

Scaling ladders and battering rams in use under Tiglath Pileser III. The enemy (above) is impaled on spikes while the army (below) fights in mountainous territory. The archer wears helmet and mail shirt, and fires from behind a huge wicker shield. Siege and mountain warfare were highly developed in the Assyrian army.

was done to create a diversion from the battering rams, but Assyrian generals could use scaling ladders in large numbers as their main method of attack. When the Assyrians could not go over the walls or through them, they tried to go under them through tunnelling. As often as not, battering rams, scaling ladders, and tunnelling were used simultaneously, and in addition to archers and contingents of supporting spearmen, the Assyrians used slingers whose high angled fire was particularly effective against defenders on the battlements and within the city.

When all else failed, or when penetration by storm appeared too costly, Assyrian armies settled on siege proper to reduce a city. The idea was simply to surround it, cut it off from all outside help and supplies, and starve it into submission. Siege proper can be dangerous. Food supplies in ancient cities were sometimes extensive enough to last for two and occasionally even three years through rationing. In the meantime the attacking army was immobilized around the fortifications, and, if the besieged city could summon allied help, the attackers might find themselves surrounded, subject to assault by the relieving force and by sallies from within the city. The Assyrians obviously preferred to avoid siege proper, and organized their army for assault.

In summary it seems fair to say that the two examples of Assyrian specialization in warfare, horse recruitment and siege operations, illustrate the organization and tactical effectiveness of the Assyrian field army. It was capable of conducting campaigns over a distance of 1,000 miles, and neither enemy army nor enemy fortifications could thwart it from achieving its strategic objective. From about 900 to 612 BC it was the supreme land force in the ancient Near East.

Strategy and Tactics: the Assyrian Army on Campaign

There is reasonably detailed evidence of the military campaigns of several Assyrian kings, and we shall look at one of them as illustrative of the war machine in action on the field. The eighth campaign of Sargon II, undertaken in 714 BC, was directed against the powerful kingdom of Urartu on the northern and northeastern frontier. The surviving report is in the form of a letter from Sargon to the god Assur, a tablet now in the Louvre.[116] Though the letter suggests that religious motives inspired the campaign, we should not be misled into assuming, as some have done, that Assyria's wars were religious crusades. Religious justifications have often been offered for war, and they were not more uncommon among the Greeks and the Romans than in the ancient Near East. Military protection of the frontiers, a concern enhanced by the possibility of booty, stimulated the grand strategy of the Assyrian kings.

As Sargon advanced northwards from his capital at Calah (near the later capital of Nineveh), he crossed a tributary of the Tigris when it was in flood. The king describes it as a 'rough passage', but in fact the ability of Assyrian armies to manage river crossings was one of their great strengths. The king then turned east towards the mountains and stopped near the frontier of the Medes to review his army. His forces encountered many difficulties as they advanced north to the area east of Lake Urmia in the vicinity of modern Tabriz. On the way they crossed 'high mountains, covered with all kinds of trees, whose surface was a jungle, whose passes were frightful, over whose area shadows stretch as in a cedar forest, the traveler of whose paths never sees the light of sun.'[117] Since the roads were 'too rough for chariots to mount, bad for horses, and too steep to march foot soldiers,' Sargon's sappers 'shattered the side of the high mountain as blocks of building stone, making a good road.' The army moved in line of column, first the chariots, then the cavalry and infantry, followed by the engineers and finally the baggage train of camels and asses.

When Sargon's army reached the kingdom of the Mannaeans (south of Lake Urmia), their king surrendered without a struggle, and 'kissed my feet'. Kings of all the districts dominated by the Medes sent him tribute, and he built a fortress to secure his line of supply, 'and stored up therein food, oil, wine and war equipment'. Advancing ever northwards against an Armenian king who abandoned his capital, the Assyrian took twelve fortified cities and eighty-four villages: 'I destroyed their walls, I set fire to the houses inside them, I destroyed them like a flood, I battered them into heaps of ruins.'

In addition to the destruction of fortifications, Sargon's strategic objective was to meet and defeat the enemy's main force, commanded by Ursa, King of Urartu: 'because I had never yet come near Ursa, the Armenian, and the border of his wide land, nor poured out the blood of his warriors on the battlefield, I lifted my hands, praying that I might bring about his defeat in battle. . . .' Ursa obliged by setting out a conventional line of archers, spearmen and cavalry. Sargon showed the decisiveness of an Alexander or a Caesar by moving his fatigued army immediately on short rations against his opponent, personally leading a chariot and cavalry assault against the enemy's line: 'I could not relieve their fatigue, nor strengthen the wall of the camp . . . what was right and left could not be brought to my side, I could not watch the rear. . . . I plunged into [the enemy's] midst like a swift javelin, I defeated him.'

It is clear that in this decisive battle Sargon, advancing in line of column, decided not to manoeuvre into line of battle, but rather to strike directly into the enemy ranks.[118] Ursa's line obviously broke as Sargon came down on it, and he pursued and destroyed the Armenian army, although Ursa abandoned his chariot and escaped on horseback.

Having achieved the objective of destroying the enemy's main force, and after wasting the countryside, Sargon began the return to Assyria by encircling Lakes Urmia and Van, where he encountered no resistance as he took several of the major strongholds of Urartu. The document shows that everywhere Sargon went, he was concerned with the logistical support of his army and with the destruction of enemy fortifications. At Uesi, southwest of Lake Van on the frontier of

Urartu, there was resistance, and Sargon took the strongly fortified site by besieging its rear while he engaged the defending force outside its gates.

On the final leg of the return Sargon sent ahead to Assyria the bulk of his army, including his chariots and infantry, and with a force of 1,000 cavalry and assault troops he crossed a high mountain pass eastwards into the kingdom of a northern Mesopotamian ruler who had defected from an Assyrian alliance. Speed and surprise were the means by which he seized the capital city of Musasir. The pass he crossed was so narrow that there was

no trail for the passage of foot soldiers . . . where no king had ever passed. . . . Their great wild tree trunks I tore down and cut through their steep peaks. . . . A narrow road, a straight passage, where the foot soldiers passed sideways, I prepared for the passage of my army between them. My chariot came up with ropes, while I, with several mounts of horses, took the lead of my army. My warriors and their horses, who go at my side, narrowed down to single file and made their wearisome way.

Surprised by the sudden attack, the city fell without resistance, and Sargon took over 6,000 captives before he returned to Assyria.

This account colourfully demonstrates the tactical flexibility of the Assyrian army. On a campaign of several hundred miles deep into enemy territory the army traversed rivers and high mountain passes, maintained its lines of supply, fought a major battle, conducted a siege of a fortified site, encircled Lakes Urmia and Van, and destroyed the countryside and the cities. Before returning to Assyria Sargon, with an élite striking force, crossed a mountain pass considered to be militarily impenetrable and seized a fortified city. The Assyrian 'wolf' was an army with cunning and vicious leadership, far better organized than any army the world had seen up to its time.

Despite Assyrian military organization, however, and the policy of terrorism (or perhaps because of it), Assyria proved unable to retain her grip on the provinces around the triangle. Possibly weakened by the efforts of national mobilization for the conquest of Egypt, Assyria in the seventh century faced rebellion by Babylon, the loss of Egypt after ruling it for less than a generation (671–650s), and the rise of the Medes of Persia. Babylon won its independence in 626, and later – in alliance with the Medes – took Assur (614) and finally Nineveh (612). There were few nations in the ancient Near East to lament the fall of the hated empire.

Persian Grand Strategy

After the fall of Nineveh, there was a period of about sixty years when Mesopotamia and Syria-Palestine were dominated by the Neo-Babylonians and the Medes of Persia. The collapse of Assyria also permitted the revival of Egyptian independence under the Saïte pharaohs and the rise in Anatolia of the powerful kingdom of the Lydians. The Greek historian Herodotus later claimed that the greatest of the Median kings, Cyaxares (*c.* 625–585), was the 'first who gave organization to an Asiatic army, dividing the troops into companies, and forming distinct bodies of the spearmen, the archers, and the cavalry, who before his time had been mingled in one mass, and confused together.'[119] This we know to be untrue, but it is an important reflection of Greek ignorance of ancient Near Eastern military practice.

When Cyrus seized the throne of Persia near the middle of the fifth century BC, the change from the Median to the Achaemenid dynasty set the stage for the emergence of the Persian Empire. It rapidly absorbed all the ancient Near East and dominated the entire area until Alexander the Great destroyed it in the last half of the fourth century. In the next chapter we shall consider in greater detail the rivalry between Greece and Persia; in the remainder of this chapter we shall examine the full range of Persian grand strategy in which the Aegean frontier was only one component.[120]

Under Cyrus (559–530) and his son Cambyses (530–522) the Persians conquered Lydia, Egypt and Babylon. Their armies reached the Jaxartes in the northeast and advanced into India. The Persian Empire became the largest territorial state the ancient Western world had ever seen, and in the age of Darius I (521–486) it was divided into provinces or satrapies, much as the Assyrian Empire had been, stretching from the satrapy of Hindush in the Indus valley to the Ionian satrapy on the Aegean, twenty provinces altogether.[121]

The military requirements for the defence of this vast empire were awesome. Persian grand strategy was much more complicated and sophisticated than any previously in the ancient Near East simply because of scale. It is more than 2,500 miles from the Aegean to the Indus, and military threats along the far northern frontiers of Persia, from the Bosporus in the northwest to India in the northeast and east, were formidable. Fortunately for Persia's kings, the southern frontier

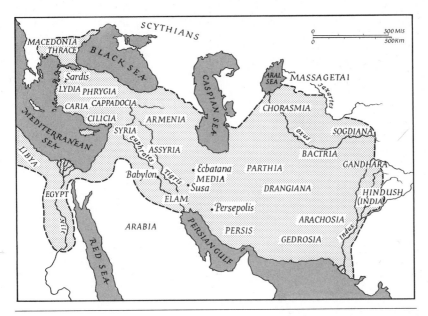

Map of the Persian Empire, c. 500 BC.

was relatively stable. The borders of Gedrosia and the Persian Gulf presented no major military challenge. The southwestern frontier along the Fertile Crescent from Babylon through Syria-Palestine to the Nile was often difficult to maintain internally in the face of rebellions, particularly in Egypt, but there were no nations beyond the frontiers to menace the military integrity of the great empire. As a result, although Persia did occasionally have to commit military forces in the region and probably maintained a small standing army in Egypt, the kings could generally rely on the prestige of their military might to hold the area.

Whereas the Assyrians had reinforced the calming influence of their armies with a conscious policy of terrorism, the Persians tried to win the approval of their subjects in the satrapies by a policy of toleration. The Old Testament reflects the joy of the Jews on the imminent arrival of Cyrus, because they expected him to allow them a large degree of religious freedom. On the whole this element of Persian grand strategy worked reasonably well in preventing rebellion and in securing the frontier provinces of the eastern Mediterranean, except in Egypt, but

81

it did not produce wildly enthusiastic adulation of Persian rule. Alexander encountered little native resistance when he marched around the east coast in the 330s BC, and virtually none that was inspired by love for Persia.

The northern frontiers were another matter. Scythians threatened from both sides of the Black Sea against the Persian frontiers in Thrace and in Armenia.[122] In the northeast Cyrus died fighting the Massagetai, and Sogdiana and Bactria were often attacked by nomadic hordes. The greatest threat came from the northwest, where Greeks and Macedonians successfully resisted a Persian attempt at conquest in the early fifth century and under Alexander in the fourth century brought the mighty Achaemenid giant to his knees. There is no doubt that from Darius I to Darius III the kings of Persia understood the limitations and the dangers of their position in the Aegean, and much of their military effort was devoted, in the end unsuccessfully, to the defence of that frontier.

The army with which they conquered and protected their empire was an impressive force.[123] In size it was competitive with armies of the Napoleonic era, and in tactical flexibility and logistical organization it far surpassed Greek armies until the time of Philip and Alexander. Based apparently on a form of imperial conscription applied in all the satrapies, the king could raise an army of around 300,000 men altogether, including the forces permanently stationed in Egypt and elsewhere. The organization of the army was based on units of ten, from myriads of 10,000 through groups of 1,000, 100, and 10, with a corresponding hierarchy of officers from myriarch to dekarch. The Persian Immortals consisted of crack troops drawn from the Persian homeland, and the force was always maintained as a standing army at its full strength of 10,000, even though military units from ancient times to today are rarely at paper strength. The Persian infantryman was armed with the bow, though he also carried a short spear and dagger, and his light shield was made of wicker. He did not wear a metal helmet, but he did have scale armour and wore trousers.

The non-Persian contingents of the army from the satrapies were as varied as the empire itself. Babylonian units fought with metal helmets and carried lances and wooden clubs; Bactrians bore the battle-axe in addition to the bow; Paphlagonians were spearmen who also used javelins. Sargatian nomads fighting on horseback used the lasso, but the main Persian cavalry was armed with the bow and with javelins.

The Persian bow was not composite and probably had a maximum effective range of 180 yards, but a few non-Persian contingents of the army possibly did use the composite bow.[124]

The army of Persia had two great weaknesses. There was no heavy infantry, or at least none to speak of, since Persian tactics generally called for a barrage of arrows from the infantry, followed by a cavalry attack, while the infantry closed with light weapons. The lack of heavy infantry made no difference on most of Persia's frontiers, but in the northwest against the Greeks it was to prove catastrophic. The other weakness, equally important, was that the national army was not a tactically cohesive force. Although it was a tactically integrated army in the sense that Persians used infantry, cavalry and skirmishers in coordination on the field of battle, it consisted of ethnic and regional levies that retained their local, tactical organization. Obviously the resultant mixture was not always tactically harmonious. In most cases this weakness was also insignificant, because Persian manpower was so overwhelming. Again, however, the Greeks benefited, especially when Philip and Alexander learned how to combine the forces of the Macedonians and their allies in a tactically unified army in which every element was familiar with the style of fighting of the units up and down the line of battle. Still, perhaps as a balance to their weaknesses, the Persians were the world's first great masters of two of the most important branches of warfare – cavalry and the war fleet – and we shall look at their achievements in each branch before we pass from ancient Near Eastern to Greek warfare.

Cavalry

Assyria, as we have seen, was the first major state to deploy cavalry units distinct from chariotry, but the chariot maintained its dominance on the field in the days of Sargon and his successors. Lydia, in the years after the fall of Nineveh, may have been the first state to rely heavily on large cavalry squadrons. Herodotus suggests that the kingdom of Croesus was famous for its horsemen and tells how even Cyrus had to resort to strategem to overcome Lydian cavalry superiority. At the battle of Sardis, before its fall, Cyrus moved his camels forward to meet Croesus' cavalry knowing that horses are naturally afraid of camels. The tactics worked, and Lydia fell to Persia, but Cyrus learned (or perhaps already knew) the potential value of cavalry.[125] The Persian army of the Achaemenid period relied heavily on it.

From that time forward to the present century cavalry was extensively used in warfare. At the beginning of this century on the Western Front in World War I the Germans had 70,000 cavalry and the French ten cavalry divisions. But the machine-gun rendered the use of cavalry too costly, and the armoured tank displaced it on the field, just as the automobile was replacing horses on the streets. As a result, students in the last half of the century find horse warfare puzzling, and some historians appear to have little understanding of how it functioned.[126]

Beginning with the Persians, the cavalry was the élite mobile striking force on the field of battle, and it retained that position until the Napoleonic era. Compared with a human being, a horse is a large and frightening beast, and it takes considerable courage for an infantryman to hold his ground as horse and rider charge against him. On the other hand, horses are easily scared, and they will not charge into an unbroken line of enemy pikemen. Rather they wheel before contact – assuming, that is, that their riders, who would be none too eager to be impaled, have not already set them about. Thus the romantic notion of the great cavalry charge into the thick of the line has recently been popularly dispelled by John Keegan in *The Face of Battle*, though military historians have always known this secret, and so too, presumably, have cavalry commanders.

I have but one caveat. It is true that cavalry will not force its way through an unbroken line, but it is also true that a line may be broken, or thrown into panic, by a cavalry attack. Under these circumstances cavalry can successfully attack infantry directly. Often one of the most difficult decisions a cavalry commander makes is to know when the enemy, despite his apparent strong formation, has become demoralized and is vulnerable to the charge. An error in judgment can be costly. A premature cavalry attack will throw the horses into panic, and the enemy can counterattack, pursue, and drive them off the field. At Issus Alexander successfully attacked the Persian line with cavalry, and we have already seen that Sargon did the same with chariotry. Normally a cavalry attack into the line must be made only where there are gaps (e.g., Alexander at Gaugamela), but one should not discount the possibility of a successful charge into an unbroken line, which, of course, does break as the charge advances.

Likewise, cavalry will not normally attack headlong into enemy cavalry. But, again, it is wrong to assume that a cavalry commander cannot ever launch a direct charge. Sometimes enemy cavalry will fall back in the face of a charge, and the trick is to know when that may be the case. Alexander was successful with such an attack at the Granicus and at the Hydaspes, as was Hannibal on his left wing at Cannae. Though the stirrup was not used in ancient warfare, the lack of it was probably not as great a handicap as many have assumed, and an ancient cavalry charge was only a little less stable than a medieval or modern one.[127]

Historically, however, the primary uses of cavalry have been for reconnaissance and for attacks against the relatively unprotected flanks and rear of the enemy. If a gap occurs in the enemy line, cavalry may charge it effectively, though it is normally important for infantry to follow in close support to press the advantage home. At Waterloo Marshal Ney, 'the bravest of the brave', who went through five mounts in the course of the battle, charged the British line without French infantry support, and all the bravery in the world could not make up for the error. The most effective use of cavalry is in pursuit, after the enemy has broken, and is in flight. The heaviest casualties in battle are ordinarily taken at this point.

The Persian kings clearly understood the tactical potential of cavalry and the proper use of it on the battlefield. The basic formation of attack, with infantry in the centre and cavalry on the wings, where it can be used against the flanks and rear of the enemy, was standard in Persia long before it was adopted by the Greeks. Despite the fact that the Persians failed to provide heavy infantry support in the centre as a base for their cavalry operations – in this respect they would learn from the Greeks – their army, with light infantry and 20,000 or so cavalry, was an imposing force.

The Origins of Naval Warfare

Another area in which the Persians were astoundingly innovative was in the projection of man's war-making capacity from the land to the sea, all the more so since Persians themselves were no sailors. Histories of naval warfare often begin with the Greeks, but the Persians organized the world's first great navy. The Athenian navy was fashioned in response to Persian grand strategy, which involved the deployment of a fleet in support of the Persian army in the Aegean sector. The Persian fleet was large (400 to 800 ships at various times from 500 to 330 BC), and it consisted, as the Greek fleets did, primarily of triremes.[128]

The origins of the trireme are shadowy and obscure. Greeks and Phoenicians in the seventh and sixth centuries BC had used the *pentekonter* with twenty-five oarsmen on each side. In its two-tiered form it is known as a bireme. Some authorities believe that the Greeks developed the trireme from the bireme sometime around 600 BC and others that it first appeared in Phoenicia or possibly in Egypt at about that time.[129] Herodotus says that Necho of Egypt, who died in 593 BC, used triremes in the canal he built from the Mediterranean to the Red Sea, and possibly Egyptians borrowed the warship from the Greeks, but present evidence is not sufficient to resolve the dispute. Whatever the origins of the trireme may be, the Persians, who certainly did not design the ship, relying heavily on their Phoenician subjects, were the first to deploy it in large numbers as part of their grand strategy for conquest and defence of their Mediterranean frontiers. In 525 Cambyses used forty triremes to support his invasion of Egypt, and in the early fifth century, after rapid growth under Darius I, whose Aegean policy was vigorous, the Persian fleet numbered 600 ships including transports.

The origins of naval warfare *per se* go all the way back to the beginning of recorded history (and perhaps into prehistory). The palette of Narmer and other evidence demonstrates that from the outset Egyptians used river warships on the Nile. As early as the Old Kingdom seagoing ships were built in Egypt, and in the New Kingdom substantial warships put to sea. There is record of a great naval battle in the Nile Delta in 1186 BC between the forces of Ramesses III and the so-called Sea Peoples. An Egyptian depiction of the battle colourfully illustrates stiff fighting in oared warships.[130] As we shall see in the next chapter, the Bronze Age civilizations of Minoan Crete and Mycenae undoubtedly also used the fighting ship, but it was not until the Iron Age, under the stimulus of the maritime cultures of Phoenicia and Greece, that the warship firmly established its place in the military history of the ancient Mediterranean, and it was the Persians, though they played no role in the development of naval technology, who first made naval operations an integral and important part of large-scale warfare.

An Egyptian warship in the reign of Ramesses III fights against the Sea Peoples and the Libyans. Oarsmen on the Egyptian vessel are protected by raised gunwales and by archers serving as marines. Note the slinger in the crow's nest.

The trireme was a marvellous fighting ship which survived challenges by Hellenistic quinqueremes and other vessels to remain the most important warship of antiquity.[131] The Persian trireme, or rather the trireme of Persia's Greek and Phoenician subjects, was somewhat lighter than mainland Greek models, but basically about the same. It was a decked galley carrying 200 men, including 170 oarsmen and 30 marines. The rowers sat below deck in groups of three (hence the name 'trireme'), one above the other in an oblique line on banks of benches on each side of the hull, and they were packed so closely together that their noses nearly touched the bottoms of the rowers in front of them. Capable of achieving speeds perhaps as high as eleven and a half knots, triremes could reach top speed from a standing start in about thirty seconds, and they were excellent for the darting and ramming tactics of the period. The trireme was designed for battle and was too crowded for normal seafaring. It stayed close to shore, and usually the crew disembarked each night. Although sails were carried for use in moving the fleet from base to battle area, they

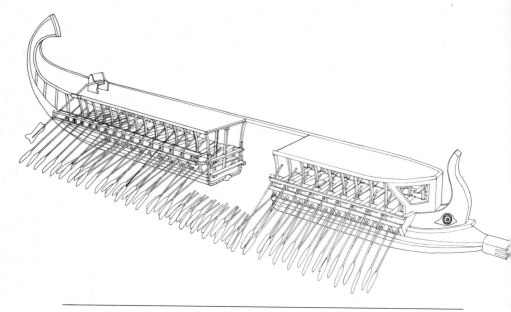

The decked trireme of the fifth century BC required 170 oarsmen close-packed in echelon. The ship was steered by a large oar on both sides of the stern, while the ram at the front could be a deadly weapon. The trireme was about 120 feet long and 15 feet wide. Leather sleeves around the oarports in the lower banks kept the water out. The top bank of 31 rowers on a side, sitting on benches above the gunwale, worked their oars on tholepins in the outrigger.

were normally left on shore for the battle itself. Herodotus says that the Persian ships sailed better than the Greek,[132] and Persian sailors were superior in naval manoeuvre on the open sea where their numerical advantage and slightly greater speed made a considerable difference.[133]

Standard naval tactics required the ability to execute several complicated manoeuvres. The most important was the so-called *diekplous* (literally, 'a passing through and out'), which was a darting movement in line ahead (in single file) by at least some of the ships of one line through the gaps in the opponent's line. Once through the line it was possible to ram and sink or disable enemy ships as they turned about to protect their rear. The faster fleet could more easily execute this gapping manoeuvre. Another possibility was envelopment, or *periplous*, an encircling attack obviously much more easily carried out by the larger fleet. The defence against both *diekplous* and *periplous* was a manoeuvre in which the defenders abandoned their line, bunched their ships and moved out radially against their attackers.[134] Often a band of about twenty marines and archers on each ship aided in assault and defence.

Although the Greeks in the period from 700 to 480 BC made significant strides in naval warfare and may have been responsible for many of the features of the Persian practice of it, it was Persia rather than one of the Greek states that first developed a major naval presence in the Mediterranean. In 490, as the Persian fleet of 600 ships approached Marathon – it is uncertain how many of them were triremes – Athens had at her disposal perhaps twenty vessels. In response to the Persian naval build-up in the Aegean, Athens and other Greek states did shortly develop major fleets of their own, but the Persian Empire had been the catalyst, and in the great clash of 480 it had the larger fleet, as it continued to have 150 years later when Alexander crossed the Hellespont.

Before turning to Greek military history it would be appropriate to look back briefly over developments in warfare around the Mediterranean from prehistoric to the end of ancient Near Eastern times. Neolithic fortifications, the emergence of the bow, the sling, and the spear, and the appearance of reasonably large, organized armies at the beginning of recorded history attest to the antiquity of war. From the pharaohs of Egypt down to the kings of Persia man honed his war-making abilities. Deployment of the column and the line, logistical organization, weapons management and development, and numerous specialized tactical units along with the techniques of siege warfare had all gradually made their appearance. Indeed most of the ingredients of warfare as it would be practised down to Napoleonic times had been forged in the ancient Near East. Under the kings of Persia an army and navy of Napoleonic proportions dominated the region, and the separate arms of cavalry, infantry, skirmishers and fleet had been refined. What Persia lacked was good, heavy infantry. The Greeks and Macedonians would fill that void, and after they adopted the other arms of ancient Near Eastern warfare, under Philip and Alexander, their armies would impose a new civilization on Persia and the Fertile Crescent.

The military inheritance of Mycenaean Greece was lost to the Classical Greeks, who lagged behind the Near East in the art of war till the time of Alexander. A soldier from the 'Warrior Vase' found at Mycenae shows that infantry pikemen played a part in Mycenaean warfare alongside the chariots.

Chapter Four

Classical Greek Warfare

Homeric Warfare

The achievements of the ancient Greeks in art, literature and philosophy are writ large on the pages of history, but warfare occupied their time and minds as much as their more humane and civilizing activities. The first monument of classical Greek civilization is Homer's *Iliad*, the most famous war poem in the history of literature. The subject of the poem is the wrath of Achilles in the Trojan War, but despite Schliemann's exciting excavations of Troy and Mycenae, the value of Homer's epic for the study of early Greek warfare remains highly controversial. It is now generally accepted that Homer provides some valuable information about Late Bronze Age warfare (1600–1100 BC) in the Aegean, but that, since he wrote probably sometime in the eighth century BC, long after the collapse of the civilizations of Minoan Crete and Mycenaean Greece, his knowledge was imperfect. His accounts of battle were shaped more often than not by the practice of warfare in his own day, in the Iron Age.

As a result, under the general rubric of Homeric warfare we must distinguish two periods – the one Homer wrote about and the one he lived in – the Bronze Age and the late Dark Age as Greece recovered from the catastrophic collapse of the Mycenaean warlords. The two periods are vastly different, and archaeology, with some help from linguistics, has provided the only basis for distinguishing between the Bronze Age and Iron Age elements in the Homeric epic. Differences of emphasis and interpretation abound, but it is generally agreed that Homer is more useful for the later than for the earlier period. Troy definitely existed, but the Trojan War remains a largely legendary event in the early history of the Greek people.[135]

Within the last generation, however, significant new discoveries have enlarged our understanding of Bronze Age warfare in the

Map of ancient Greece.

Aegean. It has become more and more apparent that the Minoans and Mycenaeans were in many respects simply an Aegean reflection of the Bronze Age civilizations of the ancient Near East, and that their practice of warfare was strikingly similar, in several respects at least, to the military developments of the period of the Egyptian New Kingdom.

From about 2000 to 1450 BC Minoans on the island of Crete developed the flourishing civilization excavated in this century by Sir Arthur Evans and others. Centred eventually at Knossos on the north coast of Crete, Minoan influences spread throughout the central portion of the island all the way south to Phaestos and northwards to the Greek mainland and some of the Aegean islands. Although Thucydides says that the Minoans maintained a maritime empire in the Aegean, or a thalassocracy, for some time modern historians have been dubious.[136] There were apparently no fortifications around the great Minoan palaces on Crete and little reflection of war in their art. Recently, though, a marvellous fresco excavated at the Minoan site of Akrotiri on Thera shows in a beautifully painted scene numerous Minoan ships, peculiarly similar to seagoing ships of the Egyptian Eighteenth Dynasty (beginning in 1575 BC).[137] Since Thera was overwhelmed by a great volcanic eruption around 1500 BC, there can be little doubt that the fresco of the ships illustrates genuine Minoan naval action, and land forces as well, but until further discoveries our knowledge of Minoan warfare will remain limited.[138]

A line of Minoan spearmen from the fresco of the ships at Akrotiri (Thera). Note the unusually long spears which in later times, before they were adopted by the Macedonians, were associated with the Egyptians.

More is known, however, about the military institutions of the Mycenaean civilization on the Greek mainland. Undoubtedly stimulated by contact with the Minoans, which became intensive in the sixteenth century BC, the highly fortified Mycenaean centres developed an obviously militaristic civilization of their own, and around 1450, perhaps after Crete was weakened by the eruption of the volcano of Thera, Mycenaean warriors seized Knossos, and power shifted to the Greek mainland. In the period 1450 to 1200 BC the Mycenaean kingdoms of Pylos and Mycenae itself, and perhaps Sparta and others, developed impressive Bronze Age armies.

Much of what is known about Mycenaean warfare is derived from the so-called Linear B tablets, discovered first by Sir Arthur Evans and deciphered by Michael Ventris in the 1950s. These tablets, in an early form of the Greek language, reveal that the Mycenaean kingdoms in the bureaucratic fashion of the ancient Near Eastern monarchies maintained an intricately organized military force, and in combination with representations in Mycenaean art it is possible to get a reasonably clear view of the military establishment.[139]

Homer knew that the warriors of Mycenaean times used bronze weapons rather than the iron ones of his day, and he obviously associated the war chariot with their military operations, but in other respects his account of Mycenaean tactics appears inadequate. Homer's war chariot was mainly a vehicle for transporting heroes to the battlefield where they dismounted and engaged in hand-to-hand combat with equally great heroes on the other side. He shows little awareness of the use of massed chariots for attacks on the flanks and rear of the enemy or for pursuit, yet the Mycenaeans themselves are likely to have used their chariots in the same way as did the Egyptians and Hittites at the battle of Kadesh in the early thirteenth century. Homer also shows only a dim awareness of the Mycenaean infantry deployed in support of chariot squadrons.[140]

The Mycenaean chariot was relatively light, in the style of the Egyptian rather than of the heavier Hittite models. A fresco from Tiryns and scenes from Mycenaean vases reveal a two-wheeled, four-spoked chariot drawn usually by two horses. Linear B tablets from Knossos show inventories of chariot bodies, wheels, bridles, blinkers and other individual items associated with the chariot, and there are also lists of fully equipped vehicles. John Chadwick, a leading authority on the period, estimates that Mycenaeans of Knossos could

field 200 chariots, though his guess may be conservative. One document alone gives a total of 246 chariot frames and 208 pairs of wheels.[141]

Much is known about Mycenaean armour. A full suit of bronze armour has been found in a Mycenaean tomb, but other evidence suggests linen garments fitted with bronze scale were more common. Shields of various sorts are depicted in the art of the period, and tablets inventory swords and daggers, possibly battle-axes, arrows and javelins, and without doubt the thrusting spear. A fascinating collection of tablets at Pylos indicates that the ruler there had at his disposal a contingent of perhaps twenty warships. [142]

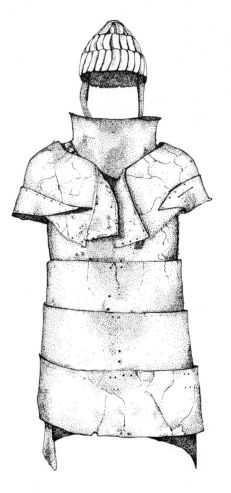

(Opposite) A Mycenaean chariot
from a fresco at Tiryns. Such scenes
in Mycenaean art reveal that the
chariot was an important part of
Mycenaean warfare as it was
during the same period in ancient
Egypt and in the kingdom of the
Hittites.

A *full suit of Mycenaean bronze*
armour, with helmet made of
boars' tusks, from Dhendrá. There
is also evidence that linen was often
used with leather and metal fittings
for armour. A suit such as the one
shown here would have been
uncomfortably warm on a hot,
Mediterranean summer day.

In my opinion there is nothing to prevent us assuming that
Mycenaean armies were much like those of the ancient Near East, and
that they relied primarily on the use of massed chariots with infantry
support. Some historians have argued that the Homeric portrayal of
chariots as vehicles mainly for the transport of warriors to the
battlefield is correct, because the geography of Greece and Crete was
too mountainous for the use of chariots in mass, but that is surely not
the case. It is true that large-scale horse operations with forces of 5,000
or more were not possible, or were at least extremely difficult, in
Greece south of Thessaly. The Persian general Mardonius in the early

fifth century was cautious about committing his cavalry on Attic terrain, but, on the other hand, the hoplite phalanx was not suited for mountainous terrain either. Despite that fact, later Greek armies were small enough to find many appropriate sites for battle on level ground. Mycenaean armies were surely not so large as to be forced to deploy their chariots in a tactically wasteful fashion merely as troop transports.

For reasons that today remain obscure, beginning as early as the fourteenth century BC Mycenaean centres on Crete were destroyed, and in the thirteenth century the process of destruction commenced on the mainland. Although at some individual sites the collapse seems to have been sudden, it was a development that stretched over a reasonably long period of time and was not complete until about 1150, when all the great Bronze Age centres (with the exception of Athens) lay in ruins. Later Greeks attributed the desolation to an invasion of Greek-speaking Dorians from the north, and subsequently Dorians did occupy much of the Peloponnese and Crete, but what actually happened remains something of a mystery.[143] The results are much clearer. Greece entered a Dark Age (1000–800 BC) in which all but the feeblest memories of Bronze Age civilization evaporated, and even the art of writing was lost.

Little is known about warfare in the Greek Dark Age, but around 800 BC the Greek world began to stir again, and in a burst of cultural activity in the eighth century laid the foundations of Hellenic civilization. The Greeks reacquired, from the Phoenicians in a new form, the art of writing, and the Homeric epics and – at the end of the century – the works of Hesiod reflect the anguish and the greatness of the fledgling new world. In the Dark Age, Greece had broken the fetters of the ancient Near East, which also suffered from an Age of Invasion in the period before and after 1000 BC. Although a revived Assyria exerted a stranglehold on the Fertile Crescent after 900 BC, the influence of the Assyrian Empire did not extend to Greece, and the Greeks were therefore free to develop their new civilization along their own lines with dramatic advances in art, literature and philosophy.

In almost every respect the freedom of Greece from ancient Near Eastern influences proved beneficial, but in military matters that was not entirely the case. We have already seen that, despite the travails of the Age of Invasion in the Near East, Assyria and then Persia maintained the continuity of an impressive military tradition that went back to the earliest civilizations and into prehistoric times. In Greece the Dark Age severance from the past was more complete, and Greeks of the eighth century started more or less anew, without benefit of the military technology and, more importantly, the strategically and tactically organized military institutions of the Bronze Age. As a result the Greek world fell far behind Assyria and Persia militarily in almost every important respect.

The warfare of the second Homeric period, the period in which Homer actually lived, benefited from only the vaguest recollections of Bronze Age fighting, and Homer's own misunderstanding of the tactical principles of Mycenaean warfare was shaped by the more or less primitive nature of Greek warfare in the eighth century BC. At the same time as Sargon was using carefully integrated contingents of infantry, chariotry and cavalry in mass in Assyria, the horse appeared in Greece as the distinctive symbol of warfare, but in a vastly different and tactically inferior way. Aristotle, speaking of this period in Greek history, said that the horseman was paramount in war, and he equated horsemen with wealthy aristocrats, since the expensive horse was a sign of wealth.[144] But it appears that the Greek mounted warrior of the eighth century used his horse mainly as a means of transport to the battlefield, and that battles of the period were fluid, free-for-all encounters in which the great aristocrats of one state duelled with those of another. Thus Homer assumed that the chariot fighting of the Bronze Age was similar to the mounted warfare of his own times. The shields worn by these mounted aristocratic grandees hung from a neck strap and could be slung over the back to cover the rear when flight seemed desirable. In comparison with the sophisticated military machine of the Assyrian Empire, Greek warfare was decidedly backward.

The Phalanx and the Fleet

Sometime between 700 and 650 BC (probably around 675) Greek states began to develop their major contribution to ancient warfare: heavy infantry, the so-called hoplite phalanx.[145] No one today knows where in Greece this first happened, but paintings on Protocorinthian pottery show indisputably that at least in Corinth the phalanx appeared by about 650 BC, and it was probably used for some time before artists began to employ it as a decorative motif on their vases. Corinth,

Sparta and Argos were quick to adopt the new formation. The hoplite phalanx consisted of spearmen several ranks deep, wearing a full panoply of heavy armour, used as shock troops, to engage the enemy head on in hand-to-hand (or spear-to-spear and shield-to-shield) combat. Until the development of the Roman legion the phalanx reigned supreme as the most formidable heavy infantry in the ancient world.

From its introduction in the early seventh century down to the conclusion of the Peloponnesian War at the end of the fifth century the phalanx underwent gradual modification, particularly in armour, but throughout the 300 years from 700 to 400 BC its tactical deployment was based on the principle of massed heavy infantry operating essentially alone without the ancillary support of light infantry, skirmishers or cavalry.[146] In the following description of the 'typical' hoplite phalanx we shall emphasize the organization, arms and deployment of the Spartan army, which, of course, was not typical, since Spartans became professional soldiers and maintained a standing army rather than using conscripts. There is little doubt, however, that in most respects the Spartan army set the standard other Greek states tried to follow. The use of heavy infantry in formation rapidly drove the 'heroic' aristocratic warrior from the field, as he could not charge with any prospect of success into a solid line of bristling spearpoints.

The most distinguishing feature of hoplite armour was a new shield, the *hoplon*, from which the infantryman took his name.[147] Originally it was a large round shield made of wood with an outer rim of bronze, but, by the end of the period, in 425, Spartans used shields covered with bronze. There were two handles, one in the centre and another on the inside edge. The infantryman inserted his left arm up to the elbow through the central handle or strap and held the leather thong at the rim in his hand. The shield was heavier and afforded more stable protection than earlier shields with only a central handle, but it could not be slung around the back. Hoplite warriors were trained intensively to keep the ranks and not turn their backs on the enemy.

In addition to the shield hoplites wore full body armour. A helmet made of bronze, covering as much of the face, head and neck as possible without reducing vision or impairing breathing, normally had a felt or leather liner. Often a crest of horsehair decorated the top and served along with the emblems painted on the shield to distinguish friend from foe. Bronze breastplates made of two pieces fitted together at the shoulders and down the sides extended nearly to the hips, while greaves protected the shins and calves. Some warriors also wore armour for arms, ankles and thighs, but there seems to have been no standard for these extras.

The offensive firepower of the hoplite phalanx consisted only of short-range or shock weapons, the spear and the sword. Since the phalanx had no intermediate- or long-range firepower whatsoever, in the form of javelins or bows, it could be used only for shock. The spear, six to eight feet long, made of wood with an iron point, was the primary weapon of the hoplite. It normally had a metal butt that could be used for stabbing a fallen enemy or to plant the spear firmly in the ground for defence against a cavalry charge. The short sword was essentially a reserve weapon to be used only when the spear was broken or dropped.

Hoplite warriors all over Greece wore the same type of armour and fought in accordance with identical tactical principles. There was a tendency over time to reduce somewhat the weight of the body armour in order to gain mobility, so by the fifth century the phalanx was not as heavy as it had been earlier, but it never came close to becoming genuine light infantry. Before the fifth century hoplites were expected to provide their own equipment, and they served without pay, except at Sparta which was organized as a military state,[148] and even there 'pay' as such was not part of the system of military reward.

The tactical use of the phalanx in the field was determined by its equipment. Because the shields on the left arm were heavy and relatively unwieldy, the right side of the hoplite was unprotected. There was an inevitable tendency for the infantryman to edge closer to the man next to him and protect his exposed right side behind his comrade's shield. The usual formation was to deploy the compact infantry in rank and file, normally but not always eight ranks deep. The organization of the phalanx was based more on the files than on the ranks, and the hoplite belonged to his file rather than to his rank, but rank and file were tactically interdependent.

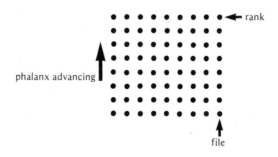

The basic idea was to maintain a solid front rank to prevent gaps for the enemy to penetrate. When a man in the front rank fell, the men in the file behind him stepped up to keep the front rank firm.

Since the phalanx easily prevailed against the 'heroic' aristocratic armies of the eighth and seventh centuries, most Greek states south of Thessaly adopted it, and Greek warfare from 675 to 490 consisted mainly of one phalanx against another. The phalanx was extremely vulnerable in flank and rear to attack by cavalry, light infantry or skirmishers, but those units were not used in the warfare of the period. The only combat possible was between one phalanx and another, and that required fighting on level ground. On hilly terrain it was too difficult to maintain an unbroken line. This style of fighting put a heavy premium on training, discipline and courage. Greek poetry of the archaic age is filled with the ethics of the new tactics – hold your place in the line, dig in, die fighting. Nothing was more disgraceful than to throw down the shield and run, not simply because it was cowardly but because it jeopardized the others in the ranks. The famous story of the Spartan mother who told her son as he left for war to come home with his shield or on it, and by implication not to throw it away in flight, illustrates the new military morality.

Since hoplite war was based on shock, many military historians have had difficulty visualizing how it functioned, and recently one scholar has argued that when two phalanxes engaged they opened their lines so that the fighters in the front could join in single combat with their opponents. But there is little doubt that Greek armies, in closely packed lines in which the warriors relied at least partly on the men on their right for protection, attempted to break the enemy line with pressure of massed ranks and files, each army thrusting its spears at the other. In the unlikely event that the soldiers stood firm consistently on both sides up and down the line, the front ranks would have been completely exhausted after thirty minutes or so of fighting, and the pressure from the rear ranks would have been crushing. But in reality, one side or the other would at some stage have showed weakness at a point in the line, and then the men in the front rank opposite followed by those in file behind would have moved vigorously ahead, using their shields to shove the enemy back. If this led to a breakdown and panic in the enemy line, the battle would have been won, but the advancing files dared not break rank for long without opening a gap in their own line. Unless the entire enemy line began to fall back, it would have been necessary for the attackers to stop the pressure and restore the ranks, returning to a spear-thrusting contest with the enemy. Presumably because the best troops were almost always on the right wing facing less good troops on the enemy's left, there would have been simultaneous advances and withdrawals from the right wings of both armies, and the final thrust to victory could not have come until the left wing of one army held off the enemy right while its own right wing advanced.[149] To be sure, late in the period a hoplite phalanx began to permit one wing to advance ahead of the rest of the line, and we shall see examples of such battles in the next chapter, but until the Peloponnesian War lines advanced mainly as a unit. There were no breakthroughs or flanking movements by a single wing.

Greek warfare of the hoplite era is unique in military history because it rested solely on shock. Until the end of the period, when Spartans began to execute a flanking manoeuvre on their right, head-on contact was the rule. In the nineteenth century du Picq argued that there is no shock in warfare (though he admitted an exception for ancient warfare), and, in this century although John Keegan does not go that far, he too emphasizes its unusual nature. The reason for its general absence is simple – men in battle are afraid; their instinct is to run. They are most afraid of shock or direct hand-to-hand fighting. As du Picq said, 'Man does not enter battle to fight, but for the victory. He does everything that he can to avoid the first and obtain the second.'[150] And in another passage:

> Discipline keeps enemies face to face a little longer, but cannot supplant the instinct of self-preservation, and the sense of fear that goes with it.
> Fear!
> There are officers and soldiers who do not know it, but they are people of rare grit. The mass shudders; because you cannot suppress the flesh.[151]

Greek and Roman armies, as du Picq conceded, did better than most in suppressing 'the flesh' or controlling fear in battle, but because fear in the face of danger is such a natural and powerful human instinct, the price paid by ancient Greek and Roman societies for their rigid discipline was high. Tight tactical organization and a strong, national, military ideology help allay fear on the field, but there is no substitute for firm discipline. Modern societies would not permit their governments to impose the brutal discipline of ancient armies. Yet, despite the discipline, we can be confident that even in antiquity when two phalanxes clashed on the field of battle the men in the ranks were frightened and easily panicked. Discipline and training could not always keep them fighting for long. In the discussion above we considered the mechanics of a drawn-out engagement, and there were some, but most hoplite battles were brief and were decided in the first clash.

One way of reducing fear in ancient as well as modern armies is to provide the troops with officers they can trust, merely one of the functions of any military command structure. Evidence for the organization of the Spartan phalanx in the last half of the fifth century permits a reasonably reliable reconstruction of its command system.[152] The chief tactical unit of the army was a battalion (*lochos*) of 100 men divided into two companies (*pentekostyes*) of 50 men each, and each company was divided into two platoons (*enomotiai*). A platoon had 25 men altogether, including the platoon leader (*enomotarch*) and a rear rank officer (*ouragos*). The platoons each consisted of three squads or files. The organization sounds somewhat complicated and confusing, but it was actually reasonably simple:

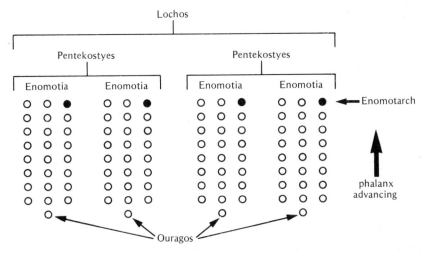

The later Spartan army consisted of six divisions, and each one (*mora*) was commanded by a general (*polemarch*) and contained four battalions. The entire army was under the command of the kings. It is doubtful that the organization was as intricate at the time of the Persian Wars, since Herodotus does not mention the *mora*. Thucydides suggests that Sparta's army was the most elaborately organized in Greece when he says, 'nearly the whole Spartan army, except for a small part, consists of officers serving under other officers. . . .'[153] Although the Athenian phalanx fought eight deep as a general rule, it was divided into ten divisions (*taxeis*) under divisional commanders called taxiarchs. Each of the ten tribes of Athenian citizens provided one division of troops, and the divisions were probably divided into battalions (*lochoi*). Ten generals (*strategoi*) were elected annually, one from each tribe, and the Athenian army suffered severely from lack of unity of command, though normally one of the ten generals would have overall command on any given day.

Because Greek armies relied so heavily on close coordination between ranks and files, and on effective use of the shield and thrusting spear, training was intensive. Soldiers learned how to move from line of column into line of battle while maintaining their ranks and files. Sparta devoted the machinery of government more or less full time to the training of the army, and all adult male Spartan citizens (the so-called Spartiates) were forbidden to engage in commerce and agriculture and required to cultivate warlike skills. Discipline was notoriously severe, and Spartan men regularly lived in military barracks until the age of thirty. Other Greek states were not armed camps, but they usually held male citizens from seventeen to fifty-nine years of age liable to service, and they had a regular training programme to keep their infantry in shape. It was less rigorous than Sparta's, and the Spartan army was deservedly feared throughout the Aegean. Since one of the main purposes of the Spartan army was to keep Sparta's serfs (helots) in subjection, however, Sparta was normally not free to use her phalanx on aggressive forays outside the Peloponnese.[154]

The Greek achievement in naval warfare was as lasting and important as in the organization of the land armies. In his famous 'Archaeology', or survey of early Greek history, in the opening chapters of his history of the Peloponnesian War, Thucydides emphasized naval warfare at the expense of the phalanx. There can be no doubt that the Greeks of the Aegean developed naval technology and tactics to a high art, but the deployment of navies in large-scale warfare in the first millennium BC was first practised by the Persians, using mainly Phoenician ships and sailors, as we saw in the last chapter. When Persia struck against Athens at Marathon in 490, the Persian army was supported by a fleet of 600 ships, and Athens was so clearly outmanned on the sea that her leaders could give no thought to the naval defence of Attica. In 499 Athens had sent twenty ships to help the Ionians in the revolt against Persia, and in 490 the Athenians had a fleet of perhaps 100 since they sent seventy against the island of Paros in the following year. Even after an intensive ship-building programme in the 480s Athens had a warfleet of only 200 ships, and the Persians effectively controlled the sea.[155] The use of a large navy in pursuit of Persian grand strategy in the Aegean forced Greek states to respond to the threat, but Persian naval strength, except for two or three generations in the mid-fifth century, was the dominant force in the Aegean from 525 to 334 BC.

Strategy and Tactics: the Persian Wars

In the fifth century BC Greek hoplite armies fought two of the most famous wars in western military history. One, at the beginning of the century, was a defensive action against a combined land and naval invasion launched against Greece by the Persians, and the other, at the end of the century, was an epochal struggle between Sparta and Athens. Because the Greek historians, especially Herodotus and Thucydides, have left amazingly detailed accounts of the fighting in those wars, they serve as a kind of historical laboratory for the study of Greek and Persian warfare in two quite distinctly different contexts. We shall examine each in turn, with occasional interruptions for analysis of the main features of warfare as it was practised in the fifth century BC.

Persian grand strategy in the Aegean had been aggressive since Cyrus first absorbed Lydia and the Greek cities of Ionia around 545 BC.[156] To defend the northwestern frontier of the Persian Empire against incursions of the Scythians Darius had crossed the Bosporus into European Thrace in 514. Then, in 499, after fruitless Persian aggression in the islands, the Greek cities of Asia Minor rose in revolt against Persian rule. Although most Greek states on the mainland ignored the plight of their fellow Hellenes in Asia, the Athenians agreed to send twenty ships and the Eretrians five. When the navy reached Ephesus, the crews disembarked, joined with the Ionians and marched to Sardis. After Sardis fell to the rebels, Athens withdrew its contingent.

It took some years for Persia to restore control over Ionia, but by 494 the Greeks had been decisively defeated. In 492 the Persian general Mardonius in a combined naval and military operation crossed the Hellespont and seized Thasos, but 300 Persian ships were destroyed in a great storm off Mt Athos. Herodotus claimed that the ultimate destination of this Persian force was Athens; if so, the storm prevented further operations.

MARATHON

In 490 Darius sent an army directly across the sea towards Eretria and Athens. In the previous year the Persian king had despatched representatives to the Greek cities demanding submission to Persia, but Athens had executed them. The Persian army assembled in Cilicia under the command of Datis and Artaphernes; numbering about 20,000 men, including perhaps 800 to 1,000 cavalry and 600 ships, the expedition sailed across the Aegean and took Eretria in Euboea after a siege of seven days. From there the Persians proceeded to Attica, where they landed in the Bay of Marathon.[157]

In this crisis Athenians debated whether to stay behind their walls or to send their army out to meet the Persians in the field. The forceful general Miltiades persuaded them to strike at Marathon, a decision that probably surprised the Persians. The Athenian army numbered approximately 10,000 men, including a small force from neighbouring Plataea. A runner, Pheidippides, was sent to Sparta for help, but the Spartans replied that they could not come until the full of the moon, several days later, when they would complete their most important religious ceremony. In the meantime the Athenians had taken up a position on the edge of the hills overlooking the Persian army encamped on the coast. As long as the phalanx used the terrain for protection, Persian cavalry could not harm it, but something had to be done relatively soon. In a closely divided debate Miltiades persuaded the other generals to attack, and he deployed the army in a thinner formation along the centre than the usual eight ranks in order to extend his own line to match that of the Persians. The wings of the phalanx were kept at least at their normal strength. To reduce the amount of time that his army would be within range of Persian arrows and to achieve tactical surprise, Miltiades ordered the phalanx to advance at the double to engage the Persians, about one mile away.

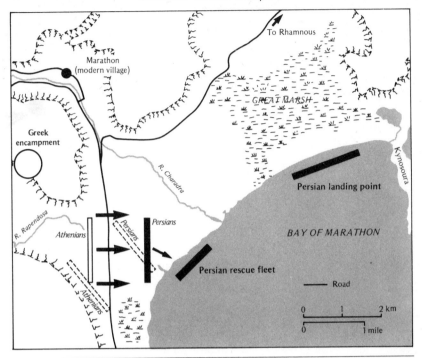

The Persians, therefore, when they saw the Greeks coming on at speed, made
ready to receive them, although it seemed to them that the Athenians were
bereft of their senses, and bent upon their own destruction; for they saw a
mere handful of men coming on at a run without either horsemen or
archers.[158]

The battle of Marathon, 490 BC.

Many historians have doubted that the Athenians could have
moved for a mile at the double with heavy armour and in formation
ready to fight, but Herodotus clearly says that they did and that they
achieved tactical surprise:

The Persians, therefore, when they saw the Greeks coming on at speed, made
ready to receive them, although it seemed to them that the Athenians were
bereft of their senses, and bent upon their own destruction; for they saw a
mere handful of men coming on at a run without either horsemen or
archers.[158]

Modern reenactments have shown conclusively that the Athenians
could not have *run* at top speed for a mile with armour, and many
historians assume that they marched until they came within range of
the Persian archers (about 180 yards), and began to run only at that
point. In that event it would have taken them about fifteen to twenty
minutes to close – not much time for the Persians to get ready. But if
they had moved from the start at the double (or at a jog), which is
infinitely easier than to run at full speed, as any jogger knows, they

109

could have closed in about eight to ten minutes (a slow jog for only one mile).

In either event the Persians had little time to deploy, yet they were able to drive back the Athenian centre and break it. On the wings, however, where the Athenians were stronger, they broke the Persian line and wheeled in to hit the Persian centre in the rear, executing a partial double envelopment. Those Persians who had not been enveloped, including the cavalry, fled to the ships, while the Greeks pursued the Persian centre, inflicting heavy casualties (6,400) with little loss (192). It took some time to kill so many and this permitted the Persians to load their horses on the transports.

Since Herodotus does not say specifically what the Persian cavalry did in this battle, and there is a Byzantine tradition that the cavalry had been withdrawn before the fight began, historians have often assumed that it played no role. But Herodotus' account strongly implies that it was involved, and a Roman historian, Cornelius Nepos, states categorically that it was. Modern military historians tend to believe that the phalanx could not have withstood a Persian cavalry attack, but Persian cavalry was light, relying primarily on the mounted archer, and it could not easily have broken the ranks of the phalanx, even on the flanks, without infantry support. By extending his line Miltiades protected against a flank attack by Persian infantry and the Persian cavalry simply was not able to turn the tide of battle.

Thus in the first major test between a mainland Greek phalanx and the Persian army the phalanx had prevailed. Nevertheless Persia had many advantages not brought to bear on the plain of Marathon. Her vast numerical superiority on land and sea had scarcely been affected by the losses of 490. Although Miltiades definitely outgeneralled Datis and Artaphernes, who did not expect the attack and seem not even to have had their army on ready alert, the Persian Empire had many able commanders, and there was every reason to believe that the Persians would return. The next campaign would be at a different level of magnitude.

THERMOPYLAE-ARTEMISIUM

For various reasons it took over ten years for Persia to seek revenge for the loss at Marathon. In the interval Darius had died (486), and his successor, Xerxes (486–465), after putting down rebellions within the empire, made ready for a full-scale invasion of Greece with the intention of occupying and annexing the Greek mainland. When the Greek states realized the extent of Persian preparations, some of them came to terms with Xerxes, but the southern states met in 481 to form a Hellenic League against the foreigners.

At Athens, resistance to Persian aggression came quickly and spontaneously, no doubt inspired by the knowledge that vengeance for Marathon would fall heavily on the city. A great ship-building programme in the late 480s enabled Athens to deploy a fleet of 200 vessels. In 481, under the urging of Themistocles, a far-sighted general who understood that the Greeks could not hope to stop Persia's land army and should focus on naval warfare, the Athenian people passed the famous Themistocles Decree, found inscribed on stone in AD 1958. The decree called for the evacuation of Athens and for total commitment to a strategy of naval defence.[159] Even the men who normally fought in the phalanx were to report for naval duty. That a major state in the age of hoplite warfare should commit itself so strongly to the revolutionary strategy of the sea reflects the tensions of the period, as well as the ability of Themistocles to foresee the strategic nature of the coming war. The Persian threat demanded dramatic measures.

Religion also played a role in forging the resolution of the Athenians. The adoption of naval strategy was in response to an oracle of Apollo at Delphi, which the Athenians had consulted when it became obvious that Xerxes would invade in force. The oracle had said,

> Safe shall the wooden wall continue for thee and thy children.
> Wait not the tramp of the horse, nor the footmen mightily moving
> Over the land, but turn your back to the foe and retire ye.[160]

Delphic oracles were often ambiguous, but Themistocles persuaded the Athenians that the wooden walls were the ships of the fleet. The decision to evacuate and to trust in the fleet was taken before the first meeting of the Hellenic League. The Athenians were able to postpone evacuation once other Greek states agreed to stop Persia in the north, but they did not abandon their faith in the navy.

In the new alliance the members – including Athens, Sparta and Corinth – pledged to cooperate against Xerxes under the overall command of the Spartans, whose warlike reputation and strength made them the only possible choice. By achieving unity of command the mainland Greeks gained an advantage that the earlier Ionian rebels had lacked. In the spring of 480, after assembling an army of 200,000 men or more, Xerxes began the march towards Greece.[161] He advanced to the Hellespont, which he bridged with ships and crossed; the Greeks were naturally impressed with the engineering skills of the Persian army, far beyond anything they had known. Persian strategy was to move into Greece with a land army so large that the Greeks would have no prospect of success against it. Such an invasion required the use of a huge fleet, since the army was too big to live off the land, and the interdependence of Persian army and fleet caused Themistocles and the Athenians to believe that victory might be won in a naval engagement. The loss of the Persian fleet would force the land army to retire. But the Athenians were unable to convince Sparta and the other states of the wisdom of this strategy.

From the beginning the Spartans were certain that the best military strategy was to build a wall across the Isthmus of Corinth and to deploy the Greek allied army behind it to halt the Persian advance. The fact that some of the allied states were north of the line was not lost on the other Greeks, especially on those cities which found themselves exposed by geography to the grip of Persia, and obvious political complications forced Sparta to set aside this plan. Spartan enthusiasm for an offensive, northward strategy was limited, and as masters of hoplite warfare, they did not share Athens' willingness to stake all on the sea. Yet the Spartans did agree to send an army to the northern border of Thessaly, mainly because it seemed possible to keep Thessaly loyal by doing so. When the force reached Tempe, however, the position proved indefensible, and the allies fell back.[162]

Thereupon they decided to halt Xerxes' inexorable advance by placing a land army at Thermopylae, where there was a narrow pass between the mountains and the sea on the most likely route of the Persian advance. In the waters nearby, off Artemisium, the Greek fleet might also hold the Persian navy, and the strategy was simply to stop the Persian colossus in its tracks. If the Greeks could block Xerxes' progress, they could reasonably assume that he would abandon the invasion, since it would have been strategically and logistically impossible for the king to keep the full Persian army and fleet immobilized for long in northern Greece. Problems would almost certainly arise in Persia as well if the invasion became bogged down.[163]

With the benefit of hindsight, the Greeks undoubtedly seem naïve to have imagined that they could stop the powerful Persian army at Thermopylae. Yet in many ways both Thermopylae and Artemisium were ideal sites for the strategy envisaged by the Hellenic League. The pass of Thermopylae was at one point wide enough only for a single cart to move through. The Persians could not extend a line of battle in such an area, and they were forced to waste their manpower in a line of column. Likewise in the constricted waters off Artemisium the lighter, faster and more numerous ships of the Persian fleet (1,200 triremes) were hampered against the Greeks (325 triremes), whose advantage in addition to the confines of the area was that they were more familiar with the coast.

The Greeks, with about 7,000 men under the command of the Spartan king Leonidas, took up their position in the pass. Only after Leonidas arrived in the region, did he learn of the mountainous path that could be used by the Persians to encircle him and attack his rear, but he posted a force of 1,000 men to guard that route. When Xerxes' army arrived at the main pass, the king could not believe that such a small number of men hoped to prevent his passage, so he waited four days in the expectation that the Greeks would withdraw rather than fight. Although the southern Greeks in the allied army did indeed panic and urge retreat to the Isthmus, Leonidas knew that the northern Greeks would defect to Persia, or Medize, as the Greeks called it, unless Sparta made a genuine effort to defend the pass. So he calmed his army, sent out a call for help, and prepared to hold his ground.

Impatient with the delay, Xerxes decided to force his way through. On the fifth day the Persians moved into the narrow pass and found that in the constricted area where they could not envelop the Greek army they could also not stand up to the heavily armed hoplites in hand-to-hand combat. The Greeks carried longer spears and were better trained in their use. At the end of the first day of fighting Xerxes committed the Ten Thousand Immortals, but they did not dislodge Leonidas and his army, not even when Persians with whips drove them from the rear. Herodotus shows that Leonidas used feinting tactics to draw Persians onto disadvantageous ground:

The Spartans fought in a way worthy of note, and showed themselves far more skilful in fight than their adversaries, often turning their backs, and making as though they were all flying away, on which the barbarians would rush after them with much noise and shouting, when the Spartans at their approach would wheel round and face their pursuers, in this way destroying vast numbers of the enemy.[164]

On the second day Xerxes hoped that the Greek army would prove exhausted by the previous effort while he easily threw in fresh troops, but Leonidas sent up the contingents of his allies in rotating waves, regularly resting his warriors, and again the Persians were thwarted. At this point Greek perfidy played a role – that evening a Greek defector hoping for reward told Xerxes of the secret path around to the rear of the Greek position, and the king despatched a unit to force this pass during the night. By dawn the Persians had reached the summit, and when the defenders stationed there earlier by Leonidas felt the sting of Persian arrows, they withdrew to higher ground to hold their position. The Persians simply ignored them, marching instead over and down towards the rear of the Greek army on the coast. Scouts brought Leonidas reports of the Persian manoeuvre, and he dismissed a large portion of his army but heroically stayed on himself with the 300 Spartans and several hundred allies to serve as a rearguard to cover the withdrawal. It was his job, and he simply did his duty. In the famous struggle on the third day Leonidas fell fighting, as did two of the brothers of King Xerxes. Attacked from front and rear, the Greek holding force was wiped out, and in their honour an inscription was later set up on the site which read: 'Go, stranger, and tell the Spartans that here we lie in obedience to their command.'

The battle of Thermopylae deservedly became part of the Spartan legend. Troops hopelessly trapped by the enemy do sometimes dig in and fight tenaciously, but that is rare. Ordinarily they break. What is remarkable about Sparta's last stand is that the best troops responded to Leonidas' orders to cover the retreat and maintained their formation in suicidal circumstances. There is no greater testimony to the rigorous Spartan system of training and discipline, a fact generally recognized by the Greeks, though too often dismissed as quixotic romanticism by rationalist historians. Many armies would have broken under far less threatening conditions than those faced by the Spartans in the pass at Thermopylae.

In the meantime, according to Herodotus, the Greeks had challenged the Persian fleet near Artemisium on the same three days as the battle of Thermopylae. Several days earlier the Persian fleet had anchored off Cape Sepias where it was not possible to beach most of the ships. A great three-day storm came up and destroyed perhaps a

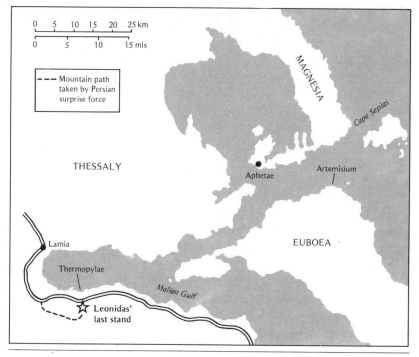

Artemisium and Thermopylae, 480 BC.

third of the Persian ships while the Greeks in safer harbour weathered the storm. Afterwards the remainder of the Persian navy sailed to Aphetae (see map), and in a skirmish the Greek fleet at Artemisium captured fifteen Persian vessels. Despite their losses the Persian fleet still outnumbered the Greek, and the Persians despatched some of their warships out around the east coast of Euboea to circle the island and hem in the Greek navy.

Herodotus says that the battle of Thermopylae, and therefore the battle of Artemisium, began two days after the Persian fleet reached Aphetae. On the first day of the naval battle the Greek fleet advanced against the Persian, and the Persians with their greater numbers attempted an envelopment (*periplous*), but the Greeks, according to Herodotus,

brought the sterns of their ships together into a small compass, and turned their prows on every side towards the barbarians; after which, at a second signal, although enclosed within a narrow space, and closely pressed upon by the foe, yet they fell bravely to work, and captured thirty ships of the barbarians. . . .[165]

Nightfall brought an end to the engagement, and on day one, as on the land, the Greeks had the advantage.

During the night a storm frightened the main Persian fleet and destroyed the contingent that had been sent around the island. On the second day Greek reinforcements arrived from Athens, and they again engaged the Persian fleet, but with indecisive results. Then on the third day the Persian navy took the offensive again, approaching the Greek fleet at Artemisium as the Spanish Armada swept through the English Channel in 1588, in a half-moon formation, hoping to execute a *periplous*. The Persians had difficulty keeping their ships in formation, and in tough fighting the Greeks avoided encirclement, so that finally the engagement ended as a draw, with heavy losses on both sides. That night news reached the Greeks of the defeat at Thermopylae, and the Greek commanders on the sea decided to withdraw.

The battle of Artemisium had not been as decisive tactically as the land battle at Thermopylae, but strategically it was every bit as calamitous for the Greeks. Xerxes had thwarted the Greek holding action on land and sea, and his fleet, though severely damaged by storms, had given the Greeks a rough fight in battle. The Persian war machine rolled relentlessly forward, and nothing now stood between it and Athens.

SALAMIS

Although the Greeks had been defeated at Thermopylae-Artemisium, their fleet fell back in good order, and the bulk of their land forces had not been committed at all, so they retained nearly their full military and naval strength.[166] Unfortunately they had no plan to deploy it, since their strategy had been simply to stop Xerxes before he reached Athens. Throughout the war Greek strategic thinking was shaped on an *ad hoc* basis as Greek forces faced one crisis after another. The Athenians favoured an aggressive naval strategy while Sparta wanted to defend the Isthmus, and Greek strategy was often based on an unhappy compromise between the two most powerful city-states.

After Artemisium, at Athens' request the fleet sailed to the island of Salamis off the coast of Attica to help in the evacuation of the city. The earlier decision to evacuate, reflected in the Themistocles Decree of

September 481, had been ignored after the Hellenic League agreed to stop the Persian advance first at Tempe and then at Thermopylae, but the failure of that strategy left Athens at the mercy of Persia. Immediate evacuation was the only alternative. The fleet ferried Athenians to Troezen, Salamis and Aegina.

Eurybiades, the Spartan commander of the fleet, assembled leaders of the various naval contingents at Salamis for a council of war. A sense of urgency weighed on the participants because the Persian army had taken Athens within nine days after Thermopylae and had burnt the city. The Greek commanders decided to move the fleet to the Isthmus, where fortifications had been completed on land, to fight another concerted land and naval engagement there, but during the night Themistocles persuaded Eurybiades to fight at Salamis. The Athenian leader believed that the waters off the Isthmus favoured the Persians, because there was room for them to fight there in an extended formation. The next day, in a second meeting of the war council, after heated debate, Eurybiades gave orders to prepare for battle. Themistocles had argued that the narrow waters off Salamis were ideal, given Greek abilities in tactical manoeuvre but limited numerical strength.

In the meantime Xerxes too had convened a council of war, and his commanders urged him to press his advantage in morale by attacking the Greek fleet immediately before it could withdraw to the Isthmus. When it finally became apparent to everyone, Greeks and Persians alike, that battle was imminent, Herodotus says that some Greek commanders realized that they had no fallback in the event of Persian victory except small islands, and they urged reconsideration of the possibility of withdrawal to the Isthmus where they could use the Peloponnese as a base. Themistocles, afraid that Greek contingents would begin to withdraw on their own, sent a night-time message to Xerxes saying that he, Themistocles, was defecting to Persia and that the king could trap the Greeks at Salamis if he moved before they abandoned their position. Xerxes then ordered his fleet in, and the Greeks were trapped. They had to fight.

Many historians have rejected as an invention this story of Xerxes and Themistocles, arguing that the two sides had already agreed to battle and that Xerxes would not have believed such an unlikely story anyway. But is it really unlikely? Athens had fallen, and the Persian high command undoubtedly knew of the dissension among Greek

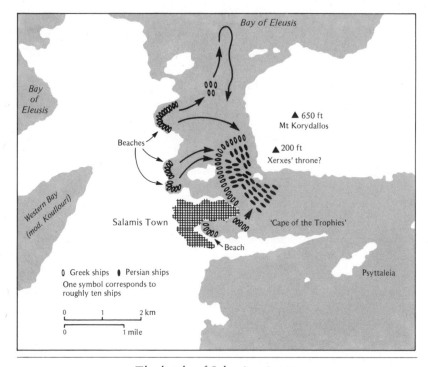

The battle of Salamis, 480 BC.

commanders on matters of strategy. Many Greek states and leaders
had already defected to Persia, and with Athens in ruins Xerxes might
easily have believed that Themistocles preferred Medizing to a
strategy of defence of the Peloponnese. It was natural, from the point
of view of the Great King, for Athenians to come to terms with Persia.

In any event Persian manoeuvres had forced a battle. To entrap the
Greeks Xerxes divided his army into three squadrons. One of them
sailed south around the island of Salamis to close the Megarian strait
in the west; another stationed itself between Salamis and the small
island of Psyttaleia (Lipsokoutali); and the third took position
between Psyttaleia and the Attic peninsula (near Mounychia). The
Persian fleet was hampered by lack of space, and the crews spent a
sleepless night under oar. When the battle began the next morning,
late in September, the Greeks moved out first to attack the Persians.
Herodotus says that the Persians had recovered their numerical
strength after the losses at Artemisium by drawing upon new

contingents from the islands, and that the Greeks had a fleet of over 300 ships. Because the Greeks embarked their hoplites, they were in a better position for boarding in the narrow waters.

As the Persian fleet advanced in line abreast to meet the Greek attack, the constriction of the waters in the channel forced them to compress their line, and some of their ships ran afoul while others fell behind. The Greeks backed water, drawing out a few of the faster Persian ships in advance of the Persian formation and then darted forward to destroy them. The Greek navy maintained formation while executing this manoeuvre, but the Persians were thrown into confusion. Having seized the initial advantage in waters inappropriate for Persian numerical strength, the Greeks vigorously attacked along their line, and the great war fleet of the Persian Empire was decisively defeated. Greek losses numbered some forty ships while 200 Persian vessels were sunk and an untold number captured.

At the time the Greeks failed to realize the extent of their victory. The next day Xerxes gave some indications of resuming the battle, but his navy had been demoralized, and the loyalty of Ionian Greeks fighting for Persia was dubious. On the second night after the battle Xerxes ordered the fleet to withdraw to the Hellespont, there to cover the retreat of his army back into Asia. Greece had been saved from the terrible power of the combined army and fleet of the Persian Empire.

PLATAEA

But the war was not yet won. Xerxes returned to Asia Minor with the bulk of his army, where he claimed victory for the sack of Athens, but he had left behind, under the able general Mardonius, a land army of some 50,000 men including perhaps 10,000 cavalry. Salamis had changed the nature of the war. No longer could Persia rely on interdependent operations of army and fleet; but an army small enough to live off the land, yet larger and much more mobile than any army the Greeks might field, still had a chance to effect the conquest Xerxes had originally intended. Throughout the winter of 480–479, Mardonius put pressure on Athens to defect, which would have given naval superiority to Persia again, while the Spartans planned to defend the Isthmus. Their strategy was more reasonable now that the Persians had no fleet and therefore no means of hitting the Greek defenders from the rear, but Athens could not acquiesce in a strategy that left her vulnerable to the Persian invaders, and she delivered an ultimatum to the Hellenic League either to move northwards against the barbarians or to witness an Athenian alliance with Persia. Only when threatened in this way did the Spartans decide to move up with the allied army to meet Mardonius at Plataea.[167]

The battle of Plataea was a complicated affair, illustrating many of the differences between Greek heavy infantry and the lighter, more mobile, Persian army. One problem for the Greeks was simply how to get at the Persian army, how to force it into battle under conditions in which the smaller heavy infantry (about 40,000 men) might avoid envelopment by the horsemen of Asia. Forced to abandon the Isthmus, the Greeks had given the strategic advantage to Mardonius.

The commander of the Greek allied army was Pausanias, a regent for an infant Spartan king. As he moved into southern Boeotia, he took up a position on the ridge of mountains extending towards the field of the Asopus river facing Mardonius, whose camp was on the other side. In fact, Mardonius had selected the battlefield, and Pausanias was reluctant to close with the Persians because to do so he would have had to move down onto the level ground and expose his flanks and rear to Persian cavalry. To force Pausanias into battle, Mardonius used his cavalry to threaten the Greek line of supply, and after several days he fouled the spring that served as the Greeks' main source of water. Meanwhile Pausanias, expecting battle almost any day, rearranged his line. Originally the Spartans had taken the place of honour on the right wing, with the Athenians on the left and the other allies occupying the centre. Mardonius had placed his best forces on his left opposite the Spartans. Since the Athenians had had experience at Marathon against Persian land forces, Pausanias decided to place them on his right and to send the Spartans to the left, but Mardonius made a comparable shift in his own line. When Pausanias saw what had happened, he put his army back into its original formation. This is one of the first occasions in military history in which the tactical confusion that frequently characterizes later warfare can be so clearly detailed.[168]

Finally, after about two weeks altogether, Pausanias decided to move his army to a different position nearer Plataea, and his men tried to execute the change under cover of night and in disarray. Seizing the opportunity Mardonius attacked at sunrise before Pausanias had ordered his line. '[Mardonius] crossed the Asopus, and led the Persians forward at a run directly upon the track of the Greeks, whom he believed to be in actual flight,' wrote Herodotus, but Mardonius

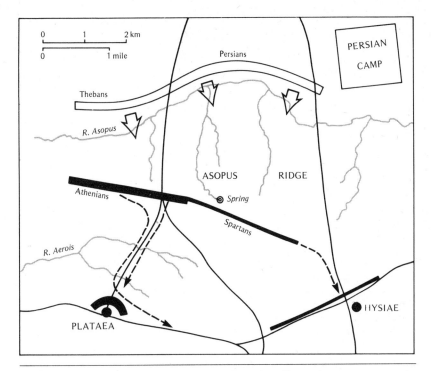

The battle of Plataea, 479 BC. The Greeks originally took a position on the Asopus ridge, but when they withdrew under cover of night to a line nearer the city of Plataea, they became confused and disoriented. The Persians attacked the following morning.

had apparently acted too impetuously before arranging his own line: 'When the commanders of the other divisions of the barbarians saw the Persians pursuing the Greeks so hastily, they all forthwith seized their standards, and hurried after at their best speed, in great disorder and disarray.'[169] On the verge of being overwhelmed, Pausanias regrouped the Spartans and closed with the Persian infantry. Mardonius personally led his cavalry, and the battle was decided when a Spartan warrior brought Mardonius down, according to one tradition by throwing a rock. The death of Mardonius sparked panic along the Persian line, and the second in command, Artabazus, abandoned the field, and led 40,000 survivors across the Hellespont. Greece had met the Persian giant face to face and driven him back into Asia.

While these events transpired on the Greek mainland, the Spartan king Leotychides led the allied fleet across the sea and carried the naval war to the eastern Aegean. On the same day as the battle of Plataea, according to tradition, the Greek fleet met the Persian near Mycale, opposite the island of Samos, where the Persians had beached their ships. The Greeks eventually disembarked, and the battle was decided on land in a clash of the crews. Victory at Mycale gave the Greeks unchallenged control of the Aegean for the next two or three generations.

The triumph of Greece over Persia has puzzled analysts since the day it became apparent. On paper Persia should have won.[170] Colossal numerical superiority, a more sophisticated logistical system, the tactical use of skirmishers and cavalry, ample intermediate- and long-range firepower, the confidence and intimidating prestige of a highly successful imperialistic tradition, and the strategic sophistication of Persian generalship combined with unity of command ought to have ensured victory. What happened? Why did the Greeks win the Persian Wars?[171]

The Greeks certainly had some advantages. They fought on their own soil, and their interior lines of supply and communication were much easier to maintain than Persia's. Patriotism, a sense of Greek against barbarian, gave them an advantage in morale, and their heavy infantry was more effective in shock. Greeks tended to explain their victory either as the triumph of the spear over the bow, that is, the superiority of their heavy infantry, or as the result of the brilliant strategic insight of Themistocles, who saw how important the navy would be in the war. Though there is merit in both views, they do not, singly or together, explain the Greek victory. Persia had the means to deal with heavy infantry by simply not engaging it on unfavourable terrain, or by overwhelming it with superior numbers, and her fleet should have beaten the Greek navy no matter how clearly Themistocles realized the strategic interdependence of Persian military and naval operations.

A passing comment in Thucydides shows that even the ancient Greeks, or at least some of them, understood the situation. He attributes to a Corinthian envoy to Sparta in 432 the observation that Persians were defeated by their own mistakes, and though this view would not have been popular in Athens or Sparta, it must surely be correct.[172] Xerxes need not have been drawn into the waters off

Salamis, nor should Datis and Artaphernes have been subjected to a double envelopment by a numerically inferior force at Marathon. It did not require military genius for Persian commanders to avoid the pitfalls of their campaigns; and they were not stupid or lacking in sufficiently sophisticated strategic and tactical insight. Many generals down to modern times have made comparable errors. Their problem was overconfidence lapsing into carelessness, an overconfidence justified by their obvious advantages and the record of Persian success in the field. But carelessness led to error, and error to defeat. The Persian Wars are testimony to the fact that at least some major conflicts are decided on the battlefield, not by the relative strengths and weaknesses of the combatants at the outset. Notwithstanding Persian mistakes, the Greeks could not have won without the morale and discipline that were the by-product of the system of training for their heavy infantry, a spirit that infected even their fleet.

Strategy and Tactics: the Peloponnesian War

Following the Persian Wars Athens built a maritime empire in the Aegean. After freeing the Ionian Greeks from Persian domination, she used her fleet to control the sea, and her power grew until the Athenian Empire became the equal in strength of Sparta's Peloponnesian League. The two armed alliances, one based on naval and the other on land forces, often clashed in the mid-fifth century, but the rivalry came to a decisive head only in 431 when the Spartan army moved into Attica in the opening campaign of the Peloponnesian War (431–404 BC). In response to this attack, Pericles, the Athenian leader, had developed a strategy to destroy Spartan power.[173]

THE FIRST PHASE – THE ARCHIDAMIAN WAR

The first phase of the war, named after the Spartan King Archidamus, who led the initial assault on Attica, was in many ways a desultory war of attrition that lasted for ten years (431–421) and ended in a stalemate. It is a military historian's nightmare, because both sides often dispersed their forces to fight small actions simultaneously all over the Greek world. But it was militarily significant in illustrating the limitations of heavy infantry and of naval power and in preparing the way for major innovations in the Greek style of warfare.

Periclean strategy for the war against Sparta is simple to describe, but it was difficult to implement. Pericles believed that Sparta's strength on land was too great for Athens to challenge, and he intended to abandon the Attic countryside to the attackers while the Athenians stayed behind their walls, connected by long walls down to the harbour at Piraeus. The fleet protected the shipping lanes necessary to provide the city with sufficient supplies, and it was large enough for part of it to be used in offensive operations around the Peloponnese. The main idea was to neutralize the Spartan army by denying it a chance to defeat Athens' own phalanx and to strike hard by sea to bring the Peloponnesian League to its knees. Periclean strategy was by no means entirely defensive, nor was it simply a strategy of exhaustion, since it did rest partly on offensive operations by sea. Needless to say, some Athenians bitterly resented standing by helplessly while the Spartan army ravaged the land, but the prestige of Pericles held the city-state to his determined course.

The strength of Athens was great. Although her land army was outclassed by Sparta's, the Athenians had 13,000 ready hoplites and an additional 16,000 for garrison duties of various kinds. Besides these forces, partly because Athens had learned from the wars with Persia, there was a cavalry of 1,200 and a contingent of 1,600 archers. The strong walls of the city and a fleet of 300 triremes combined to make Athens an impregnable bulwark against Spartan attack, and the tribute from Athenian subjects in the Aegean yielded revenues far greater than those of Sparta. Furthermore the Athenians had strategic unity of command, since they could dictate to their subjects, while Sparta's allies were more nearly equal powers, at least in the decision-making structure of the Peloponnesian League. On the other hand, Sparta, by drawing to the fullest extent upon the resources of her allies, could deploy an army of up to 50,000 and a fleet less strong than that of Athens, but sufficient for the small engagements that characterized the Archidamian War.[174]

In five of the first seven years of the war, from 431 to 425, Sparta invaded Attica and inflicted heavy damage in the peninsula, but the forays accomplished no strategic advantage. Even the great plague that swept through Athens in 430–429 and again in 427–426 did not break Athenian resolve, although it left fatalities approaching twenty-five per cent of the population in its wake, and in 429 Pericles fell victim to the disease. Yet Athens held firm, even when Sparta and

Thebes took Plataea by siege in 427. Because Spartan military action around Athens itself proved strategically indecisive, the war was determined by fighting in far-flung regions of Greece where Athenian naval resources were brought to bear.

One of the most important theatres of war was in the west, in the Corinthian Gulf, and to the north, around the island of Corcyra, the modern Corfu. When the war began, Corcyra, an ally of Athens, was already fighting with Corinth, the strongest member of the Peloponnesian League next to Sparta. Early in the war Corinth tried to subvert the Corcyrean alliance with Athens, but Athenian ships intervened, and by 425, after a bloody civil war in Corcyra, the Athenian side had massacred its opponents, and the area remained secure.

Much more interesting naval battles occurred in the Corinthian Gulf, where the Athenian admiral Phormio brilliantly won two major engagements against the Peloponnesian fleet. In 429 Sparta provoked the fighting by trying to dislodge Athens from its base at Naupactus on the Gulf. One thousand hoplites were committed on land to the region, and a Peloponnesian fleet of forty-seven ships from Corinth moved against Phormio, who was stationed near the entrance of the Gulf with twenty Athenian triremes. Phormio manoeuvred to place the enemy ships, slower than his own, in open waters, and the Corinthians, hoping to take advantage of their superior numbers and at the same time to nullify Athenian tactical expertise in the *diekplous*, formed a defensive circle. Five of the fastest Corinthian ships were inside the circle, ready to come to the support of any point on the circumference that the Athenians might attack. Phormio moved against them in line ahead, sailed around them again and again, each time driving them closer together into a smaller circle until they ran foul of each other. In exposing the sides of his vessels to the Corinthian rams he took a risk, but the greater speed and manoeuvrability of the Athenians made it a reasonable one. Then, when the wind came up to add to the Corinthian difficulties, Phormio attacked. Thucydides' description of the battle vividly illustrates the dilemma of the Corinthians:

When the wind came down [the Gulf], the enemy's ships were now in a narrow space, and what with the wind and the small craft dashing against them, at once fell into confusion: ship fell foul of ship, while the crews were pushing them off with poles, and by their shouting, swearing and struggling , with one another, made captains' orders and boatswains' cries alike inaudible, and through being unable for want of practice to clear their oars in the rough water, prevented the vessels from obeying their helmsmen properly. At this moment Phormio gave the signal, and the Athenians attacked.[175]

In this victory Phormio captured twelve Corinthian ships, and the Spartans were furious that the larger Peloponnesian fleet had not prevailed. They demanded another battle and sternly instructed their commander to win it this time! So, a month later the Peloponnesians with an enlarged fleet of seventy-seven triremes under Brasidas pressed Phormio near his base at Naupactus. To keep Phormio out of the open waters at the entrance to the Gulf, the Peloponnesian fleet moved in four lines towards Naupactus along the southern shore, and the Athenian fleet of twenty ships had to keep up with them in single file on the other side, protecting their base. Suddenly the Peloponnesian fleet executed a ninety degree turn and in line abreast moved out to trap the Athenians in a *periplous*. Since their line was four deep, it was not as long as it might have been, and eleven of the Athenian ships escaped and retreated to Naupactus. Ten of them faced about to meet twenty pursuing Corinthian vessels whose crews were already singing songs of victory and approached carelessly in a broken formation. The remaining Athenian trireme circled around and rammed and sank the leading Peloponnesian ship, whereupon the other ten Athenian vessels joined in the fight, drove off the enemy while capturing six ships and regained the ships they had lost earlier in the battle. Through initiative and daring they turned defeat into victory.

But afterwards the Spartans showed some daring of their own, and, if they had been only slightly bolder, they might have gained a great strategic advantage. When the Peloponnesian fleet returned to Corinth, as winter was approaching, Brasidas and other commanders agreed to a surprise attack on the Athenian fleet in the unprotected home harbour of Piraeus. Forty Peloponnesian triremes were based near Megara, and, although the ships suffered from neglect, crewmen of the Corinthian fleet marched over the Isthmus carrying their own oars and cushions to man those ships and attack the Piraeus. They sailed out at night, probably somewhat frightened by the boldness of their plan, and fell on Salamis first after the wind had slowed their pace. There they took three Athenian ships and began to ravage the island. This alerted the Athenians in Piraeus who manned their fleet and set out to meet the Corinthians, who in the meantime, concerned that their ships were letting in water, returned to Megara, disembarked and marched back to Corinth. Thereafter the Athenians maintained a ready alert at Piraeus, but Thucydides believed that Sparta lost a golden opportunity when its navy abandoned strategic mission and aim and diverted its course to Salamis.

There was considerable fighting in other theatres. Mytilene on the island of Lesbos revolted from Athens in 428, and Sparta agreed to send forty triremes to help and to intensify the annual attack on the Attic peninsula, but Mytilene ran out of food and surrendered before the Spartan fleet arrived. Although Athens maintained its position in the Aegean, the revolt exposed a weakness in the empire – Athens' subjects resented their subjection and were prepared to use the struggle with Sparta to their own advantage.[175]

In Sicily Athens turned the tables on Sparta. The western Greek states of southern Italy and Sicily had traditionally been close to Corinth and Sparta, and at the outset of the war Sparta called upon them for help. Although it is doubtful that much arrived, the Peloponnesian League did depend on trade with the region, particularly in grain, for its food supply, and the Athenians tried to cut it off by encouraging her allies in the area to oppose the great city of Syracuse, a staunch ally of the Peloponnesians. Athens intervened directly in 427 with a fleet of twenty ships, and in 425 increased the total to sixty. In response to this threat the leaders of Syracuse proposed a general peace in Sicily, to which the Athenian commanders agreed. Nevertheless, although Athens had generally accomplished its strategic objective by preventing aid from the western Greeks reaching the Peloponnese, the Athenians at home punished their commanders for accepting anything less than unconditional surrender.

In the first six years of the war (431–426) Periclean strategy had worked to Athens' advantage. To be sure, Plataea had fallen to Thebes and Sparta, and Attica had been at the mercy of the Spartan army, while the plague took a heavy toll; but around Corcyra and the Corinthian Gulf Athens had held its own and inflicted losses on the Peloponnesians. The aggressive naval policy in Sicily was strategically successful, the revolt of Mytilene had been crushed, and in the northwestern Aegean in the Chalcidice the city of Potidaea, a colony of Corinth, had surrendered to Athens in the winter of 430–429. Athens remained strong, and the Spartans seemed unable to use their land power effectively against the naval giant.

In 425 a surprising campaign very nearly led to Sparta's capitulation. That year, as the war in Sicily and Corcyra was nearing a close, an Athenian fleet sailing west to Sicily by way of Corcyra was driven by a storm into the harbour of the Spartan stronghold of Pylos on the southwestern corner of the Peloponnese (see map).[176] Better known in modern times as the Bay of Navarino, the ancient bay of Pylos was a major strategic site in Messenia, the heart of Spartan helot country. One of the Athenians, Demosthenes, was allowed to stay behind with five ships to seize the territory while the rest of the Athenian fleet sailed on to Corcyra, but, when the Spartans realized the danger, they recalled their army from Attica and sent units to the vicinity of Pylos. A Peloponnesian fleet of sixty ships was summoned from Corcyra, and the Spartans hoped to surround the Athenian fortifications at Pylos by land and by sea. As part of their plan they occupied the nearby island of Sphacteria by landing 420 Spartan hoplites, but the initial assault on the Athenian fortifications failed.

Meanwhile Demosthenes had sent to the Athenian fleet for help, and fifty ships finally arrived. They sailed into the bay where the Spartans were waiting for them, and in the fighting the Athenians got the upper hand and blockaded the Spartans on Sphacteria. The Spartan government sent some of their leaders, the ephors, to examine the situation, and they decided that it was hopeless. So they negotiated a truce with Demosthenes and sent ambassadors to Athens to ask for peace. Periclean strategy had very nearly worked, but the Athenians refused to negotiate. One of their leaders, Cleon, persuaded them to set conditions so harsh that Sparta had no choice but to continue the war, and shortly afterwards Cleon himself was sent to Pylos to complete the victory. He promised to do so within twenty days!

Cleon, working with Demosthenes, landed several thousand Athenians on the south end of Sphacteria against Sparta's 420 hoplites, who had taken a strong position on the north end of the island. When the Spartans were hopelessly surrounded, the surviving 292 hoplites surrendered. Of them, 120 were Spartan citizens belonging to the crack Spartan army. Thucydides makes it clear that Athens' victory at Pylos was regarded as significant all over Greece:

Nothing that happened in the war surprised the Hellenes so much as this. It was the opinion that no force or famine could make the Spartans give up their arms, but that they would fight on as they could, and die with them in their hands.[177]

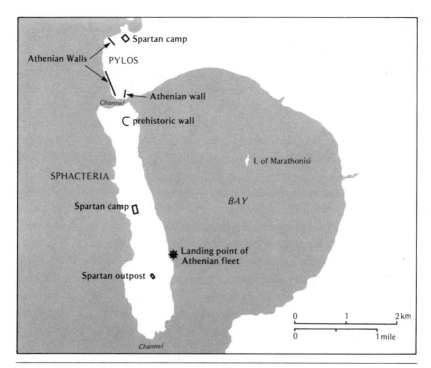

Spartan camp

Athenian Walls

PYLOS

Athenian wall

Channel

prehistoric wall

I. of Marathonisi

SPHACTERIA

Spartan camp

BAY

Landing point of
Athenian fleet

Spartan outpost

0   1   2 km

0   1 mile

Channel

Pylos and Sphacteria, 425 BC.

Athens had shattered the glory of Thermopylae, and Sparta was no longer invincible on the land. The prisoners were taken to Athens, and the Spartan government was informed that they would be killed if there were any further invasions of Attica.

Athens had achieved her success on Pylos with overwhelming manpower, but Athenian use of new, light armed infantry, the peltasts, about whom we shall learn more in the next chapter, and of archers, showed that warfare was changing and that the Greeks were beginning to see the importance of the tactical flexibility of the Persian army. Thucydides' description of the final stages of battle on Sphacteria illustrates the new style of warfare emerging in the late fifth century:

Meanwhile the main body of [Spartan] troops in the island, seeing their outpost cut off and an army advancing against them, serried their ranks and pressed forward to close with the Athenian heavy infantry in front of them, the light troops being upon their flanks and rear. However, they were not able to engage or to profit by their superior skill, the light troops keeping them in check on either side with their missiles, and the heavy infantry remaining stationary instead of advancing to meet them; and although they routed the light troops whenever they ran up and approached too closely, yet they retreated fighting, being lightly equipped, and easily getting the start in their flight, from the difficult and rugged nature of the ground, in an island hitherto desert, over which the Spartans could not pursue them with their heavy armour. . . . The shouting accompanying the onset [of the light troops] confounded the Spartans, unaccustomed to this mode of fighting; dust rose from the newly burnt wood, and it was impossible to see in front of one with the arrows and stones flying through clouds of dust from the hands of neighbouring assailants. The Spartans had now to sustain a rude conflict; their caps would not keep out the arrows, darts had broken off in the armour of the wounded, while they themselves were helpless for offence, being prevented from using their eyes to see what was before them, and unable to hear the words of command for the hubbub raised by the enemy; danger encompassed them on every side, and there was no hope of any means of defence or safety.[178]

The victory, however, proved to be a mixed blessing for Athens. Athenian intransigence persuaded the Spartans that compromise was impossible, and they renewed their efforts to win a military victory. Athens, on the other hand, was inspired by Cleon's boldness to abandon Periclean strategy to seek victory on land as well as sea. The results proved her undoing and led by 421 to a negotiated settlement.

The first act of the new Athenian strategy was a two-pronged attack by land in 424, the first from Athens against Megara and the second from the Athenian base at Naupactus against Boeotia. Sparta and the Boeotian cities thwarted both efforts, which ended in the failure of Athens' new land strategy.

In the meantime Sparta attacked the one strongpoint in the Athenian Empire that was assailable by land, the Chalcidice of the northwest Aegean coast. Early in the war Athens had taken Potidaea by siege, but other cities of the Chalcidian League, encouraged by Perdiccas, King of Macedon, continued their resistance to Athenian domination of the area. In 424 the Spartan general Brasidas marched north with an army of helots and won much territory, including the city of Amphipolis. Athens used her fleet to counterattack, and won back some of the cities, but Sparta held Amphipolis. Although Sparta and Athens, both weary of the long fighting, agreed to a truce for one year in 423, it was generally ignored in the Chalcidice. When it expired in 422, Cleon moved out from Athens with an army, and, when he reached Amphipolis, he fought a great battle with Brasidas.

Cleon approached Amphipolis before all his reinforcements had arrived, and initially did not intend to fight so much as to reconnoitre the area. Brasidas meanwhile had concealed his own army, which was ragtag and badly equipped in comparison with the fresh Athenian troops, inside Amphipolis partly to prevent the Athenians from observing their condition. The two armies were each about 5,000 strong. Ironically the Spartans, superb in the tactics of heavy infantry, had learned from Persia and from Athens the value of lighter units, and Brasidas had some at his disposal. When he saw Cleon approach carelessly close to the city from Eion in the southeast, Brasidas decided to achieve surprise by attacking the Athenians first with a handpicked force of hoplites charging on the double followed shortly thereafter by his entire army, also on the double. The initial attack was to surprise, frighten and confuse the Athenians so that Brasidas' main army could hit them before they recovered.

Meanwhile Cleon, having seen what he wanted to see, began to move his army back towards its base, and, as the phalanx wheeled to march away, it turned and exposed its unprotected right side to the enemy within the city. At that point Brasidas personally led the initial wave into the Athenian centre, causing the terror and confusion he had anticipated, and the follow-up attack of the Spartan main force broke the Athenians. The left wing of their army fled back to the base at Eion, but the right wing, except for Cleon who was killed as he fled, was surrounded on a hill and fought in reasonable order until it was finally overwhelmed. Although the Spartan victory was complete, Brasidas had been mortally wounded in the fighting.

Sparta, long weary of the war and still subject to attack from Athenian bases at Pylos and elsewhere, decided to use victory in the field to secure peace. Brasidas and Cleon, the leaders of the war party in their respective states, were gone, and at Athens the aristocratic Nicias argued persuasively for a settlement. The terms finally agreed upon in 421 provided for peace for fifty years and called for a reversion to the *status quo ante* in which both sides were to return what they had seized during the war, although a few exceptions were made to that general formula. The Thebans retained Plataea, and in compensation Athens held Nisaea near Megara, but Pylos and the captive Spartans were returned while Sparta abandoned Amphipolis.

From a military point of view the war had been quite unlike the Persian Wars. As Thucydides said, it was not decided by a few great battles, but by the dispersal of forces into many theatres where the fighting dragged on for years, partly because forces were spread so thinly that losses in any area could be made up relatively easily. The Archidamian War demonstrated that in other respects as well Greek warfare was changing. If the phalanx and the fleet continued to be the main components of Greek military institutions, contact with Persia had resulted in some changes, as we have seen.

The new, lighter and more mobile warfare was practised before it was fully understood, and in the Peloponnesian War generals and soldiers alike were mystified and surprised by its effect. One of the Spartans captured at Pylos was insulted by an Athenian ally who asked him whether those of his comrades who fell at Sphacteria were men of honour – implying that the surviving Spartans were cowards. The reply was that the arrow 'would be worth a great deal if it could tell men of honour from the rest'.[179] Warfare *was* changing. Men of honour and courage made the difference in the forward clash of man-to-man combat in shock. The bravest warriors, fighting always in the front ranks, most often fell, but intermediate- and long-range weapons penetrated the middle and rear ranks too, and sometimes men of honour were left standing while the ranks crumbled around them. Greece was beginning to catch up with the wide variety of tactical units employed in ancient Near Eastern warfare, but their incorporation into Greek fighting required a change in the code of military valour. The Archidamian War saw the initial stages of an emerging, new, military morality. Although it was still resisted by the advocates of heavy infantry, some were beginning to see that to kill from a distance, to use troops that could disengage and run away, only to return again to fight, brought a new dimension to the art of war.

THE SICILIAN EXPEDITION

The Peace of Nicias was fragile and shaky. For a few years Sparta and Athens abided by it to the extent of rarely warring directly on one another, but throughout the Greek world hostilities simmered and often flared out in renewed fighting. A minor event in Sicily led the Athenians to believe that they could intervene on that island and weaken Sparta and the Peloponnesian League without renewing the war with them directly. Although the Athenian plan was strategically bold, miscalculation and error on the tactical level resulted in a disastrous defeat and led to the resumption of the war with Sparta.[180]

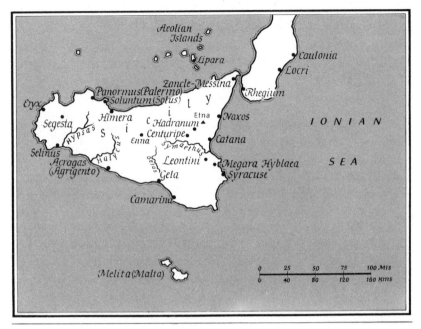

Map of Sicily.

In 416 the city of Segesta in Sicily asked Athens for help in a struggle with Selinus, an ally of the most powerful Sicilian city, Syracuse (see map). After making some enquiries the Athenians in 415 decided to intervene when they were urged strongly to do so by Alcibiades, a daring leader who was the nephew of Pericles. Nicias warned against intervention on the grounds that Sicily was too far removed from the centre of Athens' vital security interests and that the expedition would be too costly, but the assembly could not resist the bold stroke proposed by Alcibiades.

The government authorized an expedition of sixty warships under the joint command of Alcibiades, Nicias and Lamachus, a blustering, hard-nosed, Athenian general. Altogether, including triremes fitted out as troop transports, the force that sailed from Athens in the summer of 415 BC included 134 ships, 5,100 hoplites, 480 archers, 700 Rhodian slingers, 120 light armed infantry and 30 cavalry. In addition there were at least 130 smaller supply ships. Including the crews the total combatant manpower was in the neighbourhood of 27,000 men.

133

Shortly before the fleet sailed, a scandal in Athens drastically undermined Alcibiades' position. In the course of a night in June someone, or a group, had moved through the city chipping the penises off the popular statuettes of Hermes, the god of good luck and fertility. Athenians reacted in horror and fear at the sacrilege, a bad omen for the expedition, and an investigating committee was unable to discover the perpetrators, but during the enquiry witnesses claimed that Alcibiades had openly mimicked the initiation rites of an official, Athenian, secret religion, the so-called Eleusinian mysteries, associated with the worship of Demeter and Persephone. If true, the charge was criminal, and Alcibiades offered to stand trial immediately, but he was ordered to proceed with the fleet, under a heavy cloud of suspicion.

The three commanders headed for Sicily without a definite plan of action, but they achieved strategic surprise, despite inadequate security measures, because many Syracusans simply refused to believe that the Athenians would attempt such an ambitious enterprise and treated rumours of their impending arrival as a joke. At Rhegium in southern Italy Alcibiades, Nicias and Lamachus argued over strategy. Nicias took a 'strict constructionist' view of the situation, claiming that the Athenians should simply try to bring conflict between Segesta and Selinus to an end and then sail home. Lamachus wanted to sail straight to Syracuse and fight before the Syracusans could prepare for them, but Alcibiades characteristically proposed a compromise between the two extremes. He advocated a diplomatic initiative designed to encourage Syracuse's allies in Sicily to defect to Athens. Lamachus finally supported Alcibiades' plan as the better of the two alternatives, but in hindsight there is little doubt that the Athenians should have followed Lamachus' original advice to hit Syracuse hard and fast.

Sailing from southern Italy the Athenians seized Catana, about forty miles north of Syracuse, and used it as their base. Shortly afterwards, in September 415, the Athenian state ship, the *Salaminia*, arrived to arrest Alcibiades, who was thus removed from the war scarcely before it had got underway. Nicias, who dominated Lamachus, then took the entire expeditionary force to western Sicily to examine the situation around Segesta, but returned to Catana before the autumn rains, where he and Lamachus laid plans to carry the war to Syracuse by establishing an Athenian base near the Great

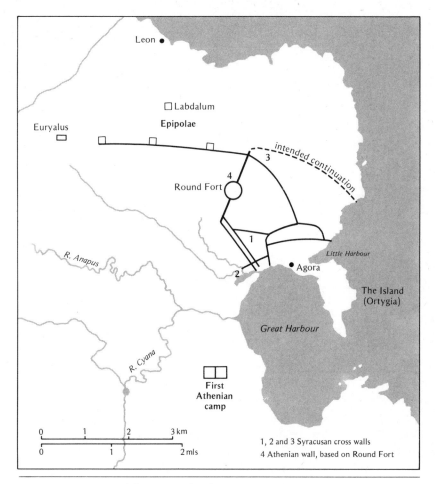

The siege of Syracuse, 415–413 BC.

Harbour of that city. High ground around the harbour would protect the Athenians from Syracusan cavalry attacks to which they were dangerously vulnerable and leave them in a strong position outside the city. Their plan, as described by Thucydides, was a marvellous subterfuge, employing a double agent:

They sent to Syracuse a man devoted to them, and by the Syracusan generals thought to be no less in their interest; he was a native of Catana, and said he came from persons in that place, whose names the Syracusan generals were acquainted with, and whom they knew to be among the members of their party still left in the city. He told them that the Athenians passed the night in the town, at some distance from their arms, and that if the Syracusans would name a day and come with all their people at daybreak to attack the armament, they, their friends, would close the gates upon the city, and set fire to the vessels, while the Syracusans would easily take the camp by an attack upon the stockade.[181]

When the Syracusans set a date (it took two days to march to Catana), Nicias and the fleet departed, careful to pass the Syracusans during the night, and moved without opposition into the Syracusan Great Harbour, where they built a camp south of the Anapus river. In a battle that followed the Athenians routed the Syracusan army, which fell back into the city, and Nicias then packed up his army and returned to Catana for the winter (October–November 415). Some military historians react incredulously to this turn of events, wondering how the Athenians could have abandoned a position so skilfully won and defended, but Thucydides says clearly that Nicias felt jeopardized by lack of cavalry and hoped to use his victory to get supplies and horses from the other Sicilian cities, which could be expected to look more favourably on the Athenian invaders now that they had demonstrated tactical superiority in the field.

Still, the Athenians had secured very little advantage in the first year of the fighting, and what victories they had achieved served mainly to convince the Syracusans to knuckle down for a hard war. They spent the winter drilling their army, repairing their fortifications, and getting as much help as possible from Corinth and Sparta. At Sparta they found an unexpected advocate in Alcibiades, who had escaped arrest on the return to Greece and fled to Athens' enemy, where he threw himself with enthusiasm into the rigours of Spartan life. He strongly urged the Spartans to help Syracuse, and in the summer of 414 they sent out a senior officer, Gylippus, who collected 3,000 men from cities in Sicily and helped train the Syracusan army in the Spartan fashion.

Meanwhile Nicias tried to take Messina, but failed, and sent to Athens for reinforcements for the campaign of 414. The native Sicels in the interior of the island joined the Athenian cause against the hated Syracuse, and Nicias with native help and reinforcements from Athens increased his cavalry arm. The Athenian strategy was to seize the high, steep plateau to the north and northwest of Syracuse called the Epipolae. From this high ground they could build walls and put Syracuse, protected by its own walls, under siege. By cover of night

Nicias sailed to Leon on the coast four miles north of Syracuse, disembarked, and attacked a major Syracusan stronghold, Euryalus, on the western end of the Epipolae. This occurred on a morning when the Syracusan army was holding a parade to bolster morale in the city, and by the time defenders arrived the Athenians were so strongly entrenched that they easily retained their position. The next day, when they marched up to the gates of Syracuse, the Syracusans stayed behind their walls and refused battle. Nicias then constructed a fort on the north central ridge of the Epipolae at Labdalum and assembled his forces. The Athenian army above Syracuse had secured a strategically strong position, and the walled city prepared for a difficult siege.

Nicias then moved across the Epipolae and built a second fort on its southern rim at a place called the Round Fort, protected by a 1000 foot rampart between it and the city. From the Round Fort the Athenians hoped to build two walls, one north and east to the sea, and another south to the Great Harbour, to tie the knot tightly around Syracuse. The fleet could be used to blockade Syracuse, and then it would be only a matter of time before the city fell. To prevent this encirclement the Syracusan army advanced against the Athenians on the Epipolae, but its morale was so low that Syracusan generals retreated without risking engagement.

Then began an incredible, maze-like race of building walls and counterwalls (see map). On the day following the retreat of the Syracusan army into the city Nicias started construction of the wall north from the Round Fort, and the Syracusans, realizing that the Athenians would have to extend a wall south as well, decided to build a counterwall westward from their city to keep the projected Athenian wall from reaching the Great Harbour. While the Athenians concentrated their energy on the northern wall, they ignored the Syracusans to the south, but finally Nicias organized a raid on a hot mid-afternoon and caught the enemy napping. After destroying the counterwall Nicias ordered construction to begin on his own southward wall which was given priority over the northern one.

The Syracusans responded by beginning another westward wall, this time further south, but Nicias attacked again as his fleet sailed into the Great Harbour, and in tough fighting Athenian forces drove the enemy back. However, the death of Lamachus on the field inspired the Syracusans to counterattack against the Round Fort, which Nicias set afire to drive off the attackers, until finally the Syracusans fell back again to the protection of their city walls. The Athenian southward wall could now be completed, and Nicias supervised the construction of a double wall, which gave him protection on both front and rear.

For various reasons Nicias left the northern wall unfinished. Perhaps success had made him overconfident, and unrest in Syracuse lulled him into the belief that the city would soon surrender. It was at this fateful moment, early in the summer of 414, that Gylippus arrived, a Spartan general with a reputation for meanness and severity. While the Syracusan assembly was considering surrender, Gylippus, with about 3,000 men, approached to within a mile or two of the city and gave orders for the Syracusan army to march out to meet him, prepared to do battle with the Athenians. Amazingly Nicias and his men had been so certain of the strength of their position that they had not taken the simplest security precautions, and the enemy was able to unite his forces while Gylippus announced that he would provide a safe-conduct if the Athenians would leave Sicily in five days! When Nicias refused to fight, Gylippus moved into Syracuse.

Nicias was totally demoralized, and Gylippus seized the Athenian fort of Labdalum while he extended his own wall across the Epipolae to counter the northward wall of the Athenians from the Round Fort. The effect, by the end of the summer, was to drive Nicias from the Epipolae (except for the Round Fort) and to force the Athenian army back onto its southern walls and the Great Harbour, thus breaking the Athenian siege. As autumn approached, Nicias sent a dreary report on this situation to the Athenian assembly and asked that the expeditionary force be withdrawn or significantly reinforced, and that in any event he be replaced. Athens sent an additional fleet under Demosthenes, who had fought at Pylos, of seventy-three triremes and more than 5,000 hoplites and skirmishers, but Nicias was not relieved of his command.

Before Demosthenes arrived, Gylippus attacked the original Athenian fleet in the Great Harbour. The Syracusans had redesigned their ships, setting the ram lower and strengthening the prow to enable them to attack Athenian vessels head on, and when the Athenians faced the new tactics, they lost courage and broke, with the sacrifice of seven ships and crews. The Syracusans prepared to finish them off the next day, but on that morning Demosthenes finally appeared with the reinforcements.

On his arrival Demosthenes realized that the Athenians were trapped in and around the Great Harbour, and he decided that they should try to reestablish their position on the Epipolae and destroy the main Syracusan counterwall. In a midnight attack the attempt failed. Then Demosthenes gave up hope and wanted to withdraw the entire force while it was still perhaps possible, but Nicias was afraid of punishment in Athens, although he finally did agree to try an escape. During the night of 27 August 413, as the Athenians prepared to leave, fate played a trick on them. There was a full eclipse of the moon, and the religious officials with the expedition saw it as an evil omen and decreed that the Athenians must wait thrice nine days for the full of the moon. By that stroke of fortune the Athenians lost their only chance for escape.

When the Syracusans realized that their enemy hoped to escape, they drew up their fleet of seventy-six ships against the Athenian fleet of eighty-six. Since there was little room in the harbour for the Athenians to use the traditional tactics of *diekplous* or *periplous*, and because the Syracusan ships could ram head on, the Athenians were badly defeated with the loss of eighteen vessels. The Syracusans then chained some of their own ships together across the mouth of the Great Harbour, and, although Nicias tried heroically to rally his men, they failed to penetrate the Syracusan line. When Demosthenes attempted to regroup the Athenians, who were in a state of panic, they refused to put to sea again.

Under these circumstances there was no alternative but to seek escape by land, in a desperate effort to reach Catana or find protection with the friendly Sicels, but the Syracusans had already blocked the roads. After several days of frantic, demoralizing marching the Athenians were surrounded, and Nicias and Demosthenes surrendered. They were put to death, probably under torture, but many of the Athenian captives faced a worse ordeal as public slaves in the stone quarries. The fortunate ones were sold as slaves to private individuals. A massive force of almost 40,000 men and nearly 200 triremes had been lost forever.

The failure of the Sicilian expedition has few parallels in history, but an obvious one is the loss of the Spanish Armada almost exactly 2,000 years later in 1588.[182] The comparison is instructive. The Spanish Armada contained about 130 ships of various sizes and shapes, 8,000 sailors, 19,000 soldiers and 2,000 oarsmen. It was slower and more cumbersome than the Athenian fleet of 415 BC, even taking into account the fact that it was armed with cannons. The distance from Spain to the English Channel is about the same as from Athens to Syracuse, and the strategic mission of the two expeditionary forces was identical – to occupy a distant island in a combined land and sea attack, though the Athenian mission was not originally as clearly formulated as the Spanish.

The Spanish Armada, unlike the Athenian expedition, met at the outset with forceful naval opposition, and its land army did not figure in the fighting, but 'acts of God' played equally important roles in the fate of the fleets. There was no lunar eclipse in 1588, but great storms damaged the Spanish vessels. On the whole both campaigns revealed the limitations of naval power exercised far from home, with few bases of support and supply between home and the area of operation. The Athenian and Spanish expeditions were sent far away by their governments in the expectation that they would be strong enough to function independently of their bases. Albeit the Spanish did hope to make use of their forces in the Netherlands, the plan required them to fight their way through the Channel to pick up their troops. Athens did eventually send reinforcements, but that was not part of the plan, and for the most part the assembly in Athens and Philip II of Spain could only sit by helplessly and anxiously await news from the distant theatre. If things went wrong, there was nothing they could do, and no real route of escape for their armadas. Both expeditions were strategically ill-advised. The Spanish Armada probably had no chance of success whatsoever, barring unlikely total panic in England, and the Athenian expedition, although it might possibly have succeeded with much better luck, could not have achieved its mission otherwise, and fortune is a thin reed on which to base a military campaign. Furthermore, had the two campaigns succeeded in attaining their initial objectives of conquest, the problems would have only just begun. Before nineteenth and twentieth century advances in communication and supply it was not easy to conquer a distant stronghold beyond the sea, but it was easier to conquer than to rule.

Though strategically unwise, the Athenian expedition to Sicily reflects a degree of military and naval sophistication more impressive, though not as technologically advanced, than that of the Spanish 2,000 years later. Nicias lacked some essential qualities of leadership, especially the strategic grasp necessary for his campaign, and he

shared a lack of enthusiasm for the whole enterprise with his later
Spanish counterpart, but he often showed signs of tactical brilliance
and of a stubborn tenacity that set him above the Duke of Medina
Sidonia. The tactical cohesion of Athenian land and naval forces was
decidedly superior to that of the Spanish, who suffered from outright
hostility between their army and navy units.

THE INTERVENTION OF PERSIA

The failure of the Sicilian expedition encouraged Sparta to reopen the
Peloponnesian War, especially since the Persians, who hoped to
reassert their influence in the Aegean, promised to provide financial
and military support. The final phase of the Peloponnesian War was
fought mainly on the sea, and several great naval battles shaped its
outcome, especially Abydus (411), Cyzicus (410), Arginusae (406) and
Aegospotami (405). Strategically the situation was relatively simple.
Sparta, with the help of Persia, was able to attempt naval domination
in the Aegean and could win the war if she destroyed the Athenian
fleet. Because of Persian reserves, the Spartans could take chances and
suffer losses. They could be beaten many times – the Athenian navy
had to be destroyed only once. The King of Persia would get Ionia
again, and naval superiority in the Aegean, while Sparta destroyed her
enemy on the Greek mainland.

The early campaigns focused on control of the Hellespont. In 411
the Spartans seized Abydus and Byzantium, but the Athenians
counterattacked, and a decisive naval battle at Abydus between a
Spartan fleet of eighty-six ships and an Athenian one of seventy-six
ended favourably for Athens. Although the battle raged back and
forth all day with heavy losses on both sides, Alcibiades, who was
back in the good graces of the Athenian government, arrived in the late
afternoon with eighteen ships, and the Spartans fell back with the loss
of thirty vessels.[183]

In 410 the action centred around Cyzicus, which the Persians
attacked by land while Sparta approached by sea. Alcibiades appeared
with the Athenian fleet of eighty-six ships and immediately set upon
the Spartan force of sixty. In the course of the battle Alcibiades
detached twenty vessels, sailed around the Spartans, and landed on
shore. The Spartan commander, Mindarus, beached his own fleet, and
in a battle on land he was killed, and his men fled. Alcibiades then
captured the entire Spartan fleet, although the crews of the Syracusan

contingent managed to burn their ships before leaving. The desperate situation of Sparta in the Hellespont is revealed in the message sent to the Spartan government after the battle of Cyzicus by the second-in-command: 'Ships lost. Mindarus dead. Men starving. Don't know what to do.'[184] The battle not only strengthened Athens' position in the Aegean, but gave a needed boost to Athenian morale.

For the next few years both sides concentrated on their position in the Aegean, and, although there was some minor fighting, nothing of great significance happened until the campaigns of 407–406 around the islands of Lesbos and Samos in the eastern Aegean.[185] With Persian help the Spartans had strengthened their fleet, and the Spartan Lysander surprised the Athenian navy, on a day when Alcibiades was off on another mission, and captured twenty-two ships. Alcibiades fled in disgrace again and no longer figured in the war.

In 406, at the Arginusae islands between Lesbos and the mainland, an Athenian fleet of 150 ships met the Spartan fleet of 120. The Athenians prevented the Spartans from executing a *diekplous*, and then pushed back and defeated the Spartan left wing, driving the Peloponnesian fleet to the island of Chios. Athens had lost twenty-five ships, but Spartan losses numbered more than seventy. After the battle a storm came up and prevented the Athenians from helping the survivors and collecting the bodies, so the assembly tried the eight admirals for negligence, despite their victory, and the six who had returned were executed, while the other two went into exile. One of those executed was Pericles, the son of Pericles! It was an ancient custom to punish generals for mistakes in the field – after all, the safety of the citizens depended on their wisdom.[186] But Athenians were especially severe, and they not only lost some good leaders but encouraged passivity, as in the case of Nicias at Syracuse, for fear of making a mistake.

The Spartan Lysander, again with Persian help, decided to carry the war once more to the Hellespont. There in 405 he attacked the Athenian fleet at Aegospotami and caught it by surprise while the crews were on land securing supplies. The Spartans captured all but nine Athenian ships and intercepted the grain fleet headed for Athens. While Lysander moved towards Athens with the fleet, a Spartan army invaded Attica, and Athens was surrounded under siege. In the spring of 404 Athens surrendered to Sparta, and was forced to destroy the Long Walls, give up the fleet and acquiesce in Sparta's control of

Athenian foreign policy. Although Thebes and Corinth demanded the complete destruction of Athens, Sparta decided that preserving the city as a rival to her allies might prove useful.

The war was over. Victory had been nearly as costly for Sparta as defeat had been for Athens, and in many ways Persia was the real winner. Ionia soon fell once again under Persian rule, and the Aegean became a Persian lake, while the Greek mainland yielded to the artless hegemony of Sparta.

The Limitations of Classical Greek Warfare

One of the obvious lessons of the Peloponnesian War, in hindsight – though there were some who learned it at the time – was the inability of the phalanx to force a decisive conclusion. The phalanx was an anomaly in warfare, and earlier even Herodotus indicated his awareness of the fact by the speech he put into the mouth of the Persian general Mardonius:

And yet, I am told, these very Greeks are wont to wage wars against one another in the most foolish way, through sheer perversity and doltishness. For no sooner is war proclaimed than they search out the smoothest and fairest plain that is to be found in all the land, and there they assemble and fight; whence it comes to pass that even the conquerors depart with great loss: I say nothing of the conquered for they are destroyed altogether. Now surely, as they are all of one speech, they ought to interchange heralds and messengers, and make up their differences by any means other than battle; or, at the worst, if they must needs fight one another, they ought to post themselves as strongly as possible [in impregnable positions], and so try their quarrels.[187]

Exclusive reliance upon heavy infantry in shock, particularly in a country as mountainous as Greece, does seem odd and has provoked even odder explanations. There has been a tendency to assume that the alternative to the strategy and tactics of heavy infantry is the use of light infantry to guard mountain passes, and that for various reasons that would not have worked. Greek heavy infantry was rational after all, many historians believe, and it did stop the Persians at Marathon and at Plataea.[188]

But that argument clearly will not do. Sole reliance on heavy infantry in shock is 'foolish' for many reasons, not the least of which is that it demands an outrageous drain on the psychic and manpower resources of its practitioners. To force men into shock under arms is the most difficult feat of war, and du Picq's observation that 'you cannot suppress the flesh', that there is no way to overcome man's understandable fear of mortal combat in shock, though overstated, reflects the very real price paid by the ancient Greeks for their manner of fighting. Sparta fielded the best armies, but suffered the greatest cost through the organization of a standing military society.

Heavy infantry by itself can only make sense in a world where other armies are also heavy infantry, but does it make sense even then? If so, it can explain hoplite warfare in Greece from 700 to 500 B C, but it does not explain why the Greeks continued to believe so strongly in the priority of heavy infantry down into the fourth century. Even in the conditions of Archaic Greece (700–500 B C) the phalanx was militarily an oddity. An integrated force of skirmishers, light infantry, heavy infantry, and light and heavy cavalry, often with special emphasis on one component or another, is more effective and less demanding on society. Heavy infantry alone simply makes no military sense and should have been easy to defeat. By the time of the Peloponnesian War light infantry and skirmishers held the phalanx at bay and sometimes defeated it, yet even then Greeks did not generally abandon their faith in the ancient formation. It is all the more amazing because in the ancient Near East integrated armies had emerged at least by the second millennium B C, and Greece's neighbours, the Assyrians and Persians, exemplified the long military tradition. And there were certainly enough horses in Greece to maintain regular, small cavalry forces.

Some have sought the explanation for this peculiar way of fighting in the political structure of the Greek states – by arguing that the use of light infantry required the arming of the lower classes, something that the wealthier hoplite class would have resisted. But there is a simpler explanation. Unacceptable as it may be to many philhellenes, the probable reason Greek states did not use other formations is that they did not know any better (and could not have) when they developed the institution of the phalanx, and that by the time they were in a position to learn from Persia, the phalanx had become too thoroughly a part of their society to be easily modified.

In the Dark Age Greece's link with ancient Near Eastern military traditions had been severed. Although Assyria and Persia represented a continuity of military development going back to earlier times, Greece, in a cultural vacuum, reverted to an almost primitive style of war characterized by champions duelling with one another in single combat. Almost any kind of formation would have proved effective in that military environment, but for various reasons the Greeks turned to heavy infantry. In their inimitable way they honed their military practices and developed the phalanx into one of history's finest heavy formations.

The phalanx, however, was more than a tactical formation. It represented a way of life, a code of manliness and morality that was much more deeply ingrained in Greece than in most military societies because the demands of heavy infantry in shock on 'the flesh' were so much greater than in integrated armies. As a social institution the phalanx was as important to the Greeks as their emerging and ever-changing political forms. The poetry of Tyrtaeus and Callinus and the advice of the Spartan mother to her son reveal the extensive influence of the military morality of the phalanx. Even in Athens and other states outside Sparta, where militarism was pronounced, all Greek men thought of themselves as warriors and were proud of it. Aeschylus, who fought at Marathon, and Socrates, who fought at Amphipolis, are notable examples.

The morality of heavy infantry made it very nearly impossible, after the Greeks came into contact with the integrated army of Persia, to imitate the obviously better military institutions of the ancient Near East. The resistance was moral and cultural and not based upon rational analysis or military science (though there *was* a science of the phalanx). The retort of the insulted Spartan survivor of Pylos showing contempt for long-range weapons was moral. The new, modern warfare of the fourth century, for the most part borrowed from Persia, as we shall see, was greeted by stiff opposition even when its advantages were obvious. The orator Demosthenes contrasted fighting of the 'fair and open kind' with the use of 'skirmishers, cavalry, archers, mercenaries and other troops' by Philip of Macedon.[189] As late as the second century BC Polybius showed the force of the older code by contrasting 'the open and honourable warfare of the ancients with the deceitfulness of his own age'.[190]

Greek victory in the Persian Wars undoubtedly also contributed to the military 'foolishness' of phalanx society. Although some Greeks realized that Persian errors made victory possible, the more common belief was that it represented the triumph of the spear over the bow or of heavy infantry over light. In naval warfare the Greeks showed more creativity, and their navy was more responsible than their phalanx for the defeat of Persia. Though there was much fighting on land during the Peloponnesian War, it too was determined at sea, and to the extent that the phalanx was made irrelevant by the fleet, Greeks could continue to believe, as they did, in the superiority of heavy infantry in land warfare. Philip of Macedon proved them wrong.

Because of the phalanx Greeks of the classical period lagged behind Persia in many other military respects. Greek fortifications and siege warfare were primitive since the hoplite phalanx was too heavy to storm the simplest barriers.[191] Blockade was the only feasible tactic against a fortified city, even a badly fortified city, unless the inhabitants could be persuaded to open its gates. The art of fortification, rendered unnecessary by the phalanx, lagged behind the ancient Near East. Spartans were proud of their unwalled city, and there were Athenians who believed that security would be greater if they tore down their walls because it would serve as an incentive to develop a phalanx as good as Sparta's.

Logistics was an equally unrefined military art among the Greeks. Small forces – and most Greek armies were small – could move without grave difficulties, but the Greeks found it almost impossible to supply the army of nearly 40,000 at Plataea in 479, even though the battlefield was only a few miles from Greek bastions on the Isthmus. Large ancient Near Eastern armies had developed logistical support systems of some sophistication, to judge by the distances they travelled, but Greek forces snaked along with far too many servants and at too slow a pace, depending as they did on ox carts for their supplies, or more often on no organized commissariat at all but on the initiative of private merchants who followed the armies and sold dear. In the Peloponnesian War there were some attempts to 'organize' the private merchants, but there was no governmental commissariat. The romantic notion of an army living off the land works only on enemy soil, when it works at all, which is why Greek soldiers were usually required to bring their own food for the first few days of a campaign until they could march into enemy country. But living off the land with armies that move as slowly as the phalanx did is no substitute for a regular logistical support system. A relatively immobile, heavy army that has no commissariat, that lives off the land, most often dies on it, as did the Athenian army in Sicily.

Later Roman armies were famous for their camps, and the ancient

Near Eastern armies of Assyria and Persia also built fortified camps in the field, but Greek armies before Alexander were unprotected at night on the march, and on the battlefield had no fortified camps to fall back upon, again because of the nature of hoplite warfare. Heavy infantry is not organized to attack enemy forces except in traditional battle array, and camps are therefore unnecessary in defence against hoplites. But in a war against an integrated army the lack of camps was a handicap. Even weapons training was regarded by the Greeks with suspicion, because the skilful use of weapons was more advantageous when the ranks were broken and the army in retreat than when fighting in formation.[192]

In every aspect of land warfare except the clash of heavy infantry Greece had much to learn from Persia. On the sea, Greeks and Persians were much more nearly equal, but greater Persian resources yielded numerical advantages difficult for the Greeks to overcome. By the Peloponnesian War there were signs of important changes in Greek warfare, but they had not yet been institutionalized and were in many respects not even appreciated, though Thucydides seems to have been ahead of his times in his lack of regard for the phalanx. Miltiades triumphed over Greek military culture at Marathon by using unprecedented tactics, but his victory over the Greek way of fighting was as much a 'near-run thing' as his victory over Persia, and no more lasting in its results.

The military revolution of the fourth century involved, amongst other things, the use of Thracian peltasts, who were lighter and faster than Greek hoplites. Their spear was normally used for throwing as a javelin, but it could also be held for thrusting. Peltasts served as skirmishers or as light infantry.

Chapter Five

The Military Revolution

In the last half of the fourth century BC Alexander the Great stormed into Asia with a superb army that defeated every Persian force in its path and eventually marched into India, where it rolled over the great army and elephants of King Porus at the battle of the Hydaspes (326 BC). This magnificent military achievement would simply not have been possible or even conceivable in the fifth century. Earlier Greeks had stopped the Persian army on Greek soil, but they lacked the cavalry and other ancillary support units necessary for an invasion of Asia. Between the end of the Peloponnesian War in 404 and the accession of Alexander the Great in 336 a military revolution in the Greek world changed the nature of ancient warfare and produced one of the finest armies in the military history of the western world. The revolution in fighting had a lasting effect in antiquity, and even the Romans on the western fringe of the greater Greek world had to come to terms with it in their own native way.

One student of this period has characterized the military revolution as the coordination of 'the infantry of the West with the cavalry of the East', a description that is accurate as far as it goes, but it does not go far enough.[193] Before Greeks and Macedonians could penetrate the heart of Persia, they had to create an integrated army – heavy and light infantry, skirmishers, and heavy and light cavalry – and to learn the means of supporting such a force logistically.[194] Furthermore, no invasion of Persia could succeed unless the attacking army had some chance of taking by storm the highly fortified strongholds on the Persian coast of the Mediterranean. Persian advantages in manpower would not permit an intruder to adopt the leisurely tactics of blockade alone. An army in blockade is vulnerable to envelopment by a relieving force and especially so in the heart of enemy territory. To take fortified sites by storm required an integrated army, but one that was supported by a corps of military engineers with far greater knowledge of the art of siege than the Greek world had produced by the end of the fifth century.

Amazingly, despite the limitations of hoplite warfare, the Greeks and Macedonians changed their way of fighting in a matter of about two generations, roughly from 400 to 350 BC. Some of the origins of this military revolution were culturally indigenous to Greece, but the influence of ancient Near Eastern warfare, represented by the military institutions of the Persian Empire, was fundamental.

One of the reasons for the military revolution was certainly the dawning realization throughout Greece of the failure of land armies to bring a decisive end to the Peloponnesian conflict. This was coupled with an awareness that light infantry posed formidable problems for the phalanx. As a result there was a great deal of experimentation with new combinations of infantry in the first half of the fourth century, although traditional and culturally ingrained reliance on the phalanx was so strong that the two most decisive battles of the period, Leuctra (371 BC) and Mantinea (362 BC), were fought by opposing phalanxes. Philip, who became king of Macedon in 359, was able to apply the new techniques in the field partly because Macedon, far to the north, had never been fully a part of Greek hoplite military culture. Although the new style of fighting was largely inspired by Persia, the borrowings were shaped in a Greek and Macedonian mould, and the new model army of the Aegean benefited from the heavy infantry of the earlier period subordinated to its most efficient role as merely one arm of an integrated tactical force.

Mercenaries

Greek mercenary troops played a decisive role in the fusion of ancient Near Eastern and Greek military institutions.[195] Mercenaries in modern warfare are generally regarded as contemptible, and the attitude sometimes unfortunately spills over into accounts of ancient warfare. Since the successful burst of nationalistic, patriotic fervour associated with the American and French Revolutions, it has been fashionable to regard foreign troops who fight for pay rather than for love of country as potentially disloyal, and in any event unlikely to display the fierce tenacity of citizens fighting for the fatherland. Because the scale of warfare has increased so dramatically in the nineteenth and twentieth centuries, and mercenaries are always difficult to recruit in large numbers, there is not in any case the same opportunity for deploying them usefully as there once was.

In the ancient world mercenaries were more often a feature of warfare, and they were frequently outstanding in the practice of their craft. They did occasionally sell out to the highest bidder and change sides at the last moment, but on the whole they served with a sense of professionalism and faced the dangers of battle with a calmer and more deadly sense of purpose than armies of raw, citizen conscripts. They were particularly useful in the specialized skirmisher arms of archers and slingers, since it took long training to become proficient in those skills, but the Persians also often found it helpful to hire relatively small (and occasionally relatively large) numbers of mercenaries to serve as hoplites. In small numbers they were used as bodyguards where their expertise in hand-to-hand fighting was important. As foreigners they were less susceptible to the blandishments of dynastic, political intrigue. In large numbers they fought in formation as shock troops in assault, a role they played more easily on Asian soil, where their opponents were less heavily armed, than in Greece. The Persians always had cavalry and light infantry to protect the flanks of their Greek mercenary phalanx.

Although mercenaries had been employed in Greece on a limited scale from relatively early times, especially by the tyrants of the Archaic Age of the seventh and sixth centuries BC, the real age of the Greek mercenary begins with the end of the Peloponnesian War. During the last phase of that conflict Greeks, particularly those associated with the Spartan cause, had worked in close cooperation with Persian governors in Asia Minor. When the war came to an end, because political and economic conditions on the Greek mainland were unsettled, many Greek soldiers drifted into the service of the wealthy Persian satraps, who had long appreciated the fighting quality of Greek heavy infantry. Mercenaries in the pay of Persia became highly instrumental in bringing back to Greece the techniques of ancient Near Eastern warfare.

XENOPHON

The first large-scale use of Greek mercenaries by Persians came in 401 BC, when the dashing Cyrus, the noblest Persian of them all, a satrap in Asia Minor and younger brother of the king, Artaxerxes II (404–359), decided to march into Mesopotamia and seize the Persian throne for himself.[196] To that end he organized his own Persian forces and recruited Greek mercenaries already serving in Asia Minor. He appealed to the exiled Spartan general, Clearchus, and to other Greek generals to assemble mercenaries (largely Peloponnesian hoplites) in Asia Minor. When they had gathered about 13,000 men, they were told only that the object of their attack was Pisidia, an untamed region of Asia Minor not fully controlled by Persia. As they reached Cilicia (and had passed by Pisidia), they began uneasily to suspect that Cyrus intended to lead them against the Great King. Cyrus obviously hoped to keep his plans secret as long as possible to catch Artaxerxes by surprise, and he calmed the mercenaries by giving them more money and by telling them that he aimed at an enemy in Syria. All were naturally suspicious, and some abandoned Cyrus at this point, but most continued on the march to the Euphrates. It was only when they reached that river that Cyrus finally admitted his real intention and again offered the Greeks more money. By then they were so deeply committed that there was little alternative, and they agreed to strike against Artaxerxes.

So far successful in his operations, Cyrus thrust into Mesopotamia where his brother waited to receive him, and the two armies came together on the field at Cunaxa about 100 miles north of Babylon. Artaxerxes had received ample early warning from Persian officials in Asia Minor, who realized from the outset that Cyrus' army was too large for a campaign in Pisidia and suspected that he planned to overthrow his brother. The king's army numbered perhaps 60,000 to 100,000 (including 6,000 cavalry and 200 scythed chariots), while Cyrus had a force of 40,000 to 80,000, including the Greeks, with only 3,000 cavalry.[197] As the armies approached one another on the east side of the Euphrates, Cyrus had to deploy from line of column into line of battle. He stationed a force of 1,000 cavalry on his right next to the river and beside them the Greeks. Cyrus himself took up position with 600 cavalry in the centre of his line, with the Persian infantry on his left and additional cavalry on the far left. It was mid-afternoon when the armies clashed, but Cyrus still did not have his entire army in line of battle.

As Artaxerxes approached in the centre of his own line, which was in better formation, Cyrus ordered Clearchus to move obliquely with the Greeks directly against the king, but the Spartan refused because

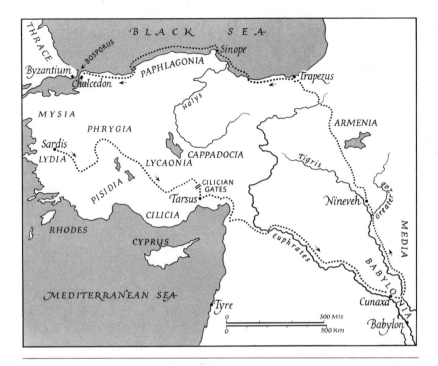

Xenophon's march, 401–400 BC.

he did not want to expose his flank to Artaxerxes' left cavalry. When the armies were within 500 to 600 yards of one another, the Greeks charged straight ahead at the double, and the Persians fell back while many charioteers abandoned their vehicles. Some of the chariots turned back against the Persians, and the Greeks opened ranks to let the others through. Overjoyed by the success on his right Cyrus charged against Artaxerxes, who was somewhat to Cyrus' left, since his line was longer. The king was attempting to envelop Cyrus' left wing when his younger brother charged into his line in the hope of killing him on the field. As luck would have it, Cyrus actually wounded Artaxerxes and knocked him off his horse, but in the ensuing confusion a Persian warrior struck Cyrus in the head with a javelin, unhorsed him, and a common soldier killed him.

Afterwards Artaxerxes attacked Cyrus' camp while the Greek army, successful on the right, pursued the retreating Persians in front of them for about three miles. The king then turned from the camp to hit the Greeks in the rear, but Clearchus faced his line about and marched back against them, forcing the king to swerve to the Greek right to avoid head on assault. To protect their flank the Greeks lined up with their backs to the river and beat off the Persian charge. Although they pursued the Persians to Cunaxa, the Persian cavalry made one last attempt to stop them but was driven back in disarray. As night fell over the battlefield, the Greeks withdrew to their original camp to find that the enemy had plundered it. As far as they were concerned, they had been everywhere victorious and did not understand where Cyrus and his men were.

The following morning bleak reality set in. The Greeks learned that Cyrus was dead and that they were trapped deep in the Persian Empire, cut off from all supplies. About midday they were instructed by messengers from the king to surrender their arms and to appear as suppliants before him. This they stubbornly and boldly refused to do, and elected Clearchus their leader now that Cyrus was dead. Since the Persians were reluctant to fight and merely wanted to get the Greeks out of the empire, Tissaphernes, the king's agent, persuaded them that he would lead them out of Babylonia and back to safety. Because the route they had come by was stripped of provisions, Tissaphernes took them across the Tigris up to the Greater Zab. There he invited Clearchus and other generals to a conference and arrested them. Although Tissaphernes expected the rest of the Greeks to surrender upon the loss of their leaders, they instead rallied and elected new generals. One of them was the Athenian Xenophon (*c.* 428–354 BC), who led them northward home, although they were by no means sure where home was. Tissaphernes merely followed closely behind, keeping on the pressure, until they moved into the mountains of Armenia. Clearchus and the other Greek generals were sent to Susa, the Persian capital, and executed.

When the Greeks finally and miraculously reached the Black Sea early in 400, they were still largely intact. Some months later, as they arrived at Chalcedon on the Asiatic side of the Bosporus, the Persian satrap in the area paid a Spartan admiral, Anaxibius, to ferry them across the strait into Byzantium. There they were employed by a Thracian prince, Seuthes, for use against barbarian tribes, but, when war broke out between Sparta and Persia in 399, they were hired by the Spartans and crossed back into Asia some 6,000 strong.

We shall return to the war in Asia, but it is important first to consider the military significance of the Cunaxa campaign. Cyrus had failed, but the Greek mercenaries had performed marvellously, and their exploit is justly famous. Some regard it as a quaint and quixotic invasion, as in certain respects it was, but in the military history of ancient Greece it was far more important than it appears at first glance, despite the failure of Cyrus to achieve strategic mission and aim. Polybius regarded this campaign as the cause of Alexander's war with Persia, because it showed the invincibility of Greek warriors deep in the heart of Persian territory and thus made an invasion of Persia seem feasible for the first time in Greek history. His statement is certainly an exaggeration (and a simplification), but it is not altogether without merit.[198]

The Greeks did learn first hand at Cunaxa the weakness of the Persian army against heavy infantry, but the real importance of the campaign was in what it told them about their own weaknesses. Clearchus had been outright insubordinate on the field, because he was afraid to expose his flank to Persian attack.[199] In head-on assault Persians could not stand up to Greeks, but a Greek army in Persia without adequate cavalry and light infantry support was in no position to force a strategically decisive defeat on the Great King. As the Greeks were pursued on their way out of Persia, they also learned the necessity for good skirmishers – slingers and archers – to protect their position. At one point Xenophon had been forced to convert Rhodian hoplites into slingers (since the sling was a native weapon on Rhodes), and they served to good advantage.[200]

Perhaps the most important lesson was in logistics. The Greeks had travelled roughly 1500 miles overland from Sardis to Cunaxa, moving twelve to fifteen miles a day under Cyrus' supply system. Xenophon's account of the campaign in the *Anabasis* shows that he, at least, was a careful student of the army on the march, and one reason for his interest was that Greek armies on their own were not capable of organizing supplies on such a scale. The logistical problems suffered by the Greeks on their return convinced them all that there was no substitute for organized supply. Equally important, they returned to share their new knowledge with other Greeks, which must have passed largely by word of mouth, but Xenophon spent the next several decades putting in writing the lessons of military action against the Persians, and his accounts influenced, directly and indirectly, the leading military figures of his age.

In addition to the *Anabasis* Xenophon wrote many other works in which he conveyed his extensive knowledge of warfare, and particularly of Persian warfare, to the reading public. Especially important for military history is his historical 'novel' on Cyrus the Great (the *Cyropaedia*).[201] The details of that story may not be strictly historical, but the picture of Persian warfare reveals a keen appreciation of the actual differences between Asiatic and Greek methods of fighting. Whether all Greek generals read Xenophon's works is doubtful, but his views became part of the military culture of the period and exercised a strong influence even on generals who did not read him. Likewise Clausewitz or Liddell Hart have left their stamp on modern war so thoroughly that it is not necessary to read them to be shaped by their views, so widely have they been disseminated in various ways in our society. For forty years, from 399 to the accession of Philip II in 359, Greeks and Macedonians absorbed the lessons of Cunaxa, until Philip organized a new army that derived much from them.

After the return of the Greeks to Europe in 399, Sparta went to war with Persia in Asia Minor. Although Spartans and Persians had been allies in the Peloponnesian War, Sparta's support of Cyrus had rendered cooperation with the government of Artaxerxes difficult, and the success of Greek troops under Cyrus made Sparta overconfident. The 6,000 Greeks remaining together from the original expedition were hired by the Spartans and deployed in Asia Minor, while a Spartan army was sent to the Hellespont where, on the Asiatic side, it achieved some success. At this juncture the Persians decided to use their naval power and placed a fleet of 300 ships under the command of the Athenian admiral Conon, who had been living in exile since his escape from the battle of Aegospotami. The newly elected Spartan king, Agesilaus, took the field in 396 BC, organized a cavalry force and defeated the satrap Tissaphernes near Sardis. Then in 395 he turned against Conon on the sea, and in the battle of Cnidus (394) the Persian navy decisively defeated the Spartans, destroying whatever naval power they had been able to organize in the Aegean. Domination of the sea ultimately gave Persia underlying control of events in Greece. During this Asiatic war Xenophon had served with Agesilaus, with whom he became fast friends, and again the Greeks, including Xenophon, had many opportunities to learn from the Persians. The deployment of cavalry by the Spartan king is an example of a lesson learned and applied in the field, but Spartan lack of siege techniques hampered their efforts – a lesson learned for the future.[202] Greeks fought as mercenaries in this war on both the Spartan and Persian sides, and the effect was to disseminate throughout the Greek world, not simply in Sparta, the changing style of fighting.

IPHICRATES

In the meantime, before the battle of Cnidus, Agesilaus had been recalled temporarily to Europe for action in the so-called Corinthian War (395–387), a war between Sparta and her allies who resented the high-handed way Sparta had treated them after their victory in the Peloponnesian War. Persia had provoked the rebellion against the Spartan hegemony in Greece by promising aid to the rebels. Militarily the war, which pitted Sparta against Corinth, Argos, Thebes, and Athens, among others, was one with many interesting and important battles, but its most significant feature was the successful development of mercenary light infantry under the Athenian general Iphicrates.

At Pylos in 425 BC, as we have seen, light armed troops had been successful against Spartan hoplites, but Athens had had an overwhelming numerical advantage against the small band of Spartans, trapped by land and sea on a barren little island. As a result it was not clear that Spartan hoplites, on more favourable terrain and in a situation more nearly tactically equal, could be defeated by light troops. During the Corinthian War Iphicrates showed conclusively that the hoplite was vulnerable to attack by light infantry.

The situation, briefly, was as follows. At the outbreak of the war in 395 Sparta's enemies gained control of the Isthmus and cut Sparta off from northern Greece.[203] So, in the following year (before Agesilaus' return), an army was sent north consisting of 6,000 Spartans and 10,000 allied infantry in addition to 600 cavalry, 300 archers, and 400 slingers. On the Corinthian side there were 24,000 hoplites and 1,500 cavalry as the two armies met on the stream of Nemea between Sicyon and Corinth. In this peculiar battle, both right wings drove off the opposing left wings, but the Spartans on the right maintained formation after their victory and wheeled about to attack the returning, victorious foes on their exposed right flank and so won a great victory.[204]

In the meantime Agesilaus had been summoned from Asia (thus satisfying Persian objectives) and was marching down through Thrace

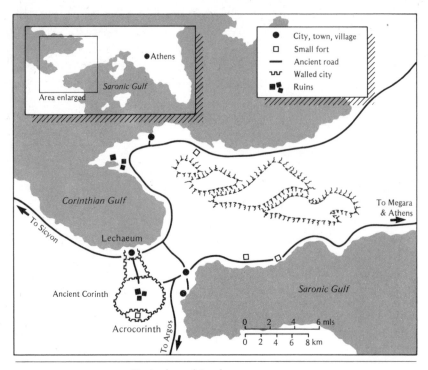

Corinth and Lechaeum, 390 BC.

and Macedonia along the route travelled earlier by Xerxes. At the battle of Coronea in Boeotia (about a month after Nemea) the two opposing right wings were again victorious, but this time they both retained formation and wheeled around to face one another.[205] Since the Thebans merely wanted to fight their way back to their retreating allies, which they ultimately did at great cost, Agesilaus made a serious mistake by not allowing them to pass and then hitting them on flank and rear, but he was left in possession of the battlefield and could justly claim victory. Sparta had opened the Isthmus, although Agesilaus crossed the Corinthian Gulf by sea.

For the next few years both sides fought indecisively to control the Isthmus – Sparta from a base in Sicyon and her enemies from Corinth. In 391 Sparta got control of the fortified port of Corinth, Lechaeum, connected to Corinth by long walls much as Piraeus was connected to Athens. Although this seemed a fortuitous development, it set the stage for Iphicrates, in 390, to deliver his fateful blow against the hoplite phalanx. One day in the summer of that year a Spartan *mora* (600 men) moved out of Lechaeum to escort a contingent of their troops around Corinth for a religious festival. After travelling three or four miles out of the base the Spartan commander sent the worshippers on with a cavalry escort. Athenian troops in Corinth decided to attack the Spartan *mora* with their light infantry, the peltasts. As Xenophon says in his account of the action,

If they [the Spartans] marched along the road, they could be shot at with javelins on their unprotected side and mowed down; and if they tried to pursue their attackers, it would be perfectly easy for peltasts, light and fast on their feet, to keep out of the way of hoplites. . . . And now as the javelins were hurled at them, some of the Spartans were killed and some wounded. . . . The polemarch then ordered the infantry . . . to charge and drive off their attackers. However, they were hoplites pursuing peltasts at the distance of a javelin's throw, and they failed to catch anyone, since Iphicrates had ordered his men to fall back before the hoplites came to close quarters. But when the Spartans, in loose order because each man had been running at his own speed, turned back again from the pursuit, Iphicrates' men wheeled round, some hurling their javelins again from in front while others ran up along the flank, shooting at the side unprotected by the shields. . . . Now, when the best men had already been killed, the cavalry came up and they once again attempted a pursuit with the cavalry in support. However, when the peltasts turned to run, the cavalry charge was mismanaged. Instead of going after the enemy until they had killed some of them, they kept, both in their advance and their retreat, a continuous front with the hoplites. So it went on, the same actions with the same results, and, while the Spartans were continually losing in numbers and in resolution, their enemies became bolder and bolder, and more and more joined in the attack.[206]

By the time it was over Iphicrates' peltasts had killed 250 of the Spartans. The defeat of a Spartan *mora* by peltasts was the wave of the future, though reflections of the hoplite morality died hard. News of the disaster caused gloom in Agesilaus' camp 'except in the cases of those whose son, father or brothers had fallen where they stood,' who 'went about like men who had won some great prize, with radiant faces, positively glorying in their own suffering.'[207] Javelins were no better at selecting 'men of honour' as their targets than the projectiles of Pylos, but Spartans were slow to learn. The fighting also shows that there was much yet to learn about the proper use of cavalry, though Xenophon and other veterans of the Asiatic campaigns were undoubtedly quick to note the error.

Iphicrates continued to make contributions to the art of Greek warfare after the Corinthian War came to an end. That war was settled by the intervention of Artaxerxes, who began to fear the Spartans, so in 387 in conjunction with Sparta he imposed a settlement which left him in control of Asia Minor and the Spartans dominant on the Greek mainland. Afterwards on several occasions the Athenian government sold the services of Iphicrates and his peltasts, and we are told by one ancient authority that his service for Artaxerxes in an Egyptian rebellion (376–373) inspired him to introduce some techniques of ancient Near Eastern warfare into Greece:

So from his long experience of campaigning in the Persian war, he thought of many excellent inventions, and paid special attention to the matter of arms. ... He made spears half as long again, and the length of the swords almost doubled. His judgement was proved right by use on active service; which made Iphicrates famous for his good ideas. He also introduced soldiers' boots which were both light and easy to take off, the boots which to this day are called 'Iphicratids' after him. He brought many other good inventions into military practice too, which it would be tedious to describe.[208]

Although the passage quoted above presents many difficulties in interpretation, two things are reasonably clear. Iphicrates introduced innovations learned in the service of Persia, and they included arming the peltasts with pikes and long swords. The long spear had been used in Egypt for some time before Iphicrates' service there, and he must have found it necessary to arm his troops with spears about twelve feet long.[209] Missile hurling troops were common enough in Persia, so Iphicrates converted his peltasts (or possibly he was commanding hoplites) into heavier units against the Egyptians. Whether peltasts later used long pikes in Greece is controversial, although there is some evidence that at least occasionally they did, but if there is any connection between Iphicrates' innovation and the creation by Philip II some fifteen years later of the Macedonian phalanx armed with the long pike, the debt of Greek and Macedonian warfare to the ancient Near East was greater than some have imagined. No ancient author says where Philip got the idea of the long pike (or sarissa), but there is little reason to doubt that it derived from Iphicrates' innovations in Egypt.

Many other mercenaries saw service with or against the Persians in the period from 404 to 359 BC. Their individual contributions to the changing forms of Greek warfare were perhaps not as significant as those of Xenophon and Iphicrates, but sheer numbers must have mattered greatly. Everywhere in Greece there were warriors, from generals to the men in the ranks, whose experience in Asia yielded new insights into the art of war. Another Athenian mercenary general of the period, Chabrias, gained nearly as much fame as Iphicrates, and he too served in Egypt in the 380s and again in the 360s, though he seems more commonly to have commanded hoplites than peltasts. Chabrias had returned to Athens from Egypt in 379, and in the following year he made his great contribution to Greek tactics in a campaign against Agesilaus of Sparta. The two armies lined up facing one another in Boeotia, with the Athenian-Theban army on a ridge. Chabrias ordered his troops to show their contempt for the Spartans (almost 20,000 strong) by standing at ease in formation, resting their shields against their knees and holding their spears upright rather than levelled against the enemy. Agesilaus decided not to force battle, partly because he did not want to fight uphill but largely because he (and presumably his troops) was disturbed by the uncommon calmness of his opponents. This display of psychological bravado was unnerving mainly because it was not common Greek practice, and one can speculate that it derived from Chabrias' experience in Egypt in the years immediately preceding the encounter.[210] The only other comparable instance of Greek troops standing at ease in the face of danger occurred in a minor episode of the Cyrus campaign. In the fourth century this may well have been an Asian practice. Xenophon's account of the battle of Cunaxa reveals that the Greeks were troubled at the outset of the fighting because the Persians facing them approached 'as silently as they could, calmly, in a slow, steady march'.[211] In mainland Greek warfare, however, it was a famous, innovative stratagem.

The widespread use of mercenaries had another important influence from the Near East. Mercenaries normally showed a professional *esprit de corps* far greater than that of conscript armies, the kind of spirit that was later embodied in the entire Macedonian army under Philip and Alexander. It was reflected most notably in the discipline and drill of mercenary units, cultivated in long training. Iphicrates was famous as a strict disciplinarian, and he kept his troops busy at all times, whether battle was imminent or not, in the manner of the later Roman legions.[212]

It is fashionable in modern times to denigrate parade-ground drill largely because the technology of modern firepower has made close-order formation unfeasible, but in ancient warfare armies fought in close order, and their performance on the parade ground, especially when it was distinctive, was often a reflection of the way they would perform on the battlefield. Its psychological effect cannot be overestimated. Although it is most clearly revealed in the impact it had on the enemy, smart execution of manoeuvres is even more important as a means of controlling the ever-present fear of battle within an army. In the final analysis the greatest danger to any warrior in the field is not the enemy – it is the fear that he will be abandoned by his support units in a flight of panic. Drill helps to overcome that inevitable fear and contributes mightily to a sense of teamwork and to a better army.

Two examples will illustrate the point. At the battle of Amphipolis in 422, Brasidas urged his own troops on by pointing out to them that Cleon's army could not even keep good formation: 'Those fellows will never stand before us. One can see that by the way their spears and heads are going. Troops which do as they do seldom stand a charge.'[213] In the fourth century Iphicrates once refused to commit badly trained troops to battle, even though he had a numerical advantage, because they could not execute some of the basic commands. Indeed, the emergence of the mercenaries and the rigorous discipline they practised denied to the Spartans the great advantage they had exercised throughout the fifth century based on the famous Spartan drill. In the *Politics* Aristotle noted the change:

Even the Spartans themselves, as we know from experience, were superior to others only so long as they were the only people which assiduously practised the rigours of discipline; and nowadays they are beaten both in athletic contests and in actual war. Their previous superiority was not due to the particular training which they gave to their youth; it was simply and solely due to their having some sort of discipline when their antagonists had none at all. . . . The Spartan training has now to face rivals. Formerly it had none.[214]

PROFESSORS OF TACTICS

In some ways the Peloponnesian War, which had created a manpower pool of warriors for mercenary service and the conditions under which they might be extensively used in Asia as well as Greece, led also to the development of a true military science. There was a recognition that warfare had become complicated – that it was, after all, more than simply holding one's place in formation, digging in and dying. A good general in earlier times selected the battlefield (preferably on the enemy's crops), pointed his army at the enemy, and let it do its job, usually fighting himself in the first rank.[215] By the late fifth century the troops, at least, knew better. Clearchus and Xenophon won their dominant positions among the Greek mercenaries of Cyrus by showing that they knew how to command, which meant many things. Included among them was the military bearing that enabled them to enforce discipline. It is surprising how troops tend towards insubordination, laxness and general indiscipline yet resent commanders who permit them to do it. Soldiers know that their ultimate safety depends on officers who can make them fight as a team, and they realize that that requires discipline. Generals also have to secure supplies. Few men in the ranks can hope to provide their own, although there is always someone who never seems to lack for them. In an age of mercenary warfare, pay is obviously important, and good generals were conscious of the fact.

On the march and in battle generals of the fourth century had much more to do than their predecessors in the fifth. Iphicrates' success with peltasts in 390 showed that war was more than the clash of hoplites on the battlefield. In earlier days armies on the march might expect easy passage through enemy territory until they met face to face with their opponent, but the use of light troops dramatically increased the dangers of the march. The battle itself was no longer decided by shock along the entire front of the line. In the Peloponnesian War the Spartans had taken advantage of the natural tendency of hoplites to drift towards their right to gain protection from the shield next to them by executing a flanking movement from their right against the enemy left.[216] In the first half of the fourth century such flanking movements had become standard in Greek warfare. This placed an added burden on generals who had to know how to rout the enemy when only one part of its line was in disarray. We have seen that Agesilaus at the battle of Coronea in 394 made a serious mistake against the enemy right wing after he had defeated the enemy left wing. In warfare, especially as it becomes reasonably complicated, generals will make mistakes, but the troops need to believe that their commander knows what he is doing, that he will not foolishly waste their lives. Nothing can demoralize an army so thoroughly as the perception of dangerous generalship, either from foolishness or recklessness, a 'gung-ho' desire to fight the enemy at all costs.

As Greek warfare became more complicated, the study of proper generalship developed into a required science and gave rise to the emergence in Greek society of the so-called professors of tactics.[217] By the standards of modern military academies early Greek military science was relatively primitive, and for various reasons it never became quite as important in the ancient world, even under the Romans, as one might have expected; but a few formal treatises on certain aspects of war were produced by ancient authors, beginning with Xenophon and Aeneas Tacticus in the fourth century BC and ending with Vegetius in the fourth century AD. History, however, was more often used as the instructor of the military arts than discrete, formal analysis along scientific lines. Cicero lamented the fact that Xenophon's *Cyropaedia* was more popular than works of Roman authors, but as governor of Cilicia he proudly proclaimed that he had put Xenophon's work into practice, and it was Cicero who revealed that Scipio always had Xenophon in his hands.[218]

Still, there were professors of tactics in the Greek world in the late fifth and early fourth centuries. Xenophon cared little for them. In his *Constitution of the Spartans* he says: 'The Spartans also carry out with perfect ease manoeuvres that professors of tactics think very difficult.'[219] Soldiers have always had contempt for 'classroom' warfare, and it is unfortunate that Xenophon is our only source for the professors of tactics. But even from his hostile account of their activities, especially in his *Recollections of Socrates*, we can see something of the work they did. The story is that Socrates encouraged a young friend who wanted to be an Athenian general to study under Dionysodorus, a professor of tactics. After the friend had done so, he returned to Socrates, who teased him for looking more like a general than he did before and then asked him what he had learned. The reply was, 'He taught me tactics and nothing else.' Socrates said, 'Tactics are fine and the army drawn up in battle positions is far better than the army not posted in battle positions.' Nevertheless, Socrates made it clear that generalship involved more than tactics: 'A general must be fully prepared to furnish the equipment necessary for war. He must be ready with supplies for the troops.' A general, Socrates goes on to say, must have cunning, kindness, cruelty, straightforwardness, deviousness, and many other qualities. He must also know how to choose between good and bad men and how to use formations as well as draw them up. Socrates then urged his friend to go back to the professor and learn these things.[220]

This one critical account of the professors of tactics contains the traditional, stereotyped criticism of the ivory-towered schoolmaster who lacks contact with the real world and has no idea how his theories might be applied. There is little reason to assume that all such instruction in tactics was as weak as that of Dionysodorus (or that he was as bad as Xenophon suggested). In any case it is an interesting illustration of the new role of warfare in Greek society, of war as an 'intellectual' activity. If Dionysodorus was not a proper instructor, the subject was nevertheless worthy of study. Warfare had emerged from the realm of morality and honour. It had become something more than a way of life to be conducted according to ancestral expectations of 'men of honour'. As the Greeks moved rapidly towards the creation of integrated armies, they began to view warfare as a complicated social activity. Warfare had become innovative rather than traditional.

Before leaving mercenaries and the professors of tactics we should note one other change in Greek warfare. In the fourth century it had become sufficiently specialized that a young Greek could aspire to a career as a general, as a leader of men on the field. In the fifth century and before, generalship had been tied to politics and the only sure path to military command was through a political career. This was not so in the fourth century. Though Athens continued to elect its generals, one could prepare for the office simply through the study of warfare, and the electorate was sufficiently aware of the difference between politics and warfare to elect at least some generals simply for their military ability.[221]

Nevertheless, specialization had not, and in antiquity would not, become so complete that only officers with military training and experience were placed in command of armies. As complicated as it was, the management of war was not in the grip of formal military academies, though there were professional generals and sometimes states sought them out and hired them. In some important circles, however, there was still a feeling in the fourth century that overall qualities of leadership were more essential in a general than military experience and training. In the *Recollections of Socrates* Xenophon tells of a bitterly disappointed candidate for a generalship in Athens who lost the election to a successful businessman who had no military experience. The defeated candidate lamented the folly of the electorate and recited his own experience in the service while displaying his many wounds to Socrates. Socrates, however, argued that one who was successful in the conduct of his private affairs probably had the qualities of leadership that would 'most likely win in war as well'.[222] Although Alexander and the generals of the Hellenistic world who succeeded him very nearly raised generalship to the level of a specialized career, and there were indications in Athens, Sparta and elsewhere in the Greek world of the fourth century that military command was becoming a career, the generalist tradition represented by Socrates continued to be a strong force, and it prevailed at Rome during the great wars of the Republic. The technology of ancient warfare, though impressive, did not require years of specialized study in military academies.

Epaminondas and Pelopidas

As Greeks began to experiment with light infantry, cavalry and skirmishers, the age of hoplite warfare came to an end, but it had one last moment of glory in the wars of the 370s and 360s between Sparta and Thebes. There is considerable irony in the fact that Spartan land power, which had been dominant in Greece from the early stages of hoplite history, was broken in the fourth century not by the newly emerging integrated armies but by another phalanx.

In two battles, Leuctra (371) and Mantinea (362) the Theban phalanx fought and defeated the legendary Spartan army, and much of the credit for Thebes' victories goes to two talented leaders, Epaminondas and Pelopidas.[223] At Leuctra Epaminondas was in command of the entire army while Pelopidas had the so-called Sacred Band of 300 crack troops. The Spartans, under Cleombrotus, encamped to the south of the flat plain of Leuctra on a ridge of hills facing the Thebans, who were also on a ridge across the plain to the north. The armies were in full view of one another. The Spartan force numbered altogether about 10,000 hoplites and 1,000 cavalry, and it included four of the six *morai* of Spartiates (about 1,800 men). The Thebans and their allies had probably only about 6,000 hoplites and 800 cavalry.[224]

Before the battle began (around midday), some of the contingents of the Theban army urged withdrawal since they could see that they were outnumbered. The Spartans, on the other hand, had been drinking, and the wine may have made them over-eager. Xenophon says that some of the Theban allies tried to flee but were driven back by Spartan cavalry and light infantry to the Theban camp. Clearly the Spartans should have let them go, but apparently they could not resist the temptation of attacking troops in flight and disarray. At the outset of the battle Cleombrotus placed his cavalry in front of the line, and Epaminondas countered by doing the same thing. Although the Spartans had a slight numerical advantage in cavalry, their force was not as experienced and well trained as the Theban cavalry. While the Spartan phalanx stood in battle formation twelve deep, Epaminondas made his unique contribution to hoplite warfare by stationing his Thebans on the left of his line (opposite the Spartiates on the Spartan right) in a formation 'fifty shields deep'. The idea, according to Epaminondas, was to 'crush the head of the serpent', to defeat the best part of the Spartan army. Thebans had traditionally fought in deeper formation than other Greeks, but Xenophon, though he does not explicitly say so, implies that Epaminondas deliberately deepened his left wing for this particular engagement: 'They calculated that, if they proved superior in that part of the field where the king was, all the rest would be easy.'[225] So the innovation of Epaminondas was twofold – to concentrate his best forces on his left directly against the Spartan right (as Mardonius had done at Plataea) and to mass them fifty deep. At the head of this formation stood the Theban Sacred Band under Pelopidas, prepared to lead the action on the Theban left wing.[226]

Cleombrotus, on the other hand, intending to use his cavalry as a screen (which explains why he placed it in front of his line rather than on his wings), hoped to execute the flanking manoeuvre that the Spartans had mastered since the time of the Peloponnesian War by moving with his right wing against the Theban left.

In the fighting at the battle of Leuctra many things went wrong, and Sparta especially suffered from bad luck and worse generalship (and possibly the wine). As Xenophon said, 'Everything certainly went badly for the Spartans, and everything, including luck, was on the side of the Thebans.'[227] Morale in the Theban army was low, except in the massed formation on the Theban left, and if the Spartan centre and left had been able to engage the Theban centre and right, they would surely have driven the Theban allies from the field. Epaminondas understood that and prepared a plan accordingly. Cleombrotus stubbornly ignored it, and though he may not have known exactly how vulnerable the Theban centre and right were, his own action combined with Epaminondas' decisiveness made it impossible for him to achieve the victory he should have won along his centre and left.

As the battle began, Cleombrotus, behind his cavalry screen, began to move to his right with the Spartans to execute the flanking movement. Epaminondas retaliated much more decisively than Cleombrotus expected. The Theban cavalry charged out immediately and threw the Spartan cavalry into flight, driving it back into the Spartan line where it interfered with and fouled the Spartan manoeuvres. Perhaps even more important than the instantaneous attack of Theban cavalry was the fact that the massed heavy infantry on the Theban left, led by the Sacred Band, followed immediately behind it in an oblique charge on the double against the extending Spartan right. For whatever reason, the Spartan centre and left did not move out to attack either the advancing Theban column or the Theban centre and right. Because the two armies did not engage except on one wing the battle was determined by the fighting there (see map).

Although the Spartan right had been thrown into confusion by the retreating cavalry and the suddenness of the Theban infantry attack while Cleombrotus was in the midst of an intricate manoeuvre, it did not break. Only Spartans had the discipline and training required to continue fighting under such circumstances, and we must marvel at their spirit and resolve. As Plutarch said in his biography of Pelopidas,

> But Pelopidas with the three hundred came rapidly up, before Cleombrotus could extend his line, and close up his divisions, and so fell upon the Spartans while in disorder; though the Spartans, the expertest and most practised soldiers of all mankind, used to train and accustom themselves to nothing so much as to keep themselves from confusion upon any change of position, and to follow any leader . . . and form in order, and fight on what part soever dangers press.[228]

Normally, when an army is thrown into confusion, it is difficult enough to reform the men in their original units; especially when they are under fire or engaged in shock. So the fighting raged, and Xenophon is surely right in saying that the ability of the Spartans to carry Cleombrotus off the field, after he had fallen from a wound that proved fatal, indicates that the Spartans, for a while, held their ground in brutal fighting. But, when Epaminondas called upon his heavy formation for 'one more step forward to please me' in a final crushing effort, the Spartans were driven back, and their army retreated to its camp. More than half of the Spartiates on the field had been killed.

Politically the battle of Leuctra was the most decisive battle in

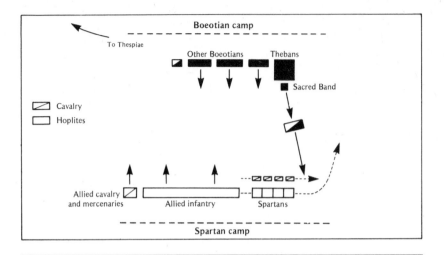

The battle of Leuctra, 371 BC.

Greek warfare since Aegospotami. It broke the Spartan hegemony in Greece and gave rise briefly to a period of Theban domination. The fact that it was decided by hoplites rather than by peltasts and skirmishers in an age when new arms had shown their effectiveness is often cited as an example of the conservative nature of Greek warfare. We have seen that Greek warfare was slow to change, but it is important to note that even in traditional hoplite tactics there are indications of new developments in the fourth century. Cavalry played an important role at the outset of Leuctra, although it was not yet used in conjunction with infantry in the classic 'hammer-and-anvil' fashion we shall see under Alexander. More important is the new emphasis on mobility in the infantry. The wars with Persia and the emergence of light armed units in Greece had led to the development of more flexible tactics. The indirect approach of attack on the flanks, the increasing use of heavy infantry on the double, the rapid development of intricate manoeuvres on the field, the use of cavalry screens or sometimes of topography to conceal formation, and the employment of fighting reserves to be used at critical moments in the battle all reveal that in heavy infantry the military revolution was having an effect. Direct, frontal assaults along the entire line had become a thing of the past as the Greeks experimented with the tactics of integrated armies while yet continuing to put their trust in heavy infantry.

About ten years later, in 362, Spartans and Thebans met again at Mantinea in the Peloponnese. By that time Pelopidas was dead. Since Epaminondas used essentially the same tactics on this occasion as he had earlier at Leuctra, and with the same results, there is no need to review the battle in detail. The heavy Theban left rolled over the Spartan right again, but as Epaminondas pressed his advantage he fell to an enemy spear.[229] Though his use of heavy infantry was tactically innovative, and his victories over the Spartan hoplite phalanx brought him great fame as the only general ever to defeat a Spartan army with another traditional phalanx, his place in the military history of ancient Greece has been overestimated. It is often said that the young Philip, who lived in Thebes as a hostage in this momentous period, learned the art of warfare from Epaminondas and Pelopidas. He did learn much from the Thebans, but, as we shall see, Philip's generalship owed more to the ideas of Xenophon, Iphicrates and Chabrias than to those of Epaminondas. As it happened, Epaminondas was the last great general of the Greek world to fight major wars with a hoplite phalanx. Though the Greeks did not know it in 362, they would soon learn that the military revolution had sealed the fate of the hoplite.

Catapults and Siege Warfare

Many of the new developments in Greek warfare of the fourth century came as the result of Greek contacts with Persia and some were indigenous to mainland Greece, but another source of innovation was the world of the Western Greeks, especially Syracuse. There, in the period from 406 to 367 BC, Dionysius I fought intermittently against Carthage for the domination of Sicily. In the course of that struggle, facing an opponent with military institutions that undoubtedly owed much to the ancient Near East, Dionysius reshaped the Syracusan army and sparked flames of military reform that spread to the Aegean.

His single most important contribution to warfare came in the year 399 BC when he assembled in Syracuse craftsmen from all over Sicily, Italy, Greece and Carthage to manufacture arms. Dionysius paid them well and helped them to set up workshops in every cranny of his city. It was in one of those shops that an unknown military engineer invented the catapult.[230] The original catapults, which spread throughout the eastern Mediterranean in the fourth century, were simple non-torsion devices, called 'belly bows' (*gastraphetes*). They were mechanical devices with triggers held against the stomach which permitted men to use two arms to pull back a composite bow stronger than anything that could be drawn with one arm alone. Their range is not known, but even if it was only 250 yards it increased the maximum effective distance of the ancient bow by twenty-five per cent or so and probably permitted better aiming, so that the increase in accuracy and range of firepower was dramatic. When they were fitted with winches and bases and given mechanical pull-back devices, they eliminated bruises to the stomach and were powerful enough to hurl stones. These machines were still called 'belly bows', and those made around 350 BC had a maximum effective range of about 300 yards with sufficient force to drive through a shield. (The word catapult means 'shield piercer'.) When they were attached to a base with a universal joint, they could be turned in any direction and adjusted for elevation of fire.

By about 370 BC catapults were in use on the Greek mainland, at least in Sparta and Athens where they had been shipped from Syracuse by Dionysius. By 350 they appear in Thessaly and in Macedon and by 340 in Byzantium. When Alexander besieged Halicarnassus in Persian Asia Minor in 334 and Tyre in Phoenicia in 332, the defenders of both cities fired catapults at the Macedonians, who returned catapult fire of their own. So in the period from 399 to Alexander's invasion of Persia in 334 catapults had become standard instruments of war in Greece and Persia.

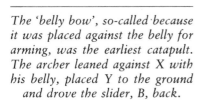

The 'belly bow', so-called because it was placed against the belly for arming, was the earliest catapult. The archer leaned against X with his belly, placed Y to the ground and drove the slider, B, back.

The invention of the more sophisticated, torsion catapult probably occurred in Macedon between 353 and 341 BC.[231] In 354 during operations in Thessaly Philip was driven away by enemy artillerymen using 'bellow bows', but in 340, at the sieges of Perinthus and Byzantium, the Macedonian king deployed torsion catapults, and they were almost certainly invented by his military engineers. The torsion catapult replaced the composite bow, using torsion springs that were normally made out of sinew or horse or human hair mounted in wooden frames. Iron levers were used for twisting the sinew or hair, and torsion catapults were much more powerful than the 'belly bows'. There was almost no limit to their size, and huge ones eventually were able to cast stones up to fifty pounds in weight. The various formulas of calibration that permitted the construction of catapults with scientifically accurate proportions were not worked out until the Hellenistic period after Alexander, but in the fourth century catapults constructed on a trial and error basis led to a major effective increase in the technology of firepower.

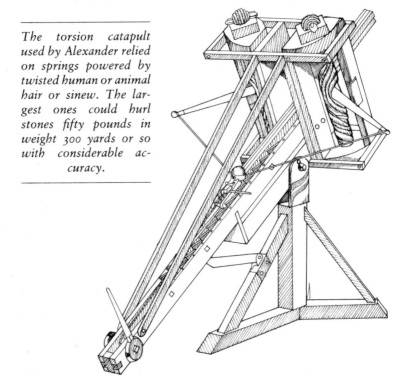

The torsion catapult used by Alexander relied on springs powered by twisted human or animal hair or sinew. The largest ones could hurl stones fifty pounds in weight 300 yards or so with considerable accuracy.

Catapults were used as field artillery on several occasions in fourth-century warfare. The first certain instance of their use in that way was against Philip in Thessaly in 354. Early in the reign of Alexander, in 335 BC, he relied upon them to cover his withdrawal across a river as he fought his way out of a difficult position near Pelium in Illyria. As Arrian described the action, 'He himself was the first across, and, setting up his artillery on the river-bank, he gave orders for every sort of missile it would take to be discharged at long range against the enemy, whom he could see pressing hard upon those of his own troops who were bringing up the rear.'[232]

Although the catapult could be usefully deployed as field artillery, and there was another instance of its use in that way by Alexander on the Jaxartes in Asia, its paramount function was for offensive and defensive fire in sieges. In the fourth century the Greeks finally caught up with the ancient Near East in siege warfare, an important part of the military revolution, and the invention of the catapult was their own contribution to that complicated branch of ancient fighting. Again it is necessary to return to Dionysius I of Syracuse, in whose workshops the catapult was invented, to find the first instance of sophisticated siege warfare in Greek military history. Significantly it was against the Carthaginians: long ago W. W. Tarn noted the ironical fact that Greeks were influenced by the ancient Near East from the west through Carthage and Sicily and back to the Greek mainland: 'What was known in Assyria was also known in Syria and Phoenicia, and so passed to Carthage; and down to 400 BC the Carthaginians knew more about sieges than any Greek.'[233] Greek sieges before 400 were merely blockades, and, though they could sometimes be reasonably complicated, as at Syracuse during the Athenian expedition, hoplites could simply not take fortified cities by storm.

That situation began to change early in the fourth century, in 397 BC, when Dionysius also adopted the ancient Near Eastern devices of siege towers and battering rams. Motya was an island fortress less than a mile off the western tip of Sicily. There was a mole or causeway, a man-made road, built into the sea linking the city with the main island, but the Carthaginians destroyed it when Dionysius approached. He began to build a new, wider one and brought up wheeled towers six storeys tall armed with catapults to drive the defenders from the fortifications. When the Syracusans reached the walls of Motya, they came up with their battering rams and forced their way inside.²³⁴ Thereafter Dionysius conducted several other successful sieges, and the art of siege warfare began to spread slowly throughout the Greek world. It was not much practised on the Greek mainland in the first half of the fourth century, mainly because the old hoplite manner of warfare continued its strong influence over Greek strategic thought, but the day was soon coming when Greeks could no longer feel safe behind their walls. On the other hand, the catapult could also be deployed effectively against attackers from behind the walls, and in 340 when Philip besieged Perinthus with catapults, siege towers over 100 feet high and battering rams, the Perinthians secured catapults from Byzantium and with additional help from Athens and Persia forced Philip to abandon the siege.²³⁵

Thus with the ability to attack fortified sites came the related ability to defend them, a reflection of the dilemma of military innovation referred to in an earlier chapter, 'the offence-defence inventive cycle'. If siege warfare, however, proved to have its limitations, it did in any event broaden significantly the strategic range of Greek and Macedonian warfare. One reflection of this change can be seen in the grand strategy of Athens in the fourth century down to its defeat by Philip in 338 at the battle of Chaeronea.

A brilliant young scholar has recently shown that Athenians of the fourth century, stripped of their naval supremacy by the Peloponnesian War and economically much weaker than in the great days of the fifth-century empire, concentrated on the development of a system of frontier defence based on an elaborate network of fortifications along the northern and western Attic frontiers.²³⁶ Taking advantage of the new light armed forces, the Athenians emphasized training in peltast tactics and the use of projectile weapons. Their fortifications were manned by these light units and were intended to stop invaders on the borders of Attica until the main Athenian force could be brought up along newly constructed or improved military highways linked with Athens. The frontier forts of the new 'fortress Attica' were sophisticated military structures containing slits or windows for the use of catapults. This system of preclusive security along the Attic frontier was first extensively developed in the 380s and 370s and continued down into the 340s. It was abandoned only when the Athenians realized that Philip's siege techniques had become so sophisticated and his army so large that their frontier fortresses could not delay his advance, and in alliance with Thebes, finally met him in the field, outside Attica at Chaeronea in 338 BC, where they were defeated.

Greek warfare had changed so drastically and rapidly during the military revolution of the first half of the fourth century, technologically and conceptually, that generals and states could not keep up with developments. The hoplite mentality remained strong, and the two most decisive battles of the period, Leuctra and Mantinea, were fought with hoplite armies, but both the Spartans and Epaminondas had used tactics that owed something to the more mobile warfare of the emerging lighter arms. By the end of the period – to be specific by the accession of Philip as King of Macedon in 359 BC – every ingredient necessary for the deployment of a fully integrated army had appeared. What was needed was someone who could put those ingredients together, and that person was Philip.

Philip and the Macedonian Army

A great deal is known about the army Alexander led into Asia in 334 BC, although there has been much controversy about certain points of organization and armament.[237] Historians assume, correctly, that Alexander's army was created by his father, Philip II, and there are some contemporary references to it in the period of Philip's reign (359–336 BC). The fullest accounts of the army, however, depend upon the more detailed descriptions of it in action under Alexander. There is a slight possibility of anachronistically assigning to Philip innovations introduced by his son, but we can be reasonably confident that Alexander's army was fashioned by Philip.

It was an integrated army that represented a fusion of the best elements of Greek and ancient Near Eastern warfare. To what extent Philip was directly influenced by Persia will remain unknown, but indirectly through the innovations of the military revolution of the early fourth century and through the influence of generals such as Xenophon, Iphicrates and Chabrias, all of whom were clearly influenced by Persian modes of fighting, the influence of the ancient Near East on the Macedonian army was strong. On the other hand, Greeks too had something to contribute to the fusion. Their heavy infantry was infinitely better than Persia's, and their tradition of training and discipline, their fighting spirit, was more intensive.

CAVALRY

The premier arm of the Macedonian army was cavalry. Cavalry had always been important in Macedon, where the hoplite phalanx was never adopted as the principal military arm as it was in the Greek states to the south. The Macedonian king was a horseman, though he sometimes fought on foot, and the best cavalry were organized as the king's Companions. The Companions wore a cuirass (a breastplate or coat of mail) and fought as shock troops rather than as skirmishers. Since they were aristocrats who had ridden from youth, their horsemanship was outstanding. Though evidence for Philip's reign is limited, based upon what is known about Alexander's army in 334, the Companion cavalry was organized into fourteen or fifteen squadrons of about 200 each, around 2,500 to 3,000 altogether. Each squadron had its own commander, and one of them, the Royal Squadron (perhaps 300 strong), was commanded by the king. Macedonian cavalry squadrons fought in a wedge formation as lancers carrying long spears (sarissas) of cornel wood and a long curving sword which they could use when needed. The wedge formation was especially good for riding through gaps in the enemy line, so the Macedonian cavalry need not be deployed simply for flanking movements. The cavalry sarissa was 9 feet long and weighed 4.2 pounds, so it was light enough to be thrown if necessary. It was in fact similar to the Napoleonic lance in size and weight, though the Macedonian weapon had an iron point on both ends. Since it was gripped at a ratio point of 3:5 (roughly 4.5 feet forward of the hand and 3.5 feet rear of it), the butt could be used for stabbing down at infantry in close quarters, or, if the forepoint was broken off, the aft point could be held up as a thrusting spear. Although ancient cavalry lacked the stirrup, the blow of the Macedonian cavalry sarissa, released by the cavalryman immediately before or on impact, so as not to unhorse the rider, had a deadly impact. As one authority has written,

Understanding the great effectiveness of even a single-pointed lance, I believe that the Macedonian lance with its second head aft is superior to anything realized later. Understanding the great skill needed to wield even a single-pointed lance, I believe that the Hellenistic lancer, with his greater range of strokes and tactics, which required greater skill and training, was superior to any subsequent lance troops. Considering that the Hellenistic cavalry had no stirrups but appear no less effective in combat than their Napoleonic counterparts, their skill and achievements appear formidable indeed. The very high level of training, and therefore cost, required to field combat-

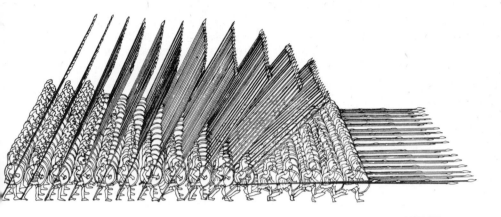

The Macedonian phalanx, here shown in its fighting formation of 256 men, the syntagma.

effective wielders of the double-pointed cavalry sarissa may in fact account for its eventual disappearance and replacement by the single-pointed lance.[238]

In addition to the Companion cavalry Philip used Thracians, Scouts (probably from Macedonia but not Companions) and Paeonians. Five of such squadrons, or 1,000 horses in all, went with Alexander to Asia. They seemed to have been armed as light cavalry with javelins, rather than the lance (except the Scouts), and they were used for reconnoitring ahead of the army and for skirmishing. Additional heavy cavalry was provided by the Thessalians, who fought on Philip's side at Chaeronea. Armed with spears, perhaps not as heavy as the Macedonian cavalry sarissa, they traditionally fought in a diamond-shaped formation which gave more mass and weight to the point of the wedge and slightly greater width at the widest extent.

THE MACEDONIAN PHALANX

The greatest single tactical innovation attributed to Philip was his organization of the famous Macedonian phalanx. Before Philip Macedonian military might rested on cavalry, but immediately upon his accession in 359 the new king, inspired partly by what he had learned as a hostage in Thebes under Epaminondas, and by his general knowledge of the changing conditions of warfare, restructured and revitalized the Macedonian infantry. He organized it as a phalanx sixteen deep and armed the phalangites with a new weapon, the long two-handed pike or infantry sarissa some thirteen feet long (and as time went by it became longer).[239] Made of cornel wood in two parts, joined by an iron sleeve, it weighed about twelve pounds. The front-rankers wore greaves, helmet and metal cuirass and carried shields approximately two feet in diameter. Rear-rankers seem to have been more lightly armed. When the Macedonian phalanx lowered its pikes for action the points of the pikes in the fifth rank projected beyond the front rank.

The Macedonian phalangites stood somewhat further apart than hoplites, since both hands were needed for the pike and it was no longer possible to seek protection from the neighbouring shield. The Macedonian phalanx was heavier and less mobile than the Greek hoplite phalanx, and it had a more specialized tactical function. Unlike the hoplites, Macedonian phalangites were normally not expected to win battles on their own. As an impenetrable heavy formation their task was to meet and pin down the enemy line while Macedonian cavalry and light infantry penetrated gaps or hit flanks and rear. The Macedonian phalanx became the anvil against which enemy forces were driven by encircling cavalry, the hammer, and smashed in battle.[240]

To enhance their prestige they became known as the 'Foot Companions' and were organized in a square sixteen deep and sixteen wide. The men in the first rank were the commanders of the men in file behind them. This square of 256 men, called a *syntagma*, fought in a battalion (or *taxis*) containing six *syntagmata* altogether, or slightly more than 1,500 men. There were twelve such battalions in the Macedonian army of Philip.

Philip trained and drilled his phalanx intensively to face in any direction by wheeling in an arc. By stepping the last eight men in the files right or left, and moving them up, Philip could double the front of his phalanx on command, or conversely, create gaps as Alexander did at Gaugamela for the Persian chariot charge. There was also an élite corps of heavy infantry, the *hypaspists*, 3,000 strong, who normally served on the right wing between the cavalry and the phalanx and were rather more lightly armed and more mobile than the regular phalangites. It is clear that the Macedonian phalangite was taught to fight in formations other than that of the phalanx and with different

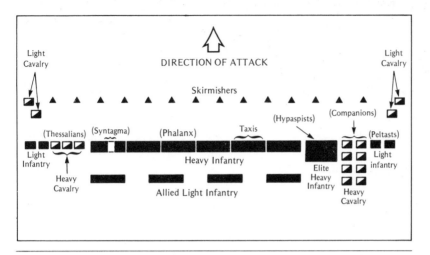

DIRECTION OF ATTACK

Light Cavalry

Light Cavalry

Skirmishers

(Hypaspists)

(Companions)

(Thessalians) (Syntagma) (Phalanx) Taxis (Peltasts)

Light Infantry

Heavy Infantry

Light infantry

Heavy Cavalry

Elite Heavy Infantry

Allied Light Infantry

Heavy Cavalry

The Macedonian order of battle under Philip and Alexander.

weapons when the conditions required it. Under Alexander they were used in sieges and in mountain warfare, where the phalanx formation would have been inappropriate.

PELTASTS AND SKIRMISHERS

The Macedonian army under Philip and Alexander also made effective use of light infantry (or peltasts) and skirmishers. Peltasts could perform the double role of both skirmishers and light infantry. The difference between the two types of warrior is that skirmishers could not close with the enemy or hold a line against enemy attack. They were mainly archers and slingers whose function was to deliver long-range firepower against the foe at the outset of battle, in the hope of demoralizing or confusing him, or to attack the enemy's line of column on the march, or his supply train. The mounted archer could serve as a cavalry skirmisher. Light infantry, normally armed with the javelin which could also be held as a spear, could sometimes serve as skirmishers in delivering the intermediate-range firepower of the javelin, particularly against hoplites, but they could also form into line and hold it, either against cavalry or on difficult and mountainous terrain against heavy infantry. Light infantry was also occasionally useful in support of cavalry attacks into gaps in the enemy line, since it was more mobile and could move in quickly behind cavalry, taking advantage of the confusion in the enemy formation. Further, light infantry could be effective in pursuit, especially in conjunction with cavalry. We have already seen how light infantry and skirmishers were effective at Pylos and under Iphicrates. Under the Macedonians they also played a role in siege operations.

Persia had always used light infantry and skirmishers effectively, and their adoption in Greek warfare was surely due to the Greek experience of fighting their great Near Eastern foe. There can be no doubt that Athens developed a corps of archers in the early fifth century directly as a result of the experience against Persia, and slingers became common too for the same reason. It is true that there had always been some archers and slingers in the Greek world, but the hoplite states ignored them until Persia showed their effectiveness.

Some Greek historians believe that the peltast was a Thracian contribution to Greek warfare, later incorporated by the Macedonians, but this view is probably incorrect.[241] It is true that the peltast was a native Thracian warrior, and that many peltasts of the fourth century were actually Thracian mercenaries, but writers such as Xenophon used the term peltast synonymously with light infantry in general, and it is clear that the inspiration for their use in Greece came from Persia. Thracians had actively fought alongside Persians against the Greeks in the Persian Wars, and peltasts were common in Persian Asia Minor. In Egypt Iphicrates had armed his peltasts with spears much longer than the hoplite ones, and when Philip fifteen years later provided the Macedonian phalangites with the sarissa, he may indirectly have imposed another ancient Near Eastern stamp on Greek and Macedonian warfare, though in this case the innovation included the transfer of the new weapon from light to heavy infantry.

In any event it was Philip who, consciously or unconsciously, wedded the best of the Greek and ancient Near Eastern military traditions. His army was fully integrated and in one respect it was vastly superior to that of the Persians. His heavy infantry, in which the Greeks had always excelled, could not be matched by Persian forces.

TRAINING, INTELLIGENCE AND LOGISTICS

We have seen that Iphicrates had a reputation for strict discipline and for keeping his troops busy even when they were not fighting. There is a story that he killed a sleeping sentry and said merely, 'I left him as I found him.'[242] One of Philip's contributions to warfare was to impose on his new integrated army a rigorous code of military professionalism based on a routine of constant drill. Early in his reign Philip is described as 'haranguing [his troops] in a series of assemblies and encouraging them in eloquent speeches to be courageous; he improved the military formation, equipped his men appropriately with weapons of war, and held frequent exercises under arms and competitions in physical fitness.' In fact, he subjected his army to the kind of training that is ordinarily reserved for commando troops in modern warfare, and there is a sense, though we should not press the point too hard, in which the entire Macedonian army was a large commando unit with shock troops and skirmishers.[243]

To aid him in the deployment of this army Philip organized the first systematic intelligence arm in Greek warfare. The Greek states of the fifth century had been interested in intelligence, and there are quaint and colourful stories of their methods of securing information of a politically, strategically or tactically delicate nature, but no Greek state of the fifth century had an organized intelligence network.[244] The systematic collection and analysis of intelligence, especially tactical, in classical Greece was probably not as highly developed as it had been in ancient Egypt or Assyria, and there is no doubt whatsoever that the Persians improved on this ancient Near Eastern tradition of spying. Herodotus in the fifth century and Xenophon in the fourth marvelled at the 'King's Eye', at his ability to know what was happening in his own empire and beyond. In the fifth century the Spartans were accused of being 'too often in ignorance of what is going on outside [their] own territory', that is, of being generally uninformed – to say nothing of their lack of organized intelligence.

Philip, on the other hand, was famous for his use of intelligence and counter-intelligence. Greeks generally reacted with moral indignation – spies, tricks and deceit were not appropriate for 'men of honour'. According to Polybius, as we have seen, Philip's use of intelligence methods contrasted sharply with the fair and open war of earlier times. The contrast is perhaps too clearly drawn, since earlier Greek states did sometimes resort to similar stratagems, but the point that Philip made them an organized and regular feature of Aegean warfare is surely sound.

Strategic intelligence on some points was readily available to Philip and Alexander as they planned the invasion of Persian Asia Minor. They would have been generally familiar with literary works conveying information about Persia, such as those of Herodotus and

Xenophon, with the reports of merchants, travellers and diplomats operating in the Persian Empire, and with the stories of the mercenaries who had served with Agesilaus, Cyrus, and other generals in Persia. In addition there were high-ranking Persians in exile at the court of Macedon who could have given Philip much useful information.

On this level it is doubtful that Philip's intelligence operations were significantly different from those of earlier or contemporary Greek states, though they were greater in scale. It is in the area of tactical intelligence and counter-intelligence that Philip made his most important contributions. As one scholar has said, 'It's clear even from the scattered evidence in our sources that no important tactical decision was made by Alexander without advance intelligence.' Another authority has written: 'No literature before Xenophon exhibits the use of the scout with a marching army;'[245] Philip, however, organized mounted scouts to move ahead of his army and relay intelligence about the route of march and the enemy's movements. Since Philip's scouts also fought in the line when battle was engaged, we do not yet have a fully specialized tactical intelligence arm, but the use Alexander made of these scouts in Asia shows how important it was to have them.

Philip was also famous for using active and passive counter-intelligence procedures to deceive the enemy. At one point he gave a false march order to one destination and actually led his men to another. Alexander once had someone dressed to look like him and remain in camp while he led part of his force on a river crossing upstream. Equally important were the efforts made to keep one's own plans secret, and the Macedonians had a rigorous system of restricting the individuals who were allowed to attend important strategic and tactical meetings. They also mounted guards to prevent information from being sent to the enemy.

It is important to note, however, that the Macedonian intelligence system was still embryonic in the days of Philip and Alexander, and that the Persian system was probably superior. The Persian king, Darius III, was always aware of Alexander's movements, and once surprised Alexander by moving with the entire Persian army into Issus, where he cut Alexander off from the rear. As Alexander advanced deep into Persia, particularly when he entered northeastern Iran and India, he was forced to improvise a more effective intelligence arm. Even so, when he left India, he had not learned of the monsoons which would delay his fleet by several months.

In the field of logistics, where the Greeks had been notoriously backward, Philip adopted the ancient Near Eastern system and applied it to his army. The result was a genuinely revolutionary change in the ability to move a large army rapidly overland for nearly unlimited distances. In a recent study of Macedonian logistics the author argues that Philip's reform set his army apart from the armies of Persia, on the grounds that Philip required his troops to carry all their own equipment and got rid of carts altogether.[246] This is based on a passage in the Roman writer Frontinus who says:

When Philip was organizing his first army, he forbade anyone to use a carriage. The cavalrymen he permitted to have but one attendant apiece. In the infantry he allowed for every ten men only one servant, who was detailed to carry the mills and ropes. When troops marched out to summer quarters, he commanded each man to carry on his shoulders flour for thirty days.[247]

The point here, however, is not that Philip abandoned the use of carts altogether. In fact both Philip and Alexander continued to use carts pulled by draft animals, as the Persians did, for the siege train, for the ambulance service, for heavy equipment and supplies, such as tents, booty, and firewood, and probably at times even for food.[248] The effect of Philip's reforms, ignoring for a moment the details of them, was to make it possible to move the Macedonian army an average of fifteen miles per day when it was on the march. If we allow for one day's rest in every five or seven days, which was necessary for the animals as well as the men, then the overall average of the army on the march was about thirteen miles per day over terrain that posed no special obstacles. For short stretches of only four or five days the pace could be quickened to an average of fifteen miles a day. These figures are for an army of 40,000 to 50,000. Smaller armies can travel faster, and specialized corps of cavalry or light infantry without the support of a baggage train can move up to forty or fifty miles a day.

Until the development of the railroad in the nineteenth century it was difficult for any army of considerable size to exceed these averages. Size matters more than one might imagine. In an army of 65,000 marching in columns ten abreast, with 6,000 cavalry five abreast, the column would extend for sixteen and a half miles. The men at the head of the column would begin marching at least two hours before those in the rear moved at all, and the latter would reach camp several hours later than the advance contingents. Halts in the course of a day's marching compound the problem. So the Macedonian average rate of march was impressive.

What Philip did in essence was to reduce drastically the number of servants attending his troops by requiring his men to carry most of their own equipment and supplies. In the hoplite states, armies regularly travelled with at least one servant per hoplite who carried the hoplite's weapons and provisions. Spartiates sometimes took as many as seven servants each on campaign. Unfortunately the servants had to eat too, and the food supplies needed for a hoplite army of 20,000 were no less than for a Macedonian army of 35,000. Furthermore the hoplite armies moved at a much slower rate, so, to put the situation in another context, allowing ten miles a day for a hoplite army, in a thirty-day campaign a Macedonian army of 35,000 could strike at a target 400 miles away on the same amount of food that would take a hoplite army of 20,000 no more than 300 miles. The vastly greater firepower of 35,000 men over 20,000 at an increase in range of thirty per cent or so suggests that Philip's adoption of Persian logistics had an impact on Greek warfare greater than that of the invention of the catapult.

Since logistics and rate of march are interrelated, Philip improved his commissariat by moving his army along at a rapid clip. That he did this consciously is clear from a statement in Polyaenus:

Philip accustomed the Macedonians to constant exercise before actual warfare by making them march often 300 stadia [ten Persian parasangs or about thirty-seven miles], bearing their arms and carrying besides their helmets, shields, greaves, spears, and their provisions, as well as utensils for daily use.[249]

On such rapid marches in a real war the baggage train would fall behind, but it would catch up eventually. It could keep up with the army if necessary, but that required using relays of draft animals.[250] All of these things the Persians had mastered. Cyrus' thrust into Mesopotamia was fast and logistically well organized. The Greek hoplites who accompanied him learned more about logistics than they had ever known before, and one of the most obvious features of Xenophon's *Anabasis* is his careful attention to the distances travelled and the time taken to travel them.

Persian logistics undoubtedly went back into Assyrian times and probably even earlier. Some historians have been critical of the Persian logistical system of the early fifth century during the Persian Wars, suggesting that the Persian army moved slowly, as indeed it did by Alexander's standards, but considering its size Xerxes performed a nearly incredible feat in taking that army into Athens. As J. K. Anderson has said, 'Nothing like the elaborate chain of bases that supported the Persian invasion of Greece in 480 BC could ever have been organized by any Greek state.'[251]

That was probably still true even in the days of Philip and Alexander, but it was not the convoy and depot system that they initiated, but rather the more rapid logistical system of the younger Cyrus. The actual organization of supply along the route travelled, outside Macedonia, was however still difficult. The army on the march could divide and move in separate groups, or advance contingents could press ahead to requisition supplies, as was often done. When conditions were adverse Philip and Alexander put their men on reduced rations, a hardship they were trained to suffer. Finally their speed was a logistical asset – if they lacked supplies they could move far enough fast enough to find new sources.

The great advantage of Philip's new logistical system can best be understood by comparing it with that of Napoleon's, with which it had remarkable similarities, as David Chandler observes in his magisterial book, *The Campaigns of Napoleon* (1966),

French armies on the march were famed for one particular characteristic besides pillage, rape and arson: their speed of movement. The far more cumbrous forces of Austria and the Holy Roman Empire never proved a match for their opponents in this respect. One reason for this lay in widely differing concepts of logistical support. Through necessity, the French lived off the countryside for the most part, 'making war pay for war,' but this at least freed them from the encumbrance of slow-moving supply convoys and a strategy based on the existence of pre-stocked arsenals and depots. They never carried more than three days' supplies. The Austrians, on the other hand, habitually marched with nine days' full rations in waggons. Small wonder that the French forces, properly led, proved capable of running rings around their slower opponents both strategically and tactically.[252]

In another passage Chandler describes this system as 'the essence of Napoleonic *blitzkrieg*'.[253] Philip and Alexander used essentially the same system (and with less care Caesar followed it too) to introduce *blitzkrieg* into the warfare of the Greek world. We have already seen that Thutmose III and Sargon II knew the strategic and tactical importance of speed. Undoubtedly Cyrus the Great knew it even better than the younger Cyrus of the *Anabasis*, but to the Greeks it was a new and revolutionary phenomenon. There is no better way to illustrate the impact of Philip's new model, integrated army than to quote from his implacable foe, the Athenian orator and statesman, Demosthenes:

I consider that nothing has been more revolutionized and improved than the art of war. For in the first place I am informed that in those days the Lacedaemonians, like everyone else, would spend the four or five months in the summer 'season' in invading and laying waste the enemy's territory with heavy infantry and levies of citizens, and would retire home again; and they were so old fashioned, or rather such good citizens, that they never used money to buy an advantage from anyone, but their fighting was of the fair and open kind . . . on the other hand you hear of Philip marching unchecked, not because he leads a phalanx of heavy infantry, but because he is accompanied by skirmishers, cavalry, archers, mercenaries, and similar troops. When relying on this force, he attacks some people that is at variance with itself, and when through distrust no one goes forth to fight for his country, then he brings up his artillery and lays siege. I need hardly tell you that he makes no difference between summer and winter and has no season set apart for inaction.[254]

Changes in warfare are often infuriating to military men, who believe that honour is inextricably related to traditional manners of fighting. The machine-gun, the airplane, and the submarine seemed peculiarly repugnant to many warriors early in this century. In 1900 the British Rear Admiral Wilson, who had been awarded a Victoria Cross, and who was in that year the Third Sea Lord and Controller of the Navy, called the submarine an 'underhand' form of warfare and labelled it a 'damned un-English weapon'.[255] At the Somme in World War I British generals wasted a generation of brave men by sending them senselessly against German machine-gun squads. It simply takes some time for a society to absorb revolutionary changes in warfare, and Greeks of the fourth century revealed the tensions of their new un-Greek style of fighting.

Chapter Six

Alexander the Great and the Origins of Modern War

Alexander the Great's generalship was so outstanding that superlatives seem inadequate to describe it. He became a legend in his own, short lifetime, and over the ages the normal vocabulary of military analysis has often been forsaken in treatments of his career. He is not the western world's only cult general – Hannibal, Caesar, Napoleon and Lee achieved that ethereal status – but as a cult figure Alexander towers above all others. Caesar and Napoleon were swept up in the mystique of Alexander every bit as much as the wide-eyed schoolboys who even today follow Alexander on his trek to the Punjab in India, amazed at his indomitable spirit, his apparent superhuman ability to hurl himself through the hordes of Asia. Neither the horsemen of Persia nor the terrifying elephants of India stayed his majestic dash to greatness and glory.[256]

Historians often find such towering figures inviting objects of attack. The 'real' Abraham Lincoln or Winston Churchill were perhaps not quite as noble, in every respect, as the Lincoln or Churchill of popular myth. It is, therefore, not surprising that the superhuman Alexander, at least in his role as king and empire builder, has been cut down to near mortal size by modern historians. Alexander's generalship has nevertheless remained largely unscathed. To be sure, historians have noted, and some have emphasized, that the army Alexander led into Asia was not of his own making. His father Philip had fashioned it, and Alexander learned much about generalship under Philip's tutelage. But Alexander was genuinely a rare, inspirational leader of men in battle, and his conception of strategy and tactics was a quantum leap ahead of any of his predecessors in the Graeco-Macedonian world. As a general Alexander is perhaps unique, a hero whom even rationalist historians can admire unabashedly.

He was not, however, so completely innovative that the roots of his generalship are totally obscure, nor was his generalship so far ahead of its time that there was no room for subsequent development and elaboration. In this chapter we shall focus on his contribution to warfare – particularly but not exclusively in strategy and tactics – on the background and nature of that contribution, and on the limitations of his generalship which help to place his overall contribution in historical perspective.

Philip had created an integrated army which was tactically more cohesive, though smaller, than the great army of Persia. Alexander's use of it on the battlefield shows that to some extent he was still the product of the age of Greek hoplite warfare. In the great cavalry battles of the Granicus and the Hydaspes his instinct was to charge head-on and to engage the enemy much as hoplite phalanxes had engaged one another in earlier days. Even in those battles, however, he was careful to coordinate his cavalry attacks with infantry support, to take advantage of his integrated army. In the great battles of Issus and Gaugamela against the Persian king, Darius III, he used genuine hammer-and-anvil tactics as he drove through the Persian line and turned against the rear of the enemy infantry.[257] Further, he showed his mastery, especially at Tyre in 332, of the techniques of siege warfare, newly developed in the Graeco-Macedonian world.

Alexander as Strategist

Alexander ascended the throne of Macedon in 336 B C when Philip was assassinated. The new king was only twenty years old, but he had been groomed for power by Philip, and two years earlier, when Alexander was only eighteen, he had been entrusted with command of Philip's left wing at the battle of Chaeronea against the combined armies of Athens and Thebes where he led the decisive charge.[258] So, despite his youth, he was not entirely inexperienced.

In the aftermath of Chaeronea Philip had united the Greek states (except Sparta) in the League of Corinth, which he dominated as 'Leader' or 'Hegemon', and proposed a crusade against Persia to liberate the Ionian Greeks from Persian domination. The possibility of successful action by a Greek army in the Persian Empire had been indicated by Greek success on the field at Cunaxa and later, in the 390s, the Spartan king Agesilaus had entertained visions of military triumph in Asia Minor. The dream of Greek victory over the armies of Asia lived on, and now Philip's integrated army, compact and mobile, was ready for a thrust into Asia Minor.

Philip's assassination on the eve of departure for the campaign called a momentary halt in the planning. Alexander turned his immediate attention towards putting down the inevitable revolts against Macedonian authority provoked by the accession of a new, young ruler. In swift, decisive campaigns Alexander reasserted control over territory to the north and west of Macedon and over the Greek states to the south. Within two years Macedonian power was reestablished, and in 334 Alexander was ready to begin the invasion of Persia.[259]

One of the greatest of modern scholars on Alexander, W. W. Tarn, is surely correct in saying, 'The primary reason why Alexander invaded Persia was, no doubt, that he never thought of *not* doing it; it was his inheritance.'[260] Officially the war was a Panhellenic crusade, an act of revenge for what Xerxes had done to Greece in the fifth century and for Persian subjugation of Greek states in Asia Minor. Specific strategic mission and aim, however, are harder to ascertain. Philip probably never intended to do more than to free the Greek cities of Asia Minor and to carve out a little extra territory for himself. Alexander, we know from hindsight, at some point decided to topple Darius III and to seize the entire Persian Empire for himself. Whether he saw that far ahead while he was still in Europe at the outset of the campaign remains uncertain. J. F. C. Fuller believed it to be 'highly improbable that when Alexander set out his idea was to subdue the entire Persian empire', but N. G. L. Hammond has recently argued that Alexander's goal from the outset was even larger than that.[261] When the king first landed on Asian soil, he cast his spear into the ground and claimed 'from the gods I accept Asia, won by the spear'. Hammond believes that Alexander intended from the beginning to become lord of all Asia – not simply king of Persia. My own opinion, for what it is worth, is that, as Alexander left Europe, he intended to destroy Persian military power, land and naval, and had not yet come to grips with the political implications of such a feat, except for what success would mean to him in Macedon and Greece. The Greeks of Asia could not long remain securely freed, even if Alexander's Ionian campaign proved temporarily successful, while Persia controlled the sea and had also the capacity to launch vast armies in counterattack.

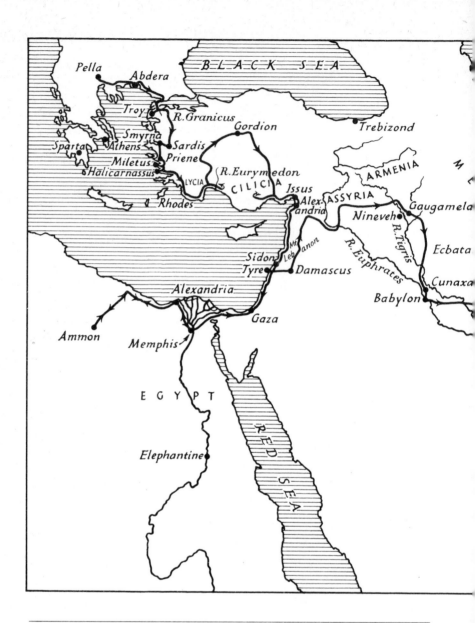

Alexander's Empire. Alexander's route is shown with a solid line, the sea voyage of Nearchus with a broken one.

Alexander's strategic plan was to meet and defeat the Persian army of Asia Minor in the field and then, after freeing the Greek cities of Ionia, to march through central Asia Minor to gain military control of

R. Oxus

R. Jaxartes

Alexandria
Eschate (Furthest)

Maracanda

SOGDIANA

Alexandria

BACTRIA

Alexandria
(Merv)

B

HINDU KUSH

Bactra

Alexandria

Alexandropolis

Kabul

PARTHIA

GANDHARA

R. Indus

R. Jhelum

Caspian
Gates

Alexandria

Bucephala

Alexandria

ARACHOSIA

Alexandria

a

AM

xandria

Alexandria
Prophthasia

Alexandria
(Kandahar)

Alexandria

CARMANIA

Persepolis

GEDROSIA

Alexandria

PERSIA

Alexandria

Patala

PERSIAN GULF

0   500

Scale of Miles

the entire area. On the sea he was at a great disadvantage; his fleet
numbered only about 180 ships while the Persian fleet was some 400
strong. Since he could not hope to defeat the Persian navy in a sea
battle, he planned to neutralize it by marching around the eastern
coast of the Mediterranean to Egypt and seizing all its coastal bases.
Then he would move into Mesopotamia to seek out and destroy the
main field army of the Persian Empire.[262]

It took four years (334–331) for Alexander to achieve this objective, and later in this chapter we shall examine in detail the major battles (Granicus, Issus, Tyre and Gaugamela) by which he succeeded in driving Darius III from the throne of Persia. After his great victory over the Persian king at Gaugamela in 331 B C he found it necessary to devote three years to a desultory, semi-guerrilla campaign against the nobles of northeastern Persia, until finally in 327 he was ready to cross the Khyber Pass into India. There in the Punjab he defeated the Indian King Porus in the battle of the Hydaspes (326 B C) and wanted to push on, impelled by a romantic notion to march to the end of the earth, a goal he believed to be within his grasp. Finally, however, before entering the Valley of the Ganges, his troops refused to go any further – by one modern estimate the route they had followed from Macedon into India had taken them some 17,000 miles. It is not surprising that in a distant, strange and fearsome land they yielded to the always strong temptation to return to the safety of home.

Alexander acquiesced, reluctantly, in their wishes and led them down the Indus, where at the mouth of the river he divided his forces in two. One part was to go by sea with the general Nearchus in a fleet specially constructed for the purpose, while Alexander led the other part by land across the barren stretches of southern Persia. This return was the most difficult part of the entire campaign.[263] Problems of supply led to the loss by thirst and starvation of a large number of his troops, and Nearchus, whose departure by sea was delayed for some months by the monsoons, suffered equally on the return journey. What had been planned as an interdependent operation between land and naval forces failed through the inability of Alexander's intelligence service to discover the secret of the monsoons. When it became apparent to Alexander, who had left the Indus according to plan ahead of his fleet, that contact with Nearchus had been lost (though Alexander did not know the reason), both forces were required to struggle back to Babylon on their own efforts. Despite great losses they succeeded.

In 323, as Alexander prepared to leave Babylon to circumnavigate the Arabian peninsula in an attempt to establish a better line of communications between Babylon and Egypt, he fell ill and died. At the time of his death he was not yet thirty-three years old, but he had become the Lord of Asia, and his extension of Greek and Macedonian influence throughout all of the ancient Near East and into India had altered the course of world history. Militarily his success had been incredible, and many attributed it to divine, superhuman qualities in the great leader. Along the way Alexander had not been reluctant to contribute to his myth. General MacArthur was not the first warrior to have a highly refined sense of public relations in the art of war.

Many of the finer points of Alexander's strategic conception will become apparent as we examine in detail the major battles, but it would not be inappropriate at this point to discuss the major criticism that has been made of Alexander as strategist. It is, essentially, that he was too bold, that he attempted more, despite his success, than a reasonable military strategist would have done. Sometimes driven as much by romantic notions of grandeur as by sound military planning, Alexander took unreasonable risks, according to this view, and was saved only by the professional discipline and *esprit* of the army his father had created.

One recent historian, in a book filled with understanding of the ancient art of war, has argued that Philip was the better strategist:

Philip had patience and knew his limitations . . . As much cannot be said of Alexander. . . . Alexander's brilliance as a tactician has blinded posterity to his less lustrous strategic powers. His motive force was again and again a restless, irrational desire (*pothos*). The soldier's art demands rational calculation. Nothing suggests that Philip lacked it. The military sense of how to fight he possessed no less than his son. The political sense of whether to fight at all is another matter. Philip seems to have possessed it in the highest degree. The case of his son requires to be considered.[264]

Certainly no one would deny that Philip was unlikely to have gone to India had he lived to lead the crusade against Persia, nor would anyone doubt that Alexander's generalship was inspired by an element of romanticism. It may be true that Philip was a more rigorous military scientist than Alexander, particularly as a strategist, but the science of war can be made to yield to the art of war where romantic notions have their place. The world's greatest generals have always been more than simply scientific practitioners of the art. If William the Conqueror had been solely a military scientist, he would not have set sail at the end of September 1066, after waiting half the summer for favourable winds. The end of September was much too late in the season to mount a cross-Channel invasion of England. Napoleon may have been overly romantic in his strategic conception, though he was clearly one of the world's greatest generals, but Alexander's romanticism led to no Waterloo. Philip's greatness as a strategist is more might-have-been than real, since he did not live to confront Darius III, and Alexander's overall success simply demonstrates what is well known in military history – that the greatest generals master military science but are not bound by it. In the history of ancient warfare Philip's creation of the new model, integrated army was a major contribution, but Alexander's use of it went far beyond his father's conception and was on balance impressively successful. In the art of war Alexander stands far above Philip.

Alexander as Tactician

THE BATTLE OF GRANICUS

When Alexander crossed the Hellespont into Asia with an army of 32,000 infantry and 5,100 cavalry, he did not have to worry about establishing a bridgehead. An additional 8,000 infantry sent two years earlier by Philip under his general Parmenio had gained control of the coast as far south as Ephesus. Dynastic unrest in Persia (Darius III ascended the throne in 336) had created the opportunity for the Macedonians to establish the bridgehead. Although a Persian counterattack led by Memnon, a Greek mercenary general in the service of Persia, had driven Parmenio out of Ephesus, Alexander's forces controlled the Hellespontine crossing. There Alexander personally visited the site of ancient Troy to place a wreath on the tomb of his reputed, distant ancestor, Achilles.

Alexander's immediate objective was to meet the Persian army of Asia Minor in the field and defeat it decisively. He was in desperate financial straits since his fleet of 182 ships (with crews of 36,000) cost him dearly, and the army of 45,000 men altogether not unreasonably expected to be paid for its efforts. Alexander, like Napoleon, intended to make war pay for itself, and a quick victory would make the task much easier.

Darius seems to have believed that his satraps in the region, with the help of Memnon, could deal with the threat, and he left the conduct of the war to them. Since the Persian generals had 20,000 cavalry and 20,000 Greek hoplite mercenaries, the king had some reason for confidence. Still, Memnon realized that the Macedonian infantry was superior to his own, and he advocated a scorched-earth policy to avoid a pitched battle and to deny Alexander any opportunity of supporting his army off the land. Memnon's advice was surely sound, but the six satraps of Asia Minor rejected it when one of them, Arsites, who governed the area in question, said that 'he would not consent to the destruction by fire of a single house belonging to any of his subjects.'

So Alexander got his wish, an early battle on the banks of the Granicus river in northwestern Asia Minor, on the third day after completing the crossing of the Hellespont.[265] The Persians had selected the site at a point where the Granicus, a fast-flowing and relatively deep river, had steep banks. Alexander had moved ahead with only 13,000 infantry and 5,000 cavalry, and in the afternoon his scouts reported that the Persians were holding the river ahead with 20,000 cavalry along their bank. Some distance behind them, on higher ground, stood the 20,000 Greek hoplites in phalanx formation. The line of Persian cavalry was about one and a half miles long. As Alexander approached he moved without delay from line of of column into line of battle with cavalry on both wings of his infantry. Parmenio, concerned that the Macedonian army would not be able to maintain its line as it moved across the river and up the opposite bank, had urged Alexander to postpone the battle to the following morning, when it might be possible to catch the Persians in an early surprise attack, but Alexander pressed on for an immediate engagement.

To avoid being outflanked Alexander extended his line to match that of the Persian cavalry. He placed the left half of his army under Parmenio and took the right for himself. The two armies facing one another across the river paused briefly in what Arrian describes as a 'profound hush' before Alexander began his attack. The special cavalry squadron of the day, under the command of Socrates, moved from Alexander's right centre towards the centre of the line and charged with some infantry support directly into the midst of the Persian cavalry. Alexander extended the rest of his right wing so that he slightly outflanked the Persian left. Although Socrates' force took heavy losses, it did its job. Alexander followed quickly behind with the Companion cavalry and broke through the Persian line. As he looked ahead, he saw that one of the Persian commanders, who had stationed themselves behind the line with picked forces, was charging down upon him. Alexander had already lost his lance, and he took one from his personal bodyguard and galloped against Mithridates, unseating him with a thrust to the face. Arrian's account shows vividly how Alexander, easily recognizable on the field with his white-plumed helmet and bodyguards, served as a magnet to draw the Persian nobles, eager for the glory of killing the Macedonian king:

Rhoesaces then rode at Alexander with his scimitar and, aiming a blow at his head, sliced off part of his helmet, which nevertheless dulled the full force of the impact. A moment later Alexander was on him, and he fell with a spear thrust through his cuirass into his breast. Now Spithridates had his scimitar raised, ready for a blow at Alexander from behind; but Cleitus, son of Dropidas, was too quick for him, and severed his shoulder scimitar and all. Meanwhile Alexander's party was being steadily reinforced by the mounted troops as one after another they succeeded in getting up out of the river and joining them.[266]

Alexander had broken the centre of the Persian line: the superiority of the Macedonian lance over the lighter Persian spear had proved decisive. When the Persian centre broke, the wings fell back too. Alexander did not make the mistake of pursuing the defeated Persian cavalry too far. Instead, he turned against the Greek mercenaries, using his cavalry to attack their flanks and rear while he led the infantry against the centre. The Greeks seem to have broken immediately, but, trapped, as they were, in a pocket with nowhere to run, the carnage was great. Only 2,000 were taken alive. Alexander lost fewer than 150 men during the entire battle, most of them in the cavalry assault against the Persian centre.

The battle of Granicus has perplexed and mystified military historians. Persian tactics seem especially inexplicable. By placing their cavalry along the banks of the river they made it impossible to do what cavalry does best – charge at the gallop. In positioning their infantry far to the rear, in a separate line, they violated the principle of integrated armies – a principle the Persians fully understood – and permitted Alexander to use a combination of infantry and cavalry, first against a line of Persian cavalry unsupported by infantry, and then against a line of infantry unsupported by cavalry.

Some historians believe that the Persians adopted an otherwise absurd battle plan because they had only one limited tactical objective – to kill Alexander.[267] By placing their cavalry along the river they hoped to concentrate on the units led by Alexander and thwart his invasion by slaying him. But it is more likely that they expected to be outnumbered by Alexander's infantry, and that they lacked confidence in their own Greek mercenaries' ability to hold against the Macedonian phalanx. If Alexander had not moved so quickly and

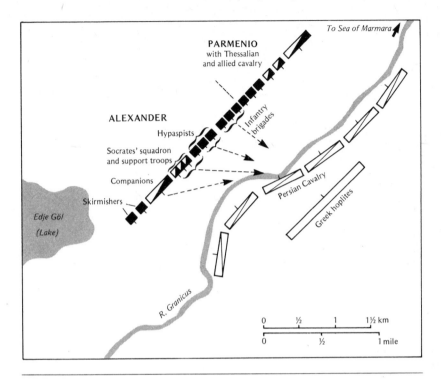

PARMENIO
with Thessalian
and allied cavalry

To Sea of Marmara

ALEXANDER

Hypaspists

Socrates' squadron
and support troops

Companions

Skirmishers

Infantry brigades

Persian Cavalry

Greek hoplites

Edje Göl
(Lake)

R. Granicus

| 0 | ½ | 1 | 1½ km |

| 0 | ½ | 1 mile |

Battle of the Granicus, 334 BC.

decisively against the Persians with only part of his army, he would indeed have been able to deploy a much larger infantry force.

On the other hand, the Persians clearly had superiority in cavalry (20,000 versus 5,000), and they had the advantage of defending a steep-sloped river bank, so they assigned this critical task to their cavalry and placed their infantry on rising ground behind it. The battle has sometimes been seen as a classic encounter of cavalry against cavalry, but this overlooks the fact that Alexander's attack, though led by cavalry, was coordinated with infantry support.

Other historians have been reluctant to believe that cavalry can effectively charge cavalry, and a popular version of this battle has Alexander feinting an attack against the extreme left of the Persian line to draw Persian cavalry from the centre.[268] In this way Alexander would have been able to attack, if not a gap in the Persian line, at least a weak point. Major General Fuller even believed that Parmenio executed a similar attack against the extreme Persian right, but the most reliable ancient source for the battle, Arrian, gives no indication of such feinting tactics. He describes, as we have seen, a furious assault in the centre of the Persian line.

One reason for this modern misunderstanding is the failure of some historians to realize that Alexander used infantry in support of his cavalry, but another is the widespread belief among military historians that a direct charge into the centre of a well-held line is no way to fight a battle. Historians in the tradition of du Picq, Liddell Hart, and Keegan more or less convey the impression that such attacks are impossible (or at least involve very heavy losses), but that is clearly not the case, not even in modern warfare.

During the sieges of Ciudad Rodrigo and Badajoz (1812) in the Peninsular Campaign Wellington used a special assault squad, called the Forlorn Hope, composed of volunteers, to lead the initial attack against a weakened point in the defender's fortitications. Such units are common in warfare. In French they are called *Enfants Perdus*. A 'Forlorn Hope' would suffer extremely heavy casualties, but, once having established a breakthrough, the rest of the army could move through relatively easily. The few survivors of the Forlorn Hope received immediate promotions and rewards and lifelong fame.[269]

Alexander's cavalry squadron of the day, under Socrates, was in effect a Forlorn Hope. It did suffer heavy casualties, but the force of its attack in the centre of the Persian line created just enough weakness and confusion for Alexander to storm through behind it with cavalry supported by infantry. These innovative tactics, reinforced by the superiority of the Macedonian lance, gave Alexander the decisive advantage at the battle of the Granicus. He would prove once again at Issus that cavalry supported by infantry can actually force a gap in the enemy line. It was not always necessary to use feinting and flanking manoeuvres to create such a gap.

After the battle, while the Persians licked their wounds and reexamined their strategy, Alexander was able to move down the coast of Ionia and free the Greek cities. Sardis, the main Persian centre in Asia Minor, fell without a fight. There was some resistance at Miletus, where the Persians trapped Alexander's fleet in the harbour, but, when the Macedonians seized the coastal fresh water supply of the Persian fleet and forced it to withdraw, Alexander decided to send most of his fleet back to Greece. Since he could not challenge the

Persians at sea, because of their superiority in numbers, he concluded that his own fleet was more a liability than an asset. Later, at Halicarnassus, the Persians again tried to stop Alexander's advance, but he stormed and took the city.[270]

He had achieved his immediate strategic objective, the liberation of the Ionian Greek states, in a stunning *blitzkrieg* of only one campaigning season. To secure his control over the area he moved into central Asia Minor where, in April of 333, he took Gordium, the heart of ancient Lydia. There he made a considerable contribution to his growing fame by solving the problem of the famous Gordian knot, a knot on the yoke of an ancient wagon in the temple of Zeus at Gordium.[271] The legend, widely known in the ancient world, was that the person who untied the knot would become the King of Asia. Alexander simply cut through it. In this skilful use of 'public relations' Alexander hoped to convince his followers that the gods favoured his mission (and perhaps intimidate the Persians). We need not be unduly cynical. Alexander was a young romantic, and he may have convinced himself, as much as he convinced others, of his destiny.

To protect his rear Alexander had left Antipater behind in Macedonia as the General of Europe, and to counter a Persian offensive on the sea Alexander ordered Antipater to protect the Hellespont and guard his line of communications. Persian counterattacks against Alexander were undoubtedly weakened by the death of Memnon and the appointment in July 333, after some delay, of the Persian Pharnabazus in his place. Darius seems to have decided to mobilize the full Persian field army and to take the offensive himself from Mesopotamia. This decision weakened Persian efforts in Asia Minor and permitted Alexander to swing down to Tarsus in August 333, encountering only minimal and half-hearted resistance at the 'Cilician Gates' along the way.

HAMMER-AND-ANVIL TACTICS: THE BATTLE OF ISSUS

The conquest of Asia Minor was complete, and the *blitzkrieg* rolled on. At Tarsus Alexander fell ill in the months of August and September, but upon recovery he decided to thrust on around the 'corner' and to carry the war down the Syria-Palestine coast of the eastern Mediterranean. By mid-October Alexander knew that Darius had mobilized a great army at Babylon, and the Macedonian king hoped to seize the coast before Darius could trap him in Asia Minor and bring the full force of Persian naval power, as well as the land army, to bear against him.

Around the first of November Alexander mobilized his army at Mallus, some miles east of Tarsus, and prepared to turn the corner. He received a report that Darius was on the plains of Syria, and when Alexander reached Issus, he and his generals decided to move on down the coast. They believed that it would be a mistake for them to march out onto the level ground of Syria, where Darius' vastly greater numbers could be used to envelop them. Instead, by clinging to the coast where the mountains came down very near to the sea, they could force Darius into battle on constricted terrain, where they would have a better chance against his large army. Therefore, Alexander pushed on south to Myriandus, about thirty miles south of Issus, in a two-day march. That night news reached Alexander that Darius had moved into Issus behind him, and that his line of retreat in Asia Minor was blocked.[272]

The news caught Alexander completely by surprise, and many military historians believe that his failure to anticipate such a move was one of his greatest mistakes. Ancient authors, on the other hand, including Arrian and Curtius, more or less suggest that Alexander had deliberately drawn Darius into a trap, but that he could not believe that the Persian king had taken the bait so soon. It was probably, however, simply a mistake on Alexander's part, although he moved decisively to correct it, and there were some hopeful elements in the new situation.

Darius had placed his army a few miles south of Issus to take up a defensive position on the banks of the Pinarus river. After spending part of the day in consultation with his generals Alexander ordered his army to countermarch back towards the enemy. The Macedonians, beginning their march at nightfall, reached the Jonah Pass nine miles north about midnight. On the following morning, probably 12 November 333 BC, a day on which the sun began to set at 5.00 pm and total darkness fell by 6.30, Alexander led his army in line of column against the Persians. As the Macedonians approached the Pinarus, they began the difficult manoeuvres from line of column to line of battle, and the fighting started sometime in the afternoon, according to one modern estimate as late as 4.00 pm, but possibly earlier.

The battleline along the Pinarus extended some two to two and a half miles from the Mediterranean coast up into the surrounding hills.

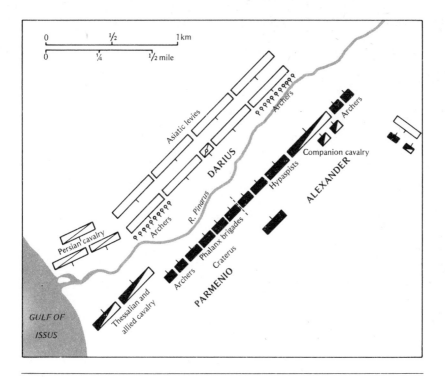

The battle of Issus, 333 BC.

Arrian claims that Darius had 600,000 men altogether, including 100,000 cavalry, but no modern historian is willing to accept such a large figure. Whatever the Persian strength (100,000 with 20,000 cavalry?), Alexander was greatly outnumbered, but because there was not much level ground he was able to extend a line as long as the Persian one. Darius had posted some of his men to the high ground on his left across the Pinarus in advance of his line. They not only protected the Persian left against a flanking attack but served as a threat to Alexander's right wing. To counter them Alexander detached a small force of skirmishers and cavalry, who drove the Persians higher into the hills and out of the action.

Darius' tactical plan was to concentrate all his cavalry on his right wing to take advantage of the level ground by the coast. He hoped to crush Alexander's left, under the command of Parmenio, in a massive charge and to wheel his cavalry around in hammer-and-anvil tactics to smash the Macedonian infantry in the rear. When Alexander saw the Persian deployment, as his army approached the Pinarus, he moved the Thessalian cavalry over to his left to strengthen Parmenio's position.

Ironically Alexander's plan was essentially the same as his opponent's, and we can see clearly in this battle how the traditions of ancient Near Eastern and Graeco-Macedonian warfare had been fused. Alexander hoped to break through Darius' left centre in a cavalry charge and to wheel around against the rear of the Persian centre in an identical hammer-and-anvil operation. As Alexander neared the Persian position, he forced his army to advance at a slow pace just as the Persians had done against Cyrus at Cunaxa. Finally, when the Macedonians were well within bow shot, probably at a distance of about 100 yards, Alexander ordered an attack on the double. With contingents of cavalry on his right, supported by infantry close behind, he charged the river at a gallop. Persian skirmishers in front of their line probably fell back in panic, creating confusion in the main infantry line on the Persian left centre, and Alexander smashed through. When Darius saw the Macedonians wheel against the centre, he panicked and fled in his chariot. Shortly thereafter he threw down his royal weapons and escaped on horseback. Unfortunately Alexander's sudden charge had opened a gap in his own right centre, and the Greek mercenary hoplites fighting for Darius moved in to attack it. Alexander had to turn against them and lost his chance to pursue the fleeing King of Persia.

On Alexander's left Parmenio faced a serious challenge, but, when the Persian cavalry saw that their centre was collapsing and realized that the king had abandoned the field, they too broke and fled. 'That was the signal for a general rout', wrote Arrian,

open and unconcealed. The horses with their heavily equipped riders suffered severely, and of the thousands of panic-stricken men who struggled in hopeless disorder to escape along the narrow mountain tracks, almost as many were trampled to death by their friends as were cut down by the pursuing enemy.[273]

Darkness prevented Alexander from conducting an extensive pursuit, but he did capture Darius' chariot, his shield, mantle and bow, as well as the king's mother, wife, infant son, and two daughters. Parmenio later seized the Persian war treasury at Damascus.

Throughout Alexander had been in the thick of the fighting. At the outset, before the armies closed, he rode up and down his line calling out to his senior and junior officers by name with words of praise and encouragement. He had actually been wounded – not seriously – by a sword-thrust to the thigh. On the following day he rewarded with money and promotions those of his men who had distinguished themselves in the battle. There can be no doubt that this victory over Darius and the Persian army inspired the Macedonians with confidence in the ability of their young king to triumph over every obstacle.

One of the most knowledgeable modern authorities on the military career of Alexander, N. G. L. Hammond, has recently argued that the king must have led an infantry brigade into Darius' line at the outset of battle on the grounds 'that cavalry never delivered a frontal charge on an infantry line'.[274] We have seen, however, that general principles of that sort always have their exceptions. Actually the rule in this case ought to be stated differently: A cavalry charge directly into a heavy infantry formation cannot be successful if the infantry holds and does not panic. The trick is to know when the infanty line will break in the face of a charge. Alexander gambled that a sudden attack (and probably one in which he was driving Persian skirmishers back into the infantry ranks) would demoralize and break the enemy. We need not dismount Alexander (only to remount him again for the later phase of the action, as Hammond does) at the battle of Issus.

Alexander at the battle of Issus – a detail from the 'Alexander Sarcophagus' from Sidon (c. 310 BC).

THE SIEGE OF TYRE

The victory at Issus was strategically decisive because it gave Alexander more than a year to complete the conquest of the Mediterranean coast before facing Darius in the field again at Gaugamela. One of the most impressive features of Alexander's generalship was his knowledge of when, and when not, to pursue. After Issus he maintained strategic mission and aim by continuing his march around the Mediterranean to neutralize the Persian fleet by denying it use of its land bases. As he headed southward, the great Phoenician cities of Byblus and Sidon surrendered to him.

The succession of easy conquests ended at Tyre, a highly fortified island city with a circumference of nearly three miles and walls up to 150 feet high. Situated about half a mile off the coast, Tyre was also protected by water about twenty feet deep around its edges. Confident that they could withstand a siege, the Tyrians proposed to offer Alexander neutrality rather than submission, but he believed that he could not leave such a strong naval base uncontrolled, so he ordered his army to take the city.[275]

In January 332 the army began construction of a 200-foot wide mole from the coast to the city. As the construction neared the city, the Tyrians began to attack Alexander's men with catapults and from their ships. Alexander responded by constructing two 150-foot towers

The siege of Tyre, 332 BC.

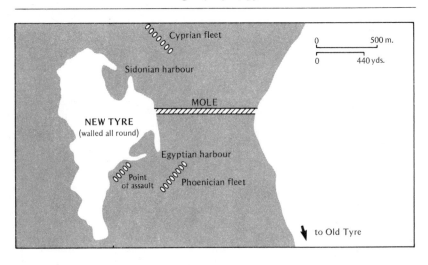

at the end of the mole, protected by rawhide screens against flaming Tyrian arrows and armed with catapults to return fire against the city and against the ships. Finally the Tyrians towed a specially converted horse transport ship loaded with combustibles against Alexander's towers and burnt them down. The king responded by ordering his men to widen the mole in order to build more towers on it.

It was at this point that Alexander's naval policy began to pay dividends. The Phoenician contingents of the Persian fleet which belonged to those cities that had defected to Alexander arrived off the coast and joined the king. Finding himself in possession of about 200 ships Alexander was able to blockade Tyre and protect his mole from attacks by sea. He then used some ships against other parts of the Tyrian wall and discovered that by tying them together he could use them as platforms for battering rams. To prevent the Macedonians from anchoring the ships Tyrian frogmen dived underwater and cut the ropes, but Alexander then switched to chains. He also had to remove great boulders that had been dropped by the Tyrian defenders to impede his operations.

As the siege progressed, Alexander's troops faced all the ingenious devices of defensive siege warfare, including the use of red-hot sand and boiling oil from the walls above. The Tyrians even built towers of their own on top of their walls, until finally the Macedonians working from the sea with battering rams breached a section of the south wall. The siege had gone on for seven months when this happened, and Alexander in July 332 ordered a massive assault against the city on the breach in the wall, against the two Tyrian harbours, and from the end of the mole. As the Macedonians swarmed inside, behind a Forlorn Hope made up of some of the Royal Hypaspists, infuriated by their frustrations and suffering, embittered because the Tyrians had earlier thrown Macedonian captives from their walls, they showed no quarter. Over 8,000 Tyrians were killed and 30,000 sold into slavery. One of the most famous sieges in ancient warfare had come to an end, and Alexander had demonstrated how thoroughly Greeks and Macedonians had finally mastered the ancient Near Eastern art of the siege.

When he moved on towards Egypt Alexander encountered resistance again at Gaza, but built a great mound of earth around its high walls and stormed it, though not until he had been wounded in the shoulder by a bolt from a catapult.[276] Again there was great bloodshed, and the survivors, mainly women and children, were sold into slavery. The human toll of Alexander's conquests was mounting. The way to Egypt now lay open, and, when the Macedonians arrived in November 332, there was no opposition or loss of life. The entire eastern coast of the Mediterranean belonged to the King of Macedon, who was not yet twenty-five years old. *Blitzkrieg* had changed the world.

HAMMER AND ANVIL: THE BATTLE OF GAUGAMELA

Alexander spent the winter of 332–331 in Egypt, preparing to move with his army into Persia to challenge Darius in the heart of his empire. The victory at Issus had driven Darius back into Persia and given Alexander the opportunity to complete his neutralization of the Persian fleet. In the meantime Macedonian admirals had gained control of the sea, and Alexander was able to use it to reinforce his army in Egypt. Antigonus, who had been left behind by Alexander in Asia Minor, successfully defended Macedonian conquests by staving off Persian counterattacks.

After Issus Darius had sent envoys to Alexander offering him an alliance in return for the captured members of the Great King's family. Alexander had replied haughtily:

Your ancestors invaded Macedonia and Greece and caused havoc in our country, though we had done nothing to provoke them. As supreme commander of all Greece I invaded Asia because I wished to punish Persia for this act – an act which must be laid wholly to your charge. . . . First I defeated in battle your generals and satraps; now I have defeated yourself and the army you led. . . .

Come to me, therefore, as you would come to the lord of the continent of Asia. . . . Come then, and ask me for your mother, your wife, and your children and anything else you please; for you shall have them, and whatever besides you can persuade me to give you.

And in future let any communication you wish to make with me be addressed to the King of all Asia. Do not write to me as an equal. . . . If, on the other hand, you wish to dispute your throne, stand and fight for it and do not run away. Wherever you may hide yourself, be sure I shall seek you out.[277]

Later, during the siege of Tyre, Darius made a more concrete proposal: 10,000 talents ransom for the members of the royal family, the cession of all Persian territory west of the Euphrates, marriage with Darius' daughter, and alliance. In consultation with the Macedonian generals Parmenio is supposed to have said, 'I would accept, were I Alexander,' and Alexander replied, 'So too would I, were I Parmenio.' Alexander's view of the offer was certainly correct. Darius had proposed to give him scarcely more than he had already taken for himself, and there was no secure defensive frontier for Alexander's eastern empire as long as Persia remained strong in Mesopotamia.

Recently a leading authority on Greek warfare has argued that Alexander should have made a dash on Persia after the fall of Tyre, and he believes that Alexander's entry into Egypt was militarily unnecessary and the result of 'mystical imaginings rather than military calculations'.[278] But there were sound reasons for rounding off the conquest of the Mediterranean coast, and Alexander made good use of the months after Tyre for reinforcing his army. It would probably have been folly, regardless, to have begun an invasion of the Persian heartland so late in the summer without opportunity for logistical planning.

In any event, in the spring of 331 Alexander left Egypt for the long march into Persia.[279] Countermarching up the Syrian-Palestine coast, where he could now easily supply his army of 47,000 by sea, he finally swung over towards the Euphrates, which he reached in early August. There he learned that Darius was waiting for him far to the south with a large army outside Babylon. But Alexander would not be drawn down the Euphrates, where the problems of supply were great, simply to fight Darius on level terrain ideal for the Persian army. Instead, after bridging and crossing the river, Alexander actually turned north for a while before swinging east, keeping the foothills of the Armenian mountains on his left in country which offered pasturage for the horses and supplies for the army.

Darius finally abandoned his position at Babylon and moved north across the Tigris, which he hoped to use as his line of defence against Alexander. When Alexander learned from captured Persian scouts of Darius' intention, he made a forced march to the Tigris and crossed it unopposed north of Darius' camp. Then, after resting for several days, the Macedonians headed south and in four days made contact with an advanced Persian cavalry force. From the captives Alexander learned that Darius was nearby with the full Persian army. For four days the Macedonians rested and fortified a camp for the baggage and camp followers, so that when Alexander set out at the end of that time, it was with a streamlined, highly mobile striking force. Three or four miles from his own camp, on the plain below, Alexander first caught sight of the Persian camp, again three or four miles away. The date was 30 September 331 BC, and the battle of Gaugamela, a nearby village, would be fought on the morrow, 1 October.

Although Alexander had turned Darius' position by crossing the Tigris to the north, Darius had succeeded in selecting his own ground for the battle. Some of the Macedonian generals wanted to move immediately to attack the Persians as soon as they were spotted, but this time Alexander let Parmenio persuade him to delay for a day so that reconnaissance units could inspect the ground between the two armies. In the interval the Macedonians constructed a field camp in their new position.

The Persian army was enormous. Although Arrian's figure of more than 1,000,000 may be rejected out of hand, it is possible that Darius had somewhere between 100,000 to 250,000 men on the field. Whatever his strength, it was significantly greater in cavalry and in infantry than Alexander's 47,000. Furthermore, Darius had some dramatic surprises in store for Alexander. In addition to the huge force of cavalry and infantry the Persian king deployed four squadrons of scythed war chariots, each fifty strong, consisting of two- and four-horse teams. He also had fifteen Indian war elephants. The elephants apparently did not figure in the battle – we hear no more of them until they were taken later in the Persian camp – but Darius planned to rely heavily on the chariots, his secret weapon.

The Persian line was naturally much longer than the Macedonian. As the two armies approached one another with cavalry on both infantry wings, Alexander noticed that the ground in front of the Persian chariot squadrons had been levelled, and he ordered his army to advance obliquely to the right to force the chariots onto uneven terrain. Darius almost certainly hoped for a double envelopment, a massive cavalry attack around both wings of the Macedonian army, and to terrify the Macedonian infantry in the centre with a chariot attack.

To prevent the envelopment of his left wing under Parmenio Alexander had put it in echelon formation. His plan, similar to the one he had used at Issus, was for Parmenio to fight a holding, defensive battle on the left while he looked for an opportunity to break through the Persian line with Companion cavalry from the right, and to catch Darius again between the hammer of the Macedonian cavalry and the anvil of the phalanx. When Darius saw that Alexander's army was

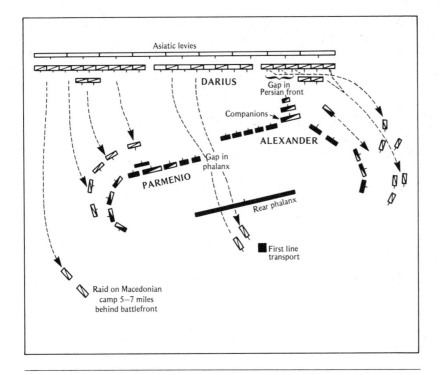

Asiatic levies

DARIUS

Gap in
Persian front

Companions

ALEXANDER

Gap in
phalanx

PARMENIO

Rear phalanx

First line
transport

Raid on Macedonian
camp 5—7 miles
behind battlefront

The battle of Gaugamela, 331 BC.

moving obliquely right, the Persian king ordered cavalry units on his far left to advance against Alexander's right. Alexander responded by sending some cavalry squadrons out to meet them, and a furious small engagement began. At that point Darius signalled the chariot attack, but Alexander's skirmishers, mainly javelin men, stationed in advance of his line, since they did not fight in precise formation, were able to wheel aside and disable either the drivers or the horses as the chariots came crashing down on the Macedonians. For the chariots that got through, the Macedonians opened ranks and cavalry grooms in the rear rode them down. The secret weapon had misfired. Macedonian skirmishers and parade ground drill combined to win the day.

Darius then ordered a heavy attack on Alexander's left wing. There Parmenio was outflanked, and, when units of the Persian line also broke through the Macedonian left centre, Alexander's situation became desperate. His army was saved simply because the Persians who had breached the line and those who were turning the flank continued on to loot the Macedonian camp rather than wheeling to hit the Macedonians in the rear. Still, Parmenio had been overwhelmed and was on the verge of defeat.

When Darius pressed his advantage by attacking Alexander's right, some of the Persian cavalry units dashed ahead and by so doing created a gap between Persian left infantry and cavalry. Alexander saw the gap develop and immediately wheeled to charge it in a wedge formation. As he broke through, he turned against the centre of the Persian line, heading straight for Darius who was stationed in his own centre. By this time Macedonian infantry had poured into the gap behind the cavalry, and Darius panicked, as he had done at Issus, and fled.

Unfortunately, Alexander could not pursue. Parmenio needed help, since the Persians fighting against him did not know their king had fled, and Alexander had to fight his way through a crowd of retreating Persians, some of them still in formation, to come to the relief of his left wing. 'The ensuing struggle', wrote Arrian, 'was the fiercest of the whole action.' By the time Alexander arrived to help Parmenio, Parmenio's Thessalian cavalry had counterattacked, and the whole Persian army was in rout. Alexander then attempted to catch Darius, but it was too late. The King of Persia had escaped with his life, though not with his honour.

The Macedonian army had performed superbly, and Alexander's use of it had been masterful. Darius was destroyed by his defeat at Gaugamela. Alexander now had possession of the heart of Persia and was able to take Babylon and Susa without resistance. Persepolis was defended by a Persian army of 40,000, but Alexander took it too, forcing his way through, or at least around, the heavily defended Persian Gates. In January 330 BC he fired the Achaemenid palace at Persepolis and declared the crusade against Persia at an end.[280] From this point on he acted as the King of Asia, not as the Hegemon of the League of Corinth. Greek allies were allowed to return home, but those who wanted to stay in his service as mercenaries were permitted to do so.

For his part Alexander intended to complete the conquest of Persia. In early summer he set out for Ecbatana, whither Darius had fled, and then pursued the Persian king up towards the Caspian Sea, at which point the nobles of northeastern Iran decided to kill their king in whom they had lost all confidence. During the years 329–327 BC Alexander fought a tough guerrilla war against those nobles in the strange and far-off lands of Bactria and Sogdiana.[281] It was during this campaign that he married Roxana, the Bactrian princess. Though the tensions of the distant campaign and the king's increasing haughtiness as Lord of Asia (combined with a serious drinking problem) led to some grave dissension within the ranks of his army, and Parmenio, among others, was executed, Alexander held his force together until finally he overwhelmed his opposition.[282]

THE BATTLE OF THE HYDASPES

When he had Persia firmly in hand, Alexander set out in 327 across the Khyber Pass into India.[283] His campaigns in India and the return to Babylon are filled with points of interest to military historians, but in this survey of ancient military history we shall focus on the one, great battle of the Hydaspes in the Punjab which ranks alongside Issus and Gaugamela as among his major battles.[284]

His opponent on the Hydaspes river, a tributary of the Indus, was King Porus, a 'giant' around seven feet tall, whom Alexander came to admire after the battle. Porus commanded an army of at least 30,000 infantry, 4,000 cavalry, 300 chariots, and 200 elephants. Though Alexander's total force in India may have been about 75,000 fighting men, on the day in May 326 when he fought Porus' army he had only about 5,000 cavalry and perhaps 15,000 infantry under his immediate command.[285]

Porus' position on the Hydaspes, blocking Alexander's advance, was formidable. The river itself was deep and turbulent, filled with the run-off of the Himalayan snows. The war elephants were a special hazard for Alexander. In addition to their psychological effect – the huge beasts undoubtedly frightened Alexander's men – they could be particularly useful against the Macedonian cavalry. Horses are by nature frightened of elephants and must be trained to them.[286] If Alexander attempted a head-on assault across the river, a difficult operation under any circumstances, the Indian elephants would frighten and stampede his horses on their rafts. Arrian summarized the situation nicely:

It was clear to [Alexander] that he could not effect the crossing at the point where Porus held the opposite bank, for his troops would certainly be attacked, as they tried to gain the shore, by a powerful and efficient army, well-equipped and supported by a large number of elephants; moreover, he thought it likely that his horses, in face of an immediate attack by elephants, would be too much scared by the appearance of these beasts and their unfamiliar trumpetings to be induced to land – indeed, they would probably refuse to stay on the floats, and at the mere sight of the elephants in the distance would go mad with terror and plunge into the water long before they reached the further side.[287]

As a result Alexander decided to attempt a ruse. He began moving his cavalry up and down his side of the river every night for several nights running. Macedonian cavalrymen were encouraged to make as much noise as they could during these manoeuvres, so that Porus with his elephants had to follow them. After a few days Porus tired of the hopeless chasing and stayed in his own camp.

Alexander then left his general Craterus behind holding his original base with more than 5,000 troops and some cavalry squadrons, while he moved with the rest of his army eighteen miles north under cover of darkness and during a rainstorm. His counter-intelligence operations in this campaign are impressive. He had earlier spread a rumour that he intended to wait until the river receded before crossing. He even had someone dressed to impersonate him in the main camp. All of this was intended to lull Porus into inactivity, and it seems to have succeeded.

The point Alexander had selected for crossing was at a bend upstream where the river was divided into two channels by an island. He instructed Craterus to cross the river and hit Porus in the rear if the Indian general turned to meet the Macedonian main striking force, but only if Porus withdrew all elephants from his main camp. Should elephants be left behind to defend the crossing (as actually happened), Craterus was to wait until the Indians had been driven back by the force under Alexander's command.

On the following morning Alexander crossed the river to the north (with difficulty, in water nearly shoulder high) and rode ahead with his cavalry while the infantry followed some two and a half miles behind. When Porus learned from his scouts that Alexander was attempting to cross the river, he sent his son northwards with 2,000 cavalry and 120 chariots to defend the bank, but the Indians were too late. As they came into view Alexander charged against them in successive charges, squadron after squadron, and drove them in panic from the field. Porus' son was killed, and the Macedonians succeeded in capturing all the chariots.

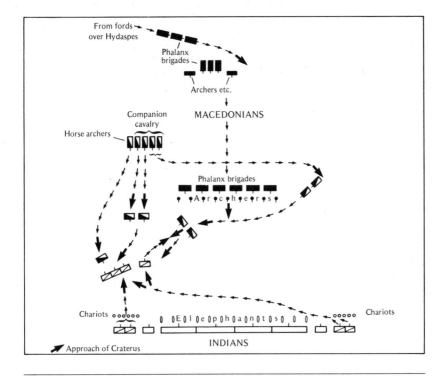

From fords over Hydaspes

Phalanx brigades

Archers etc.

Companion cavalry

Horse archers

MACEDONIANS

Phalanx brigades

Chariots

Chariots

Approach of Craterus

INDIANS

The battle of the Hydaspes, 326 BC.

Porus then decided to move in force against Alexander, but he left behind a small guard with some elephants to prevent Craterus from crossing. With 30,000 infantry, 4,000 cavalry, 300 chariots and 200 elephants, Porus outnumbered Alexander, who had only 6,000 infantry, although his 5,000 cavalry gave him a decisive advantage in that arm. Selecting ground that was not too muddy from the recent rain, Porus extended a line slightly over two miles long while Alexander's would have been less than half that, with his infantry eight deep.[288]

Porus had 2,000 cavalry and two chariot squadrons 150 strong on each wing. The 200 elephants were lined up some fifty feet apart in front of the Indian infantry. Alexander bunched his cavalry on his right and prepared to bear down on the Indian left cavalry where Porus was in command. He detached a small cavalry force (about 1,000) under Coenus to move left against the Indian right cavalry, but since he expected Porus to move his right cavalry over to the left wing, to defend against Alexander's massed attack, Coenus was instructed to come in behind the Indians when that happened.

Alexander first sent forward the mounted archers from his right, who disposed of the Indian chariots and disrupted the Indian left cavalry with a barrage of long-range firepower. He then moved out with the Companions in line of column in an encircling and flanking attack against the Indian left, hoping to draw the Indian cavalry away from its infantry support. Porus brought his right cavalry over, in front of his line, and Coenus moved across the field between the two opposing infantries to hit it in the rear.[289] As a result Porus was not able to integrate his two cavalry wings before Alexander came down hard against him. Conjointly with the final massive assault the Macedonian infantry moved to prevent Porus from deploying his elephants against Alexander's cavalry. His skirmishers were particularly useful against the elephants, 'shooting down the drivers', according to Arrian,

and pouring in a hail of missiles from every side upon the elephants themselves. It was an odd bit of work – quite unlike any previous battle; the monster elephants plunged this way and that among the lines of infantry, dealing destruction in the solid mass of the Macedonian phalanx, while the Indian horsemen, seeing the infantry at one another's throats, wheeled to the assault of the Macedonian cavalry.[290]

But Alexander's men drove the enemy cavalry back again upon the elephants.

By this time the elephants were boxed up, with no room to manoeuvre, by troops all round them, and as they blundered about, wheeling and shoving this way and that, they trampled to death as many of their friends as of their enemies.

Finally the Indians broke and fled. Seizing this opportunity Craterus crossed over the river and was able to use his fresh troops for pursuit, and the slaughter was great. Porus was wounded and captured; when he was taken before Alexander, the Macedonian asked him how he wanted to be treated. 'As a king', Porus replied, and Alexander was so impressed by the answer that he restored the Indian to his kingdom. They became fast friends.

Throughout this campaign Alexander's generalship had been outstanding. He acted with speed and decisiveness, yet with careful planning and attention to logistics. The fact that he had crossed the

Indus and fought a major battle and still maintained a line of communications that reached all the way back to Macedonia is perhaps the most remarkable thing of all. He was certainly overextended and would feel the effects of that on the return journey to Babylon, but in the Punjab he was not totally adrift in an unknown world, hopelessly cut off from his bases in Persia and beyond. Had he decided to return by the route he had travelled, he would have faced few difficulties. The geographic and strategic conception of the Greek world had been broadened beyond the wildest dreams of Pericles and Epaminondas.

Alexander at Waterloo:
His Place in the History of Warfare

After Alexander warfare would never be the same. He had carried the art to a level of sophistication that would rarely be equalled and even more rarely excelled for more than 2,000 years from his own day to the age of Napoleon. Technological change, particularly the introduction of gunpowder in the Late Middle Ages and for that matter advances in the theory of catapult fire later in the ancient world, made some things possible that Alexander could not have known. But they did not significantly alter the state of the art that he had so effectively refined.

Obviously, not every refinement of pre-industrial war can be attributed to Alexander. Generals still had to learn the restraint to stay out of the thick of the fighting. Alexander's example of bravery on the field inspired his men to incredible efforts, but his boldness led to several serious and potentially lethal wounds, and his manner of fighting at the front made it difficult and nearly impossible for him to change his tactical plan once he had committed his army to battle. Though this criticism of his generalship is valid, however, it can also be overdrawn. In warfare down to Napoleon there were many generals who exposed themselves to great risk, including Caesar and Wellington. Marshal Ney was famous for his courage under fire, and other generals of the Napoleonic era placed themselves in jeopardy. General Pakenham, who had led a famous charge at Salamanca (1812) in the Peninsular Campaign, died in the battle of New Orleans (1815), and General Ross, after burning Washington D.C., fell in the attack on Baltimore. Napoleon, as we shall see, damaged his own cause by staying too far in the rear at Waterloo.

The hammer-and-anvil tactics of Alexander's integrated army have remained basic in warfare down to the present day. Although Alexander never achieved a classic double envelopment, as Hannibal did at Cannae, the double envelopment is simply a variation of hammer-and-anvil tactics, albeit a difficult one to execute successfully. To illustrate the importance of hammer-and-anvil tactics in warfare generally we can point to MacArthur's campaign from Hollandia to Leyte in the Philippines during World War II, which has been described as 'extremely daring, more daring and far more complicated than those of Patton in Europe,' and as 'the most brilliant strategic conception and tactical execution of the entire war.' MacArthur, in his *Reminiscences*, said of this campaign: 'Leyte was to be the *anvil* against which I hoped to *hammer* the Japanese into submission in the central Philippines – the springboard from which I could proceed to the conquest of Luzon, for the final assault against Japan itself.'[291]

Another feature of Alexander's generalship that is justly admired is his regard for his men. 'No conqueror had so few casualties in battle,' writes N. G. L. Hammond, 'and the reason was that Alexander avoided "the battle of rats" by using his brains not just to win, but to win most economically.'[292] Among modern generals MacArthur again stands out for his clear understanding that generals have an obligation, simply as generals and not for political reasons, to devise plans for victory at little loss in life. Some of Alexander's success in this area stemmed also from his realization that an army well trained, strictly disciplined and highly motivated was less likely to take needless casualties.

The best way to appreciate the qualities of Alexander's generalship (and of his army) is to compare him in some detail with another well-known general. For this purpose I have selected Napoleon – not arbitrarily, but because the comparison has often been made, in passing, by military historians. David Chandler, the most famous student of Napoleon's generalship in our generation, has said, 'Napoleon, indeed, was a military phenomenon, the greatest soldier of modern history and possibly the greatest of all time, his only serious rivals for the title being Alexander the Great of Macedon and the Mongol Emperor Genghis Khan.'[293] Historians of Alexander have also noted similarities. E. W. Marsden in a book on Alexander's strategy observed that 'both faced a remarkably similar strategic problem', as one prepared to invade Persia and the other Russia. 'In

Russia,' he added, 'Napoleon failed. Alexander succeeded in the conquest of Persia. Napoleon, whose secretary read Arrian aloud to him in Egypt, apparently did not derive therefrom the secret of success.'[294]

The comparison between the two generals is not far-fetched. By the Age of Napoleon the practice of war had obviously changed in many ways since the time of Alexander, but closer examination will reveal that the changes were not as great as one might imagine, and it will also illustrate the enormous contribution of Alexander to the art of war. I propose, then, to look at the battle of Waterloo (1815), first to consider what might have happened had Alexander been in Napoleon's place as commander of the French army, and then to consider how Wellington might have fared had he faced Alexander's own Macedonian army. I have selected Waterloo – again not arbitrarily – because it was one of the most significant battles in modern history and because, as David Chandler says, 'only Gettysburg has been written about as often'.[295] The reader naturally will have to make some allowances, but the only important one I ask for is to set aside the consideration of the psychological impact of exploding gunpowder on Alexander and his men. There is no way of knowing what that might have been, though I am prepared to concede that it would have been great.

For reasons of economy we shall begin with the problems confronting Napoleon on the morning of 18 June 1815, the day of the battle. The strategic complications that had brought him to that point are simply too intricate for consideration here. By that morning two things were obvious – the battle would be fought that day on ground selected by Wellington, and Napoleon had to defeat Wellington before Blücher and the Prussians nearby could join forces with him.[296]

Napoleon was optimistic and estimated the odds at nine to one in his favour. Plans were made by his staff for dinner in Brussels that evening. During a meeting at 9.00 am Napoleon contemptuously dismissed all possibility that Wellington, the 'Sepoy General', and his army could withstand the French attack and turned aside the suggestion that reinforcements be summoned from the French army to his right under Grouchy. David Chandler has suggested that this conversation led Napoleon to delay the onset of battle – the first shot was not fired until about 11.30 am, and the main battle did not begin until 1.00 pm.

The ridge that Wellington hoped to hold just south of Waterloo was about two miles long, and the British had earlier secured control over two strongholds somewhat in advance of their line. One, Hougoumont on the right, was a château with an orchard. The other, La Haie Sainte, in advance of Wellington's centre, was a farm with orchard, garden and stables. Napoleon's plan was to storm Wellington's position in a series of frontal attacks, and Marshal Ney was given tactical command of the French army while Napoleon stayed in the rear with the Imperial Guard, which was to be thrown into the fighting at the decisive moment. As David Chandler says, 'The Emperor was seeking a quick victory of an unsophisticated type.' Napoleon himself is supposed to have said that 'in half an hour I shall cut them to pieces'.[297]

The heart of Wellington's line was defended by two ranks of musketeers with cavalry and artillery support. Ney began the battle by attacking Hougoumont in advance of Wellington's right. What had probably been planned as a diversion to draw strength away from the British centre became a bloody slug-out lasting all day long and diverting more French than British troops in the end. An entire French division with artillery support was still fighting around Hougoumont by 8.00 pm after the rest of their army had been driven from the field.

At about 1.00 pm French artillery began to lay down a barrage of fire almost 700 yards away from the centre of Wellington's line. Since the British troops were able to protect themselves behind the ridge selected by Wellington, French guns did little damage. On the whole artillery was not an important factor in the battle of Waterloo. Four French infantry divisions under d'Erlon, about 17,000 strong, proceeded to move against the British in heavy battalions 200 men wide and twenty-seven ranks deep. Although the French infantry offered an inviting target to British guns, d'Erlon moved up, passed La Haie Sainte, and carried the attack towards the British line. At a critical moment Wellington's cavalry under Lord Uxbridge charged against the French infantry, driving off d'Erlon's cavalry support and forcing his infantry back with heavy losses. But one of the British cavalry regiments, the Scots Greys under Sir William Ponsonby, pursued too far, blew their horses, and the French lancers chewed many of them up in pursuit. Ponsonby was dismounted and killed. The first French attack had been thwarted, but Wellington had suffered heavy cavalry losses.

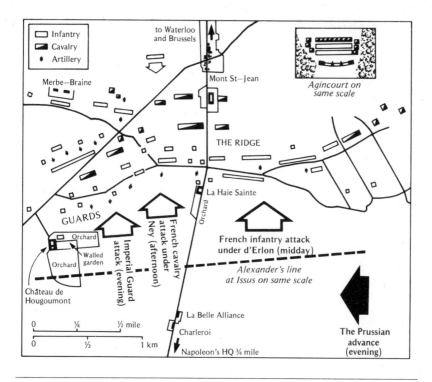

Legend:
- □ Infantry
- ◨ Cavalry
- ♦ Artillery

to Waterloo and Brussels

Merbe–Braine

Mont St–Jean

Agincourt on same scale

THE RIDGE

La Haie Sainte

GUARDS

Orchard

French cavalry attack under Ney (afternoon)

French infantry attack under d'Erlon (midday)

Imperial Guard attack (evening)

Orchard

Walled garden

Orchard

Château de Hougoumont

Alexander's line at Issus on same scale

La Belle Alliance

The Prussian advance (evening)

Charleroi

0 — ¼ — ½ mile

0 — ½ — 1 km

Napoleon's HQ ¾ mile

The battle of Waterloo (1815), with Agincourt (1415) and Issus (333 BC) on the same scale. Ancient battles were larger and more sophisticated than is generally known.

At about 4.00 pm, despite problems at La Haie Sainte, Ney decided to lead a great cavalry charge into Wellington's position. Five thousand cavalry were mobilized for the attack, and Ney personally led the charge against British infantry squares in Wellington's right centre. They advanced along an 800-yard front over muddy ground and, remarkably, without infantry support. Ney apparently believed that he had seen signs of weakness in the British line and was so anxious to take advantage of the situation that he failed to coordinate a proper attack. For a full hour wave after wave of French cavalry pounded against the British squares, but Wellington's troops held. Compounding his error, at 5.00 pm Ney threw in the remaining French cavalry, another 5,000 horsemen, but again the British held firm, though the pressure on their squares was intense.

In the meantime Blücher was getting nearer. Although the French cavalry had been driven back, around 6.00 pm Ney finally took La Haie Sainte and asked Napoleon to bring up the Guard (about 6.30). At last, at about 7.00 pm, Napoleon personally led the Guard, his élite infantry, to within 600 yards of the line where he turned it over to Ney. By this time the Prussians were appearing on the field. Around 7.30 the Guards, in heavy and deep formation, moved against Wellington's right centre with cries of '*Vive l'Empereur*'. As they approached to within twenty yards of the British line, Maitland's Brigade rose from concealed positions on the ridge and delivered heavy fire at point-blank range into the deep French formation. A bayonet charge broke the Guards, who were also exposed to fire along their flanks. By using fire and bayonets intermittently Wellington's army drove the French from the field. Pursuit was entrusted to Blücher. Napoleon had to hide within one of his own squares until his staff whisked him away, hopelessly defeated and crushed.

This battle, so decisive in European history, has been refought many times by armchair generals, and we must do it once again, using it as a standard by which to judge Alexander's generalship and his contribution to the art of war. How might Alexander have fought this battle had he been in Napoleon's shoes? First we should remember that the scale of the battle, in troop strength and geographically, would not have daunted Alexander. He had fought opponents more numerous than Wellington's army along lines of about the same length. Gunpowder would have been new to him, but he had some experience in using catapults as field artillery, at somewhat less range and destructive power. In fact neither French nor British artillery proved decisive at Waterloo. The battle was determined when cavalry and infantry, singly or in combination, closed with the enemy. The big guns at Waterloo could not prevent that from happening.

All military historians agree that Napoleon and Ney made several critical mistakes on the day of Waterloo, and we can safely assume, based on what we know of Alexander's career, that he would not have made any of them. It is of course theoretically possible that he might have had a bad day too, just as Napoleon did, but, unlike Napoleon, Alexander never actually had such a day in his own experience. In any event, the point is not to prove that Alexander was a better general than Napoleon – merely that Alexander had brought the art of war to a nearly modern level some 2,000 years before the French emperor.

We know that Alexander understood the proper use of an integrated army, a concept he and his father had borrowed from the ancient Near East and had improved through the development of good heavy infantry, the Macedonian phalanx.

Napoleon's first mistake was in delaying the initial attack against Wellington for so long, a mistake compounded by the fact that Prussians were coming to relieve the British. Everything we know about Alexander suggests that he would not have been so sluggish and indecisive. At the Granicus and at Issus Alexander moved from line of column into line of battle and attacked his enemy without delay. In his other battles he always moved vigorously, once he was in tactical range, to close with the enemy. Furthermore Alexander would not have mounted an attack either with cavalry or with infantry unsupported by the other arm. Ney's use of cavalry unsupported by infantry remains to this day almost inexplicable. Finally, Alexander would not have stayed behind his line the way Napoleon did. Wellington and Ney exposed themselves to risks all day long. Ney went through five horses on the afternoon of the battle, but Napoleon was so far behind his line that he could not intervene in tactical operations. He is reported to have been angry when Ney organized the French cavalry for the initial charge, but the Emperor was too far away to prevent it. Although Napoleon's presence on the field, according to Wellington, 'was worth 40,000 men' (a statement that could be made equally well of Alexander), at Waterloo he dissipated this effect by remaining too far to the rear. That is a mistake that Alexander could not conceivably have made.

To appreciate the full force of Alexander's achievement we must consider, briefly, what he might have done against Wellington with the Macedonian army rather than the French. Setting aside the psychological impact on the Macedonian army of exploding gunpowder, it is doubtful that Alexander's army would otherwise have been decisively affected by British firepower. Although Napoleon's forces attacked in even deeper formation than the Macedonian phalanx, and were therefore a more inviting object of attack for British artillerymen, artillery did not prevent the French from getting within twenty yards of the British line in the fateful final assault. Presumably Alexander's troops might have done that also.

Likewise the infantry musket was not an especially formidable weapon. Useless at 100 yards, it had some effect at fifty, but the injunction to 'wait until you see the whites of their eyes' was widely applied in Napoleonic warfare, and the Guard had approached to within twenty yards before Wellington turned his own forces against it. At a distance of twenty yards the Macedonian phalanx with its thirteen-foot lances would have been a greater threat to Wellington than Napoleon's Guards. It is of course possible that British firepower might have broken their ranks just as it did, in conjunction with a bayonet charge, against Napoleon's Guard. But a bayonet charge against the Macedonians would have been futile. Since it took several seconds to reload a musket, and the British had only two lines of musketeers, Macedonians within a range of fifty yards or less, trained as they were to charge at the double when necessary, could have closed with devastating effect against the British infantry. Assuming that they could have withstood the initial barrage of fire in which, admittedly, they would have taken heavy losses, Macedonian phalangites would have been vastly superior to British infantrymen in hand-to-hand combat.

Alexander's skirmishers would have been more effective at Waterloo than they were in antiquity. Bows and slings had a longer effective range than muskets, and, since warriors of the early nineteenth century wore little armour, arrows and slingstones would have done relatively more damage. The likely performance of Macedonian cavalry against British stirrups is perhaps more debatable, but the quality of Macedonian horsemanship was high, and the Macedonian cavalry lance was a fearsome weapon. French lancers caused the British so much trouble on the field at Waterloo that in the following year the British organized their own lancer units.

Obviously one cannot say categorically that Alexander's Macedonian army would have driven Wellington from his ridge in 1815, but the battle might have been a near-run thing. I am well aware that such comparisons can be odious and have only limited utility. Battles, happily, cannot be refought. As David Chandler says of Waterloo,

Any attempt to analyse the outcome . . . of this celebrated campaign and battle must differentiate between psychological and physical factors; states of morale and quality of leadership come under the first category, numerical strength, weaponry, tactical doctrine and organization belong to the second. The ultimate result cannot be attributed to any one particular cause – it was the product of a combination of factors, both tangible and intangible, as is the result of any battle. To achieve a wholly just evaluation is practically impossible. . . .[298]

It is even more difficult to compare the practice of war in one age with that of another, but no achievement of one period can be fully evaluated without some comparison, tacit or specific, with a comparable achievement elsewhere. Whatever Alexander's performance on the field of Waterloo might have been, he had brought warfare 2,000 years earlier to a high water mark. The Romans later made improvements in the organization of infantry, but no other ancient general made as many basic contributions to warfare as Alexander the Great.[299]

We have surveyed the origins of warfare from prehistoric times down to the fourth century B C. Beginning with the invention of tactics – the use of the column and the line in prehistory – down to the sophisticated application of hammer-and-anvil tactics by the integrated army of Macedonia, developments had generally been slow. The ancient Near East played a greater role than is often realized in producing integrated armies, but Greek heavy infantry was superior to its Persian counterpart. When Philip and Alexander combined the two traditions in the Macedonian army, the result was a style of warfare that continued, despite some technological and organizational changes, down to the Age of Napoleon. Only in the twentieth century, with the advent of enormous armies, airplanes, submarines, machine-guns, rapid-fire small arms, and now nuclear weapons, has warfare changed fundamentally.

Notes

Chapter One

1 Quoted in Keegan 1976, p. 141. There is much on Mercer in Howarth 1969.
2 Keegan 1976, p. 197.
3 Engels 1978.
4 Keegan 1976, p. 171.
5 Eccles 1965.
6 Turney-High 1971, p. 23.
7 Quoted in Keegan 1976, p. 150 (italics mine).
8 Keegan 1976, pp. 173–4.
9 In addition to Turney-High 1971, see Quincy Wright, *A Study of War* (Chicago 1942), I, pp. 53–100; Joseph Schneider, 'Primitive Warfare: A Methodological Note', in Leon Bramson and George W. Goethals, eds., *War: Studies from Psychology, Sociology, Anthropology* (New York 1964), pp. 275–83; Robert Carniero, 'A Theory of the Origin of the State', *Science*, 169 (1970), pp. 733–8; and David Webster, 'Warfare and the Evolution of the State: A Reconsideration', *American Antiquity*, 4 (1975), pp. 464–70; Wenke 1980, pp. 357–61.
10 Turney-High 1971, p. xiii.
11 Wenke 1980, pp. 357–61.
12 For a brief, recent survey see Boyce Rensberger, 'Ancestors, A Family Album', *Science Digest*, 89, no. 3 (April 1981), pp. 34–43, and *The First Men*, Time-Life Series, 'The Emergence of Man' (New York 1973). More detailed works are cited in the following notes.
13 William James, 'The Moral Equivalent of War', in Bramson and Goethals, eds., *War*, pp. 21–31.
14 Sigmund Freud, *Civilization and Its Discontents* (London 1930), p. 86, and 'Why War?' (the letter to Einstein) in Bramson and Goethals, eds., *War*, pp. 75–7.
15 In Bramson and Goethals, eds., *War*, pp. 269–74.
16 Raymond Dart, 'The Predatory Transition from Ape to Man', *International Anthropological and Linguistic Review*, 1 (1954), 207–8.

17 Dart 1959, p. 113.
18 Ardrey 1961, 1966, 1970 and 1976. See also Desmond Morris, *The Naked Ape* (London and New York 1967), and *The Human Zoo* (London and New York 1969).
19 Lorenz 1966.
20 Montagu 1976, and Leakey 1979.
21 Richard E. Leakey and Roger Lewin, *People of the Lake: Mankind and Its Beginnings* (New York 1979), p. 233.
22 Lorenz 1966, p, 239.
23 See Franz Weidenreich, 'Six Lectures on Sinanthropus', *Bulletin Geological Society of China*, 19 (1939), and Kenneth P. Oakley, 'On Man's Use of Fire, with Comments on Toolmaking, and Hunting', in S. L. Washburn, ed., *Social Life of Early Man* (New York 1961), pp. 176–93. See also Montagu 1976, pp. 109–11.
24 *Atlas of Primitive Man in China* (Beijing 1980), pp. 32–55.
25 Alice M. Brues, 'The Spearman and the Archer', in Yehudi A. Cohen, ed., *Man in Adaptation: The Biosocial Background*, 2nd edn (Chicago 1974), pp. 285–95.
26 Kenneth P. Oakley, *Man the Tool-Maker*, 4th edn (London and Chicago 1964), p. 72. See also Grahame Clark, *The Stone Age Hunters* (London 1967), pp. 23–37, and Jacques Bordaz, *Tools of the Old and New Stone Age* (New York 1970).
27 Grahame Clark and Stuart Piggott, *Prehistoric Societies* (London and New York 1965), p. 60.
28 For the statistics see Hadingham 1979, pp. 255–8. For the argument of sexual significance and for the best reproductions of cave art see André Leroi-Gourhan, *The Art of Prehistoric Man in Western Europe* (London 1968). The best general discussion is Ucko and Rosenfeld 1967. See also P. R. S. Moorey, ed., *The Origins of Civilization* (Oxford 1979), pp. 105 and 114.
29 On the origins of the bow see Gad Ransing, *The Bow: Some Notes on Its Origin and Development* (Acta Archaeologica Lun-

densia, ser. 8, no. 6: Lund 1967), and Manfred Korfmann, *Schleuder und Bogen in Südwestasien von den Frühesten Belegen bis zum Beginn der historischen Stadtstaaten* (Antiquitas, 3, Band 13: Bonn 1972). See also Bridget Allchin, *The Stone-tipped Arrow* (London 1966).

30 See works cited in n. 29 above. For evidence of Late Palaeolithic date see William Reid, *Arms Through the Ages* (New York 1976), pp. 9–11. See also Hardy 1976, pp. 11–27.

31 Neolithic rock art has been found all over the world. For the art of the Spanish Levant see Johannes Maringer and Hans-Georg Bandi, *Art in the Ice Age: Spanish Levant Art: Arctic Art* (New York 1953); Andreas Lommel, *Landmarks of the World's Art: Prehistoric and Primitive Man* (New York 1966), pp. 47–8; and Tom Prideaux, *Cro-Magnon Man* (in 'The Emergence of Man' series, Time-Life: New York 1973), pp. 145–51. See also Burchard Brentjes, *African Rock Art* (trans. by A. Dent, New York 1969); Robert R. R. Brooks and Vishnu S. Wakankar, *Stone Age Painting in India* (New Haven 1976); Torgny Säve-Söderbergh, ed., *The Rock Drawings* (*The Scandinavian Joint Expedition to Sudanese Nubia Publications*, 4 vols.: Odense 1970); and Muvaffak Uyanik, *Petroglyphs of South-Eastern Anatolia* (trans. by Halük V. Saltikgil, Graz 1974).

32 I am assuming a maximum range of 100 to 150 yards for the earliest simple bows, but that may be too high. Ordinarily they would have been used at a much closer range than that, often nearly point-blank.

33 The best work on this subject has been done in New World archaeology. See Dennis Stanford, 'Bison Kill by Ice Age Hunters', *National Geographic*, 155, no. 1 (Jan. 1979), pp. 114–21, which contains a section on the use of the spear-thrower (or atlatl) and on how a mammoth was butchered.

34 Turney-High 1971, pp. 26–8.

35 For the excavation reports see Fred Wendorff, ed., *The Prehistory of Nubia* (Dallas 1968), vol. II, pp. 954–95. There is an excellent discussion of the remains in Hoffman 1979.

36 David Howarth, *Waterloo: Day of Battle* (New York 1969), p. vii.

37 See James Mellaart, *Çatal Hüyük: A Neolithic Town in Anatolia* (London 1967), and, for a slight revision of the earlier dating, *The Archaeology of Ancient Turkey* (London and Ottowa 1978), pp. 9–22.

38 On the sling see Korfmann (cited in n. 29 above), and K. G. Lindblom, *The Sling, Especially in Africa: Additional Notes to a Previous Paper* (Stockholm 1940). See also V. Gordon Childe, 'The Significance of the Sling for Greek Prehistory', *Studies Presented to David M. Robinson* (St Louis 1951), pp. 1–5, and Korfmann's article, 'The Sling as a Weapon', *Scientific American*, 229, no. 4 (Oct. 1973), 34–42.

39 James Mellaart, *Excavations at Hacılar* (Edinburgh 1970), vol. I, p. 158, and *Çatal Hüyük*, p. 217.

40 See Korfmann (n. 29, above), pp. 6–16, and Lindblom (n. 38, above).

41 Xenophon, *Anabasis*, III, 3, 6–20; 4, 1–18. Hogg (1968) says 'The range of the sling in the hands of an expert was approximately 500 yards under suitable weather conditions.' Most slingers under battlefield conditions would probably not have done even half that well.

42 Quoted in Lindblom (n. 38, above), p. 26.

43 Quoted in Lindblom (n. 38, above), p. 6.

44 Yadin 1963, vol. I, pp. 9–10, and Adcock 1957, p. 16.

45 Vegetius, II, 23. See also G. R. Watson, *The Roman Soldier* (London 1969), pp. 60–61.

46 Caesar, *BC*, III, 4.

47 See Korfmann (n. 29, above), pp. 6–16.

48 Mellaart 1975, p. 277.

49 *Ibid.*, p. 278.

50 Charles L. Redman, *The Rise of Civilization: From Early Farmers to Urban Society in the Ancient Near East* (San Francisco 1978), pp. 215–16.

51 The best discussion is De la Croix 1972, pp. 12–14. See also Paul Lampl, *Cities and City Planning in the Ancient Near East* (New York 1968).

52 See Kathleen Kenyon, *Digging Up Jericho* (London 1957); Margaret Wheeler, *Walls of Jericho* (London 1956); and Yadin 1963, I, pp. 32–35.

53 For population figures the best discussion is Peter Dorell, 'The Uniqueness of Jericho', in Roger Moorey and Peter Parr, eds., *Archaeology in the Levant: Essays for Kathleen Kenyon* (Warminster 1978), pp. 11–18.

54 Mellaart 1975, pp. 48–51.

55 See the various essays in Jack R. Harlan, Jan M. J. De Wet, and Ann B. L. Stemler, eds., *Origins of African Plant Domestication* (The Hague 1976).

56 See article by Dorell in n. 53, above.

57 Mellaart, *Çatal Hüyük*. For the revised dating see Mellaart, *The Archaeology of Ancient Turkey*, p. 13.

58 De la Croix 1971, p. 14.

59 Turney-High 1971 p. 124.

60 Obviously I do not mean to suggest that Neolithic and Bronze Age warriors are identical, but merely that 'heroic' feats of warfare occurred in both periods.

Chapter Two

61 The excellent handbook used at the United States Military Academy at West Point by Elmer C. May and Gerald P. Stadler (1980)

begins with a chapter on the Greek hoplite.

62 B. H. Liddell Hart, *Strategy* (New York 1954), begins with the Greeks, and his *A Greater Than Napoleon: Scipio Africanus* (London 1926) reveals his admiration for the achievements of ancient warfare. See also Fuller 1960 and the same author's *Julius Caesar Man, Soldier, and Tyrant* (London 1965).

63 Yadin 1963. See also Oakeshott 1960.

64 For advances in Greek logistics in the fourth century BC see Engels 1978.

65 For the standard view see James H. Breasted, *A History of Egypt* (New York 1909), p. 84, or John A. Wilson, *The Culture of Ancient Egypt* (Chicago 1951), p. 82. W. B. Emery, *Archaic Egypt* (Harmondsworth 1961), pp. 112–18, gives a slightly more balanced view.

66 Sir Alan Gardiner, *Egypt of the Pharaohs* (Oxford 1961), p. 404.

67 Gardiner, *Egypt of the Pharaohs*, p. 394.

68 For these figures and others consult R. Ernest Dupuy and Trevor N. Dupuy, *The Encyclopedia of Military History* (New York 1970), *passim*.

69 Yadin 1963, I, pp. 6–13.

70 Jac Weller, *Weapons and Tactics; Hastings to Berlin* (New York 1966), p. 18.

71 Littauer and Crouwel 1979.

72 Yadin 1963, I, pp. 7–8.

73 *Ibid.*, I, pp. 10–11.

74 Turney-High 1971, p. 7.

75 Eccles 1965, pp. 45–6. See also Hart, *Strategy*, pp. 335–6.

76 For a survey of their views see the essays on them in Earle 1943. Though Hart was a severe critic of Clausewitz on many points, he too thought in terms of winning victories through 'indirect' offensive attacks.

77 (Baltimore 1976), pp. xi–xii.

78 See especially R. O. Faulkner, 'Egyptian Military Organization', *Journal of Egyptian Archaeology*, 39 (1953), 32–47; A. W. Lawrence, 'Ancient Fortifications', *Journal of Egyptian Archaeology*, 51 (1965), 69–94; and Schulman 1964.

79 Emery, *Archaic Egypt*, pp. 112–18.

80 Gardiner, *Egypt of the Pharaohs*, p. 94–8.

81 Faulkner, *Journal of Egyptian Archaeology*, 39 (1953), 32–6.

82 *Ibid.*, 33–4.

83 *Ibid.*, 36–41.

84 In addition to Faulkner on this point see the somewhat different views of Schulman 1964, p. 21, for discussion and additional bibliography.

85 On the 'Walls of the Prince' see Lawrence, *Journal of Egyptian Archaeology*, 51 (1965), 71.

86 *Ibid.*, 71.

87 Gardiner, *Egypt of the Pharaohs*, pp. 148–72. See also John Van Setera, *The Hyksos*

(New Haven 1966).

88 Lawrence, *Journal of Egyptian Archaeology*, 51 (1965), 88.

89 On the Egyptian army see also Yadin 1963, I, pp. 111–14, and Robert Laffont, *The Ancient Art of Warfare*, I (Paris 1966), pp. 16–31.

90 See Eccles 1965, *passim*.

91 U. S. Grant Sharp, *Strategy for Defeat* (San Rafael 1978), though focussing primarily on the air war over North Vietnam, contains some discussion of General Westmoreland's strategy in the south.

92 On Megiddo see Yadin 1963, I, pp. 100–103, and George Steindorff and Keith C. Seele, *When Egypt Ruled the East* (Chicago 1957), pp. 53–6. See also R. D. Faulkner, 'The Battle of Megiddo', *Journal of Egyptian Archaeology*, 28 (1942).

93 This quotation and those that follow are taken from Yadin 1963, I, pp. 100–103.

94 On the battle of Kadesh see Gardiner 1960, and the still useful study by Breasted (1903). See also Simon Goodenough, *Tactical Genius in Battle* (London 1979), pp. 29–32, and Yadin 1963, I, pp. 103–10.

95 For example, at Munda Caesar threw himself into the front ranks and said afterwards that he had often fought for victory but at Munda he had fought for his life (Plut., *Caesar*, 56). As we shall see in Chapter Six, Alexander also performed similar feats of courage on the field.

96 Hans Goedicke, 'Considerations on the Battle of Kadesh', *Journal of Egyptian Archaeology*, 52 (1966), 71–80, believes that the division of Sutekh was not part of the army under Ramesses near Kadesh. It had advanced separately up the coast, and the mercenaries who arrived in the nick of time from the west were attached tactically to that division.

97 See David Howarth, *Waterloo: Day of Battle* (New York 1969), p. 142: 'The Duke had been in the thick of it all the time, riding along the line and taking shelter inside the squares each time the cavalry charged.' On the battle see also Chandler 1980.

98 On the chariot see above, n. 71, and Yadin 1963, I, pp. 4–5, 37–40.

99 Yadin 1963, II, pp. 253–87, and Herzog and Gichon 1978. See also John Ellis, *A Short History of Guerrilla Warfare* (New York 1976), p. 9.

Chapter Three

100 Gibbon, of course, did not use the word 'polite' in the sense of 'well behaved' but in its literal sense of 'polished and cultivated'. For the comparison between Assyria and Rome see, among others, A. T. Olmstead, *History of Assyria* (Chicago 1923), pp. 645–55, and in a different context A. Leo Oppenheim, *Ancient Mesopotamia* (Chicago 1977), p. 90.

Notes

101 For a survey of developments in this period see Samuel Noah Kramer, *The Cradle of Civilization* (New York 1969), pp. 51–9, and Oppenheim, *Ancient Mesopotamia*, pp. 163–7. See also Georges Roux, *Ancient Iraq* (Harmondsworth 1964), pp. 234–9.

102 See the excellent article by James Muhly, 'How Iron Technology Changed the Ancient World and Gave the Philistines a Military Edge', *Biblical Archaeology Review*, 8, no. 6 (Nov./Dec. 1982), 40–54, for discussion and additional bibliography.

103 Yadin 1963, II, 291–302.

104 W. G. Lambert, *Babylonian Wisdom Literature* (Oxford 1960), pp. 146–7 (quoted in Muhly, above, n. 102).

105 See the discussion of these three fronts by Oppenheim, *Ancient Mesopotamia*, pp. 165–7.

106 *Ibid.*, p. 167.

107 Luckenbill 1926, II, p. 152.

108 Luckenbill 1926, I, pp. 144–5.

109 W. Manitius, 'Das stehende Heer der Assyrerkönige und seine Organization', *Zeitschrift für Assyriologie und vorderasiatische Archäologie*, 24 (1910), 97–149; pp. 185–224, remains the standard treatment though it is long out of date. See also H. W. F. Saggs, 'Assyrian Warfare in the Sargonid Period', *Iraq*, 25 (1963), 145–154, and J. E. Reade, 'The Neo-Assyrian Court and Army: Evidence from the Sculptures', *Iraq*, 34 (1972), 87–112.

110 See H. F. W. Saggs, *The Greatness That Was Babylon* (London and New York 1962), p. 254.

111 Postgate 1974.

112 *Ibid.*, p. 17.

113 General Sir Evelyn Wood, *Cavalry in the Waterloo Campaign* (London 1895), p. 14. See also David Chandler, *The Campaigns of Napoleon* (New York 1966), pp. 351–6, and M. Adolphe Thiers, *History of the Consulate and the Empire under Napoleon* (Philadelphia 1865), vol. 5, p. 566.

114 On this point see the discussion in Littauer and Crouwel 1979, pp. 11–12.

115 Yadin 1963, II, pp. 313–28.

116 The classic discussion is by F. Thureau-Dangin, *Une Relation de la Huitième Campagne de Sargon* (1912). The translation may be found in Luckenbill 1926, II, pp. 73–99. See also Georges Contenau, *Everyday Life in Babylon and Assyria* (New York 1966), pp. 149–54, and Olmstead, *History of Assyria*, pp. 229–42.

117 Luckenbill 1926, II, pp. 73–99 and for the following quotations on the campaign.

118 For discussion of attacks in line of column by French armies in the revolutionary period see Chandler, *The Campaigns of Napoleon*, pp. 67–8.

119 Hdt., I, 103 (translation Rawlinson, New York 1875).

120 On Persia see especially A. T. Olmstead, *History of the Persian Empire* (Chicago 1948), Richard N. Frye, *The Heritage of Persia* (Cleveland 1963), and J. M. Cook, *The Persian Empire* (London and New York 1983).

121 Hdt., III, 89–94.

122 On the Scythians see Tamara Talbot Rice, *The Scythians* (London and New York 1957).

123 On the Persian army see Olmstead, *History of the Persian Empire*, pp. 230–47; Hignett 1963, pp. 40–55; Burn 1962, pp. 321–36; and an old but still useful book, Grundy 1901, *passim*.

124 Hdt., VII, 61–99.

125 Hdt., I, 80.

126 Keegan 1976, *passim*, is excellent on cavalry warfare. For the Greek and Persian period see Tarn 1930, pp. 50–100, and Adcock 1957, pp. 47–53.

127 See the excellent article by Paul Rahe, 'The Military Situation in Western Asia on the Eve of Cunaxa', *American Journal of Philology*, 101 (1980), 79–96.

128 On the Persian fleet see Hignett 1963, pp. 51–5.

129 See Morrison and Williams 1968, pp. 129–31, and Casson 1971, p. 81, n. 19, for opposing views. See also Alan B. Lloyd, 'Triremes and the Säite Navy', *Journal of Egyptian Archaeology*, 58 (1972), 268–79, who accepts a Greek origin for the trireme, and Lucien Basch, 'Phoenician Oared Ships', *The Mariner's Mirror*, 55 (1969), 139 ff., 227 ff. See also Lloyd's reply, 'Were Necho's Triremes Phoenician?' *Journal of Hellenic Studies*, 95 (1975), 45–61, and their exchange in *Journal of Hellenic Studies*, 100 (1980), 195–9.

130 R. O. Faulkner, 'Egyptian Seagoing Ships', *Journal of Egyptian Archaeology*, 26 (1941), 3–9. See also Yadin 1963, II, pp. 251–2.

131 In addition to items cited in notes 128–130 above, beginners will find useful the article by Vernard Foley and Werner Soedel, 'Ancient Oared Warships', *Scientific American*, 244, no. 4 (April 1981), 148–63. See also Chester G. Starr, 'The Ancient Warship', *Classical Philology*, 35 (1940), 353–74.

132 Hdt., VIII, 10.

133 Hdt., VIII, 60. See also my article, 'Herodotus and the Strategy and Tactics of the Invasion of Xerxes', *American Historical Review*, 72 (1966), 102–15.

134 Morrison and Williams 1968, pp. 135–43 and 313–20.

Chapter Four

135 For a general account of the problems see Greenhalgh 1973, esp. pp. 156–72. The bibliography is enormous. Other important works include G. S. Kirk, 'War and the Warrior in the Homeric Poems', in J-P.

Vernant, *Problèmes de la Guerre en Grèce Ancienne* (Paris 1968), pp. 93–117; J. V. Luce, *Homer and the Heroic Age* (London and New York 1975); D. L. Page, *History and the Homeric Iliad* (Berkeley 1959); and Snodgrass 1964.

136 See esp. Chester G. Starr, 'The Myth of the Minoan Thalassocracy', *Historia*, 3 (1955), 282–91.

137 Compare the ships of the Theran fresco with the Egyptian ship illustrated in R. O. Faulkner, 'Egyptian Seagoing Ships', *Journal of Egyptian Archaeology*, (1941), plate IV. Avner Raban, 'The Thera Ships: Another Interpretation', *American Journal of Archaeology*, 88 (1984), 11–19, appeared too late for use in the text above.

138 The refusal to think of the Minoans as anything but totally peaceful people dies hard. See Christos G. Doumas, *Thera: Pompeii of the Ancient Aegean* (London and New York 1983), pp. 129–33.

139 John Chadwick, *The Mycenaean World* (Cambridge 1976), pp. 159–79.

140 On this point see Chester G. Starr, 'Homeric Cowards and Heroes', in Arther Ferrill and Thomas Kelly, eds., *Chester G. Starr Essays in Ancient History* (Leiden 1979), pp. 97–101.

141 Chadwick, *The Mycenaean World*, p. 167. See also p. 170 for discussion of chariot tablets at Pylos.

142 Chadwick, *Mycenaean World*, p. 173.

143 Carol Thomas, 'A Dorian Invasion? The Early Literary Evidence', *Studi micenei ed egeo-anatolici*, 19 (1978), 77–87, and N. G. L. Hammond, *Migrations and Invasions in Greece and Adjacent Areas* (Park Ridge 1976).

144 Greenhalgh, 1973, p. 142; Aristotle, *Politics*, 1297b.16–19.

145 The bibliography is unending. Readers will find references to the most important works in J. Salmon, 'Political Hoplites?' *Journal of Hellenic Studies*, 97 (1977), 84–101. See also A. Snodgrass, 'The Hoplite Reform and History', *Journal of Hellenic Studies*, 85 (1965), 110–22.

146 Adcock 1957, pp. 14–28, and Connolly 1981, pp. 37–50.

147 For armour see the up-to-date review in P, Cartledge, 'Hoplites and Heroes', *Journal of Hellenic Studies*, 97 (1977), 12–15; Snodgrass 1967, pp. 48–88; and Connolly 1981, pp. 51–63.

148 On pay see Pritchett 1971, I, pp. 3–29.

149 See A. J. Holladay, 'Hoplites and Heresies', *Journal of Hellenic Studies*, 102 (1982), 94–103, and Cawkwell 1978, pp. 150–3, whose views are those referred to in the paragraph above.

150 du Picq 1921, p. 94 (written in French in the 1860s).

151 *Ibid.*, p. 48.

152 See Anderson 1970, pp. 225–51, who cites the ancient evidence, and Connolly 1981, pp. 37–8.

153 Thuc., V, 66. On the Spartan kings as military commanders see Carol Thomas, 'On the Role of the Spartan Kings', *Historia* 23 (1974), pp. 257–70.

154 For Spartan policy see W. G. Forrest, *A History of Sparta 950–192 B.C.* (London 1968), p. 39.

155 Jordan 1975, and Morrison and Williams 1968, *passim*.

156 On the Persian Wars generally see Hignett 1963 and Burn 1962. See also Green 1970. There is an interesting popular account by Ernle Bradford, *The Battle for the West: Thermopylae* (New York 1980). For the Ionian revolt see Donald Lateiner, 'The Failure of the Ionian Revolt', *Historia*, 31 (1982), 129–60.

157 For the battle of Marathon see the excellent article by Gordon Shrimpton, 'The Persian Cavalry at Marathon', *Phoenix*, 34 (1980), 20–37, and the full discussion in Hammond 1973, pp. 170–250. On the range of the ancient bow see Wallace McLeod, 'The Range of the Ancient Bow', *Phoenix*, 19 (1965), 1–14, and 26 (1972), 78–82.

158 Hdt., VI, 112. See also W. Donlan and J. Thompson, 'The Charge at Marathon: Herodotus 6. 112', *Classical Journal*, 71, (1976), 339–43, and 'The Charge at Marathon Again', *Classical World*, 72 (1979), 419–20.

159 N. G. L. Hammond, 'The Narrative of Herodotus vii and the Decree of Themistocles at Troezen', *Journal of Hellenic Studies*, 102 (1982), 75–93. Some scholars believe this decree to be a fake. For that view see C. Habicht in *Hermes*, 89 (1961), 1–35.

160 Hdt., VII, 141.

161 The problem of numbers in Herodotus is impossible to resolve with certainty. I have followed what seems to be the trend in recent scholarship to regard his figures for the fleets as generally reliable and to scale down the figures for the Persian army. Some scholars reduce his figures for the fleets, but they usually retain his ratio of Persian to Greek warships.

162 N. Robertson, 'The Thessalian Expedition of 480 B.C.', *Journal of Hellenic Studies*, 96 (1976), 100–20.

163 See my 'Herodotus and the Strategy and Tactics of the Invasion of Xerxes', *American Historical Review*, 72 (1966), 102–15, and J. A. S. Evans, 'Notes on Thermopylae and Artemisium', *Historia*, 18 (1969), 389–406.

164 Hdt., VII, 211.

165 Hdt., VIII, 11.

166 On Salamis see Hammond 1973, pp. 251–310; W. Marg, 'Zur Strategie der Schlacht von Salamis', *Hermes*, 90 (1962), 116–19, and W. K. Pritchett, 'Salamis Revisited', *Un-*

iversity of California Publications in Classical Studies, 1 (1965), 94–102.

167 See W. K. Pritchett, 'Plataea Revisited', *University of California Publications in Classical Studies*, 1 (1965), 103–21, in addition to the works cited in n. 156, above.

168 It is not as easy to move large numbers of soldiers as is often assumed. Wellington once said, 'If thirty thousand men were drawn up in close order in Hyde Park, there are not three men in Europe who could get them out again.' See Anderson 1970, p. 103.

169 Hdt., IX, 59.

170 So says Hignett 1963, p. 50, though he goes on to argue for the superiority of the spear over the bow.

171 Chester G. Starr, 'Why Did the Greeks Defeat the Persians?' in Arther Ferrill and Thomas Kelly, eds., *Chester G. Starr Essays on Ancient History* (Leiden 1979), pp. 193–204.

172 Thuc., I, 69, 5.

173 Grundy 1948; G. E. M. de Ste. Croix, *The Origins of the Peloponnesian War* (Ithaca 1972); Kagan 1974.

174 Thomas Kelly, 'Thucydides and Spartan Strategy in the Archidamian War', *American Historical Review*, 87 (1982), 25–54, and A. J. Holladay, 'Athenian Strategy in the Archidamian War', *Historia*, 27 (1978), 399–427.

175 Thuc., II, 84 (translation Crawley, and for subsequent quotations).

175a John Wilson, 'Strategy and Tactics in the Mytilene Campaign', *Historia*, 30 (1981), 144–63.

176 Wilson 1979.

177 Thuc., IV, 40.

178 Thuc., IV, 33–4.

179 Thuc., IV, 40.

180 For the Sicilian campaign see Kagan 1981, Green 1970, and W. Liebeschuetz, 'Thucydides and the Sicilian Expedition', *Historia*, 17 (1968), 289–306. See also C. A. Powell, 'Religion and the Sicilian Expedition', *Historia*, 28 (1979), 15–31.

181 Thuc., VI, 64.

182 For the Spanish Armada I have relied upon Garret Mattingley, *The Defeat of the Spanish Armada* (Boston 1959), and David Howarth, *The Voyage of the Armada: The Spanish Story* (New York 1981).

183 See A. Andrewes, 'The Generals in the Hellespont', *Journal of Hellenic Studies*, 73 (1953), 2–9.

184 Xen., *Hell.*, I, 1 (from Xen., *A History of My Times*, transl. Rex Warner (Penguin Books, Harmondsworth 1966)). See also Edmund F. Bloedow, *Alcibiades Reexamined* (Wiesbaden 1973), pp. 46–55, and A. Andrewes, 'Notion and Kyzikos: The Sources Compared', *Journal of Hellenic Studies*, 102 (1982), 15–25. See also R. J. Littman, 'The Strategy of the Battle of Cyzicus', *Transac-*

tions of the American Philological Association, 99 (1968), 265–72.

185 Noel Robertson, 'The Sequence of Events in the Aegean in 408 and 407 B.C.', *Historia*, 29 (1980), 282–301.

186 See Jennifer Tolbert Roberts, *Accountability in Athenian Government* (Madison 1982), pp. 124–41, and A. Andrewes, 'The Arginusae Trial', *Phoenix*, 28 (1974), 112–22.

187 Hdt., VII, 9.

188 The most important discussions are Anderson 1970, pp. 1–9; P. Cartledge, 'Hoplites and Heroes', *Journal of Hellenic Studies*, 97 (1977), 18–24; and A. J. Holladay, 'Hoplites and Heresies', *Journal of Hellenic Studies*, 102 (1982), 97–103.

189 *Third Philippic*, 48–51.

190 Anderson 1970, p. 1.

191 Lawrence 1979 and Winter 1971.

192 Anderson 1970, p. 86.

Chapter Five

193 Paul A. Rahe, 'The Military Situation in Western Asia on the Eve of Cunaxa', *American Journal of Philology*, 101 (1980), 88.

194 For Greek, as opposed to Macedonian, logistics see Pritchett 1971, I, pp. 30–52, and Anderson 1970, pp. 43–66.

195 On mercenaries generally see Parke 1933 and Griffith 1968.

196 In addition to the *Anabasis* of Xenophon, see J. K. Anderson, *Xenophon* (London 1974), pp. 73–145.

197 Numbers remain notoriously difficult, even in the fourth century, especially when Persians are involved. See George Cawkwell's balanced assessment in his introduction to Rex Warner's translation of Xenophon's *The Persian Expedition* (Harmondsworth 1972), pp. 36–8. Xenophon says that Artaxerxes had 900,000 troops on the field with another 300,000 on the way. Anderson, *Xenophon*, pp. 99–100, argues for smaller numbers than Cawkwell. In the text above the numbers are respective, that is, if Artaxerxes had 100,000 then Cyrus had 80,000.

198 Polyb., III, 6.

199 Though Clearchus had sound reasons for refusing to obey Cyrus, they do not justify his insubordination. He did have some cavalry protection on his flank, and it is simply unacceptable, as Clearchus the Spartan should have known, for a ranking officer to disobey the commander-in-chief in the midst of battle.

200 Xen., *Anab.*, III, 3–4.

201 In fact, there is a great deal of information on military matters in most of Xenophon's works including the *Hellenica*, the *Recollections of Socrates*, and the *Constitution of the Lacedaemonians*, to say nothing of his works on horsemanship.

202 Xenophon's *Agesilaus* is a sympathetic account of the Spartan king, but it also contains much valuable information on the military history of the early fourth century. For Agesilaus' strategy see Ober 1980, Chap. II, and Charles D. Hamilton, 'The Generalship of King Agesilaus of Sparta', *Ancient World*, 8 (1983), 119–27.

203 See Hamilton 1979.

204 The best discussions of the battle of Nemea are in Anderson 1970, pp. 141–50, and W. K. Pritchett, 'The Battle Near the Nemea River in 394 B.C.', in *Studies in Ancient Greek Topography, Part II, Battlefields* (Berkeley 1969). See also Hamilton 1979, pp. 220–2.

205 See Pritchett 1969, pp. 85–95; Anderson 1970, pp. 151–3; and Hamilton 1979, pp. 225–6.

206 Xen., *Hell.*, IV, 5, 10–16 (trans. Warner, n. 184, above). For a discussion see Anderson 1970, pp. 123–6, and Hamilton 1979, pp. 285–6.

207 Xen., *Hell.*, IV, 5, 7, (trans. Warner, n. 184, above).

208 Diodorus, 44, 1–4, quoted in G. T. Griffith, 'Peltasts, and the Origins of the Macedonian Phalanx', in Harry J. Dell, ed., *Ancient Macedonian Studies in Honor of Charles F. Edson* (Thessaloniki 1981), p. 161, with commentary.

209 Anderson 1970, pp. 129–31. Griffith, 'Peltasts', p. 166, suggests that Iphicrates commanded hoplites not peltasts in Egypt.

210 Anderson 1970, pp. 89–90. Cornelius Nepos wrote biographies of both Iphicrates and Chabrias.

211 Xen., *Anab.*, I, 8.

212 Anderson 1970 p. 90. On *esprit de corps* see Parke 1933, p. 54.

213 Thuc., V, 10, 5–6.

214 Arist., *Politics*, 8.3, 4 13338b (trans. Barker, London 1946). See the discussion in Pritchett 1974, II, p. 209.

215 Adcock 1957, pp. 6–7.

216 Thuc., V, 71.

217 Anderson 1970 pp. 94–5, 105.

218 Cic., *Brutus*, 112; *Ad Fam.*, IX, 25, 2; *Tusculan Disputations*, II, 62. See also Anderson, *Xenophon*, pp. 2–6.

219 XI, 8.

220 III, 1–4 (trans. Anna S. Benjamin, *Recollections of Socrates* (Indianapolis 1965)).

221 On generalship as a career see Parke 1933, p. 39.

222 III, 4.

223 On this period generally see Buckler 1980.

224 The best discussion of the battle is Buckler 1980, pp. 62–9, and 'Plutarch on Leuktra', *Symbolae Osloenses*, 55 (1980), pp. 76–93. See also Anderson 1970, pp. 192–220. A. M. Devine, 'Ernbolon: a Study in Tactical Terminology', *Phoenix*, 37 (1983), 201–17, offers a fascinating proposal that Epam-

inondas used a wedge formation on his left wing.

225 Xen., *Hell.*, VI, 4, 12 (trans. Warner, n. 184, above).

226 The position of the Sacred Band is highly controversial. I follow Buckler 1980, pp. 63–4, though some historians believe that the Sacred Band was stationed at the rear of Epaminondas' column. For that view see Anderson 1970, pp. 216–17.

227 Xen., *Hell.*, VI, 4, 5 (trans. Warner, n. 184, above).

228 Plut., *Pelopidas*, 23 (Dryden).

229 For a full discussion of Mantinea see Anderson 1970, pp. 221–4, and Buckler 1980 pp. 213–19. On the importance of Epaminondas generally see C. Mitchell James, *Epaminondas and Philip II: a Comparative Study of Military Reorganization* (PhD dissertation, Univ. of Kentucky 1980).

230 Marsden 1969, pp. 48–56. Beginners may wish to consult Werner Soedel and Vernard Foley, 'Ancient Catapults', *Scientific American*, 240, n.3 (March 1979), pp. 150–60. See also Lawrence 1979, pp. 43–9.

231 Marsden 1969 p. 60.

232 Arrian, *Anab.*, I, 6, 8 (from Arrian, *The Campaigns of Alexander*, trans. Aubrey de Sélincourt (Penguin Classics, rev. edn 1971), copyright © The Estate of Aubrey de Sélincourt 1958, reprinted by permission of Penguin Books Ltd). All subsequent references to Arrian are to this edition.

233 Tarn 1930, p. 102.

234 See J. I. S. Whitaker, *Motya* (London 1921), p. 75ff., Marsden 1969, pp. 99–100, and Lawrence 1979, pp. 37–8, 42–4.

235 Marsden 1969, pp. 100–101.

236 Ober 1980.

237 A sample of numerous treatments of Alexander's army includes Fuller 1960, pp. 39–54; Hammond 1980, pp. 24–34; and Connolly 1981, pp. 68–75. See also, more specifically on Philip, Cawkwell 1978, pp. 150–65, and Hammond and Griffith 1979, pp. 405-49.

238 Peter A. Manti, 'The Cavalry Sarissa', *Ancient World*, 8 (1983), 80, who cites the evidence.

239 N. G. L. Hammond, 'Training in the Use of the Sarissa and Its Effect in Battle', *Antichthon*, 14 (1980), 53–63. See also M. Markle, 'The Macedonian Sarissa, Spear, and Related Armor', *American Journal of Archaeology*, 82 (1978), 483–97.

240 There is an excellent discussion of Macedonian hammer-and-anvil tactics in May and Stadler 1980, p. 27. For the importance of hammer-and-anvil tactics in warfare generally see *Encyc. Brit.* (1942 edn) under 'cavalry'.

241 See Best 1969, and the article by Griffith cited in n. 208, above.

242 On Iphicrates as a disciplinarian see Anderson 1970, p. 121.

243 Hammond 1980, pp. 27 (for the quotation above) and 33 for commando training.

244 Dvornik 1974; Chester G. Starr, *Political Intelligence in Classical Greece* (Leiden 1974); and Donald Engels, 'Alexander's Intelligence System', *Classical Quarterly*, 30 (1980), pp. 127–40. See also Jack Balcer, 'The Athenian Episnopos and the Achaemenid "King's Eye"', *American Journal of Philology*, 98 (1977), 252–63.

245 Engels, *Classical Quarterly*, 30 (1980), 129–30, and Pritchett 1971, I, p. 132. In the fifth century Spartans were famous for keeping some military information secret. See Thuc., V, 68.

246 Engels 1978, pp. 11–25. See also the review of that book by Ernst Badian, 'Alexander's Mules', *The New York Review of Books*, 26, no. 20 (20 Dec. 1979), 54–6.

247 Front., *Strat.* 4, 1, 6 (Loeb edn, 1925).

248 See Hammond 1980, p. 308, n. 10.

249 Polyaenus, 4, 2, 10.

250 Hammond 1980, p. 34.

251 Anderson 1970, p. 53.

252 David Chandler, *The Campaigns of Napoleon* (New York 1966), p. 45.

253 *Ibid.*, p. 160.

254 Demosthenes, *Third Philippic*. 48–51 (quoted in Fuller 1960, p. 48).

255 Edwyn Gray, *A Damned Un-English Weapon, The Story of British Submarine Warfare 1914–18* (London 1971), pp. 12–14.

Chapter Six

256 For Alexander's generalship see the items cited above in n. 237. See also Bosworth 1980, and Atkinson 1980.

257 See above, n. 240.

258 For the battle of Chaeronea see Hammond 1973, pp. 534-57.

259 For the military details of the first two years of his reign see Hammond 1980, pp. 35–64.

260 Tarn 1948, p. 8.

261 Fuller 1960, p. 89, and Hammond 1980, pp. 67–8.

262 Ulrich Wilcken, *Alexander the Great*, with a Preface by Eugene Borza (trans. by G. C. Richards, New York 1967), p. 77.

263 See the excellent account of Alexander's troubles in the Gedrosian desert in Engels 1978, pp. 135–43.

264 Cawkwell 1978, pp. 164-5.

265 See N. G. L. Hammond, 'The Battle of the Granicus River', *Journal of Hellenic Studies*, 100 (1980), 73–88, whose notes contain a full bibliography of modern studies of the battle. For the quote in the text above from Arrian see Arrian, I, 13, in *The Campaigns of Alexander* (n. 232 above).

266 Arrian, I, 15 (n. 232 above).

267 For this popular view see Tarn 1948, p. 16.

268 Fuller 1960, p. 151.

269 For the forlorn hope, which is normally spelled in lower-case letters, see W. F. P. Napier, *History of the War in the Peninsula*, vol. IV (London n.d.), pp. 89 and 112, and C. W. Robinson, *Wellington's Campaigns*, 3rd edn, part II (London 1906), p. 221: 'Assaulting columns at sieges were, speaking generally, composed at this period of a storming party led by its forlorn hope. . . .'

270 For the siege of Halicarnassus see Fuller 1960, pp. 200–206.

271 For the manner in which he untied it see Hammond 1980, p. 88.

272 For the battle of Issus see Fuller 1960, pp. 154–62, and Hammond 1980, pp. 100–110, and the commentaries of Bosworth and Atkinson cited above in n. 256.

273 Arrian, II, 11 (n. 232 above).

274 Hammond 1980, p. 104.

275 For Tyre see Fuller 1960, pp. 206–16, and Hammond 1980, pp. 112–15, and again see the commentaries in n. 256, above.

276 For Gaza see esp. Fuller 1960, pp. 216–18.

277 Arrian, II, 14 (n. 232 above).

278 Cawkwell 1978, p. 164.

279 In addition to the various works cited in the notes above see Marsden 1964.

280 Eugene N. Borza, 'Fire from Heaven: Alexander at Persepolis', *Classical Philology*, 67 (1972), 233–45.

281 See Fuller 1960, pp. 234–45, and Hammond 1980, pp. 150–86.

282 E. Badian, 'Alexander the Great and the Loneliness of Power', *Studies in Greek and Roman History* (Oxford 1964), pp. 192–205, and 'The Death of Parmenio', *Transactions of the American Philological Association*, 91 (1960), 324–8.

283 For the route see Engels 1978, pp. 107–10, and Stein 1929.

284 For other Indian campaigns see Eggermont 1975.

285 For troop strength see Hammond 1980, p. 203, and for the length of the line at the Hydaspes, pp. 207–8.

286 Scullard 1974.

287 Arrian, V, 10 (n. 232 above).

288 The best account is by J. R. Hamilton, 'The Cavalry Battle at the Hydaspes', *Journal of Hellenic Studies*, 76 (1956), 26–31. See also Fuller 1960, pp. 180–99, and Hammond 1980, pp. 204–11.

289 I differ from Hamilton on this point. Since Porus' left cavalry was in front of his elephants when Alexander attacked, and since the right cavalry joined him shortly before Alexander drove the Indians back into the elephants, the Indian right cavalry must have

crossed in front of the main line and not behind it.

290 Arrian, V, 17 (n. 232 above).

291 William Manchester, *American Caesar: Douglas MacArthur 1880–1964* (New York 1978), pp. 445–6, quoting first Vincent Sheean and then MacArthur. The italics in MacArthur's comment are mine.

292 Hammond 1980, p. 256.

293 Chandler 1980, p. 32.

294 Marsden 1964, p. 1. See also Wilcken, *Alexander*, p. 84.

295 Chandler 1980, p. 9.

296 For the account that follows I rely heavily on Chandler 1980, but I have read extensively on the battle. Readers should consult the works listed in notes 2, 97, and 113, above.

297 Chandler 1980, p. 128.

298 *Ibid.*, p. 187.

299 See also the assessment of Colonel T. A. Dodge (1890), p. 662: 'As a captain, Alexander accomplished more than any man ever did. He had no equal predecessor who left him a model for action. He showed the world, first of all men, and best, how to make war. He formulated the first principles of the art, to be elaborated by Hannibal, Caesar, Gustavus Adolphus, Turenne, Prince Eugene, Marlborough, Frederick and Napoleon.'

Select Bibliography

Adcock, F. E., *The Greek and Mac-edonian Art of War* (Berkeley 1957).

Anderson, J. K., *Ancient Greek Horse-manship* (Berkeley 1961).

——*Military Theory and Practice in the Age of Xenophon* (Berkeley 1970).

——*Xenophon* (London 1974).

Ardrey, Robert, *African Genesis* (New York and London 1961).

——*The Territorial Imperative* (New York and London 1966).

——*The Social Contract* (New York and London 1970).

——*The Hunting Hypothesis* (New York and London 1976).

Atkinson, J. E., *A Commentary on Q. Curtius Rufus' Historiae Magni Books 3 and 4* (Amsterdam 1980).

Best, J. G. P., *Thracian Peltasts and Their Influence on Greek Warfare* (Groningen 1969).

Binford, Lewis, *In Pursuit of the Past* (London and New York 1983).

Bosworth, A. B., *A Historical Com-mentary on Arrian's History of Alex-ander* (Oxford 1980).

Breasted, James H., *A Study in the Earliest Known Military Strategy* (Chicago 1903).

Buckler, John, *The Theban Hegemony 371–362 B.C.* (Cambridge, Mass. 1980).

Burn, A. R., *Persia and the Greeks* (London and New York 1962).

Casson, L., *Ships and Seamanship in the Ancient World* (Princeton 1971).

Cawkwell, G. L., *Philip of Macedon* (London 1978).

Chandler, David, *Waterloo: The Hund-red Days* (London 1980).

Connolly, Peter, *Greece and Rome at War* (London 1981).

Croix, Horst De la, *Military Con-siderations in City Planning: For-tifications* (New York 1972).

Dart, Raymond, *Adventures with the Missing Link* (New York 1959).

Delbrück, Hans, *History of the Art of War within the Framework of Political History*, vol. I, trans. W. J. Renfroe Jnr (Westport, Conn. 1975).

Dodge, T. A., *Alexander*, 2 vols. (Boston 1890).

du Picq, Ardant, *Battle Studies: Ancient and Modern Battle* (New York 1921).

Dvornik, Francis, *Origins of Intelligence Services* (New Brunswick 1974).

Earle, Edward Meade, ed., *Makers of Modern Strategy* (Princeton 1943).

Eccles, Henry E., *Military Concepts and Philosophy* (Rutgers 1965).

Eggermont, *Alexander's Campaigns in Sind and Baluchistan and the Siege of the Brahmin Town of Harmatelia* (Louvain 1975).

Engels, Donald W., *Alexander the Great and the Logistics of the Macedonian Army* (Berkeley 1978).

Fuller, J. F. C., *The Generalship of Alexander the Great* (London 1958 and Rutgers 1960).

Gardiner, Sir Alan, *The Kadesh Inscrip-tions of Ramesses II* (Oxford 1960).

Green, Peter, *The Year of Salamis* (London 1970).

——*Armada from Athens* (London 1971).

Greenhalgh, P. A. L., *Early Greek Warfare: Horsemen and Chariots in the Homeric and Archaic Ages* (Camb-ridge 1973).

Griffith, G. T., *The Mercenaries of the Hellenistic World* (Groningen 1968: originally published in 1935).

Grundy, G. B. *The Great Persian War* (London 1901).

——*Thucydides and the History of His Age* 2nd edn (Oxford 1948).

Hadingham, Evan, *Secrets of the Ice Age: The World of the Cave Artists* (New York and London 1979).

Hamilton, Charles D., *Sparta's Bitter Victories: Politics and Diplomacy in the Corinthian War* (Ithaca, N.Y. 1979).

Hammond, N. G. L., *Studies in Greek History* (Oxford 1973).

——*Alexander the Great: King, Commander and Statesman* (Park Ridge, N.J. 1980).

Hammond, N. G. L., and Griffith, G. T., *A History of Macedonia*, vol. II (Oxford 1979).

Hardy, Robert, *Longbow: A Social and Military History* (London and New York 1976).

Herzog, Chaim, and Gichon, Mordechai, *Battles of the Bible* (London and New York 1978).

Hignett, C., *Xerxes' Invasion of Greece* (Oxford 1963).

Hoffman, Michael A., *Egypt Before the Pharaohs* (New York 1979).

Hogg, O. F., *Clubs to Cannon: Warfare and Weapons Before the Introduction of Gunpowder* (London 1968).

Humble, Richard, *Warfare in the Ancient World* (London 1980).

Jordan, Borimir, *The Athenian Navy in the Classical Period* (Berkeley 1975).

Kagan, Donald, *The Archidamian War* (Ithaca 1974).

——*The Peace of Nicias and the Sicilian Expedition* (Ithaca, 1981).

Keegan, John, *The Face of Battle* (London and New York 1976).

Lawrence, A. W., *Greek Aims in Fortification* (Oxford 1979).

Leakey, Richard E., *Origins* (London and New York 1979).

Littauer, M. A., and Crouwel, J., *Wheeled Vehicles and Ridden Animals in the Ancient Near East* (Leiden 1979).

Lorenz, Konrad, *On Aggression* (trans. M. Wilson, London and New York 1966).

Luckenbill, D. D., *Ancient Records of Assyria and Babylonia*, 2 vols. (Chicago 1926).

McCartney, Eugene S., *Warfare by Land and Sea* (New York 1963).

Marsden, E. W., *The Campaign of Gaugamela* (Liverpool 1964).

——*Greek and Roman Artillery: Historical Development* (Oxford 1969).

May, Elmer C., and Stadler, Gerald P., *Ancient and Medieval Warfare* (West Point 1980).

Mellaart, James, *The Neolithic of the Near East* (London and San Francisco 1975).

Montagu, Ashley, *The Nature of Human Aggression* (New York 1976).

Morrison, J. D., and Williams, R. T., *Greek Oared Ships 900–322 B.C.* (Cambridge 1968).

Oakeshott, R. Ewart, *The Archaeology of Weapons* (New York 1960).

Ober, Josiah, *Athenian Reactions to Military Pressure and the Defense of Attica, 404–322 B.C.* (PhD dissertation, University of Michigan 1980).

Parke, H. W., *Greek Mercenary Soldiers* (Oxford 1933).

Postgate, J. N., *Taxation and Conscription in the Assyrian Empire* (Rome 1974).

Pritchett, W. K., *The Greek State at War*, 2 parts (Berkeley 1971 and 1974).

——*Studies in Ancient Greek Topography*, 4 parts (Berkeley 1965–82).

Rodgers, W. L., *Greek and Roman Naval Warfare* (Annapolis 1937).

Sandars, Nancy, *The Sea Peoples* (London and New York 1978).

Schulman, Alan R., *Military Rank, Title and Organization in the Egyptian New Kingdom* (Berlin 1964).

Scullard, H. H., *The Elephant in the Greek and Roman World* (London and Ithaca, N.Y. 1974).

Snodgrass, A. M., *Early Greek Armour and Weapons* (Edinburgh 1964).

——*Arms and Armour of the Greeks* (London and Ithaca, N.Y. 1967).

Stein, Sir Aurel, *On Alexander's Track to the Indus* (London 1929).

Tarn, W. W., *Alexander the Great* (Cambridge 1948).

—— *Hellenistic Naval and Military*

Developments (Cambridge 1930).

Turney-High, H. H., *Primitive War: Its Practice and Concepts*, 2nd edn (Columbia, S.C. 1971).

Ucko, Peter J., and Rosenfeld, André, *Palaeolithic Cave Art* (London and New York 1967).

Warry, John G., *Warfare in the Classical World* (New York 1980).

Wenke, Robert J., *Patterns in Prehistory* (Oxford 1980).

Wilson, John, *Pylos 425 B.C.* (Warminster 1979).

Winter, F. E., *Greek Fortifications* (Toronto 1971).

Yadin, Yigael, *The Art of Warfare in Biblical Lands in the Light of Archaeological Study*, 2 vols. (London and New York 1963).

Illustration Credits

All maps by Hanni Bailey, except p.64 (S. Ebrahim) and pp. 190–1 (H. A. Shelley); all battle plans by Martin Lubikowski; the following drawings by Schelay Richardson: pp. 18, 25 (right), 29 (right), 32, 35–7, 40, 41 (above), 42, 49, 73, 76, 88, 90, 94, 96, 97, 100, 101, 148, 171, 172, 179, 203. Other credits: after Connolly 1981: pp.171, 172; after P. Levi, *Atlas of the Greek World* (1980): p.177; after Maringer and Bandi 1953: pp.21, 22; after Mellaart 1967: pp.24, 25 (left), 31; after C. Redman, *The Rise of Civilization* (1978): p.29; after *Scientific American*, vol. 244, no. 4 (1981): p.88; after Yadin 1963: pp.26, 39, 41, 43, 44, 75.

Index

Index